# Digital Television

## Satellite, Cable, Terrestrial, IPTV, Mobile TV in the DVB Framework

## Third Edition

Hervé Benoit

ELSEVIER

AMSTERDAM • BOSTON • HEIDELBERG • LONDON
NEW YORK • OXFORD • PARIS • SAN DIEGO
SAN FRANCISCO • SINGAPORE • SYDNEY • TOKYO

Focal Press is an imprint of Elsevier

Focal Press

| | |
|---|---|
| Senior Acquisitions Editor: | Angelina Ward |
| Publishing Services Manager: | George Morrison |
| Project Manager: | Mónica González de Mendoza |
| Assistant Editor: | Kathryn Spencer |
| Development Editor: | Stephen Nathans-Kelly |
| Marketing Manager: | Amanda Guest |
| Cover Design: | Alisa Andreola |

Focal Press is an imprint of Elsevier
30 Corporate Drive, Suite 400, Burlington, MA 01803, USA
Linacre House, Jordan Hill, Oxford OX2 8DP, UK

**Library of Congress Cataloging-in-Publication Data**

Benoit, Hervé.
  [Télévision numérique. English]
  Digital television : satellite, cable, terrestrial, iptv, mobile tv in the dvb framework/Hervé Benoit. – 3rd ed.
    p. cm.
  Includes bibliographical references and index.
  ISBN 978-0-240-52081-0 (pbk. : alk. paper) 1. Digital television. I. Title.

TK6678.B4613 2008
621.388'07–dc22

2007046661

**British Library Cataloguing-in-Publication Data**
A catalogue record for this book is available from the British Library.

ISBN: 978-0-240-52081-0

For information on all Focal Press publications
visit our website at www.books.elsevier.com

08 09 10 11 12   5 4 3 2 1

Printed in the United States of America

# Contents

Contents

Contents

# Preface

This book does not aim to make the reader an expert in digital television (which the author himself is not). Rather, its purpose is to describe and explain, as simply and as completely as possible, the various aspects of the very complex problems that had to be solved in order to define reliable standards for broadcasting digital pictures to the consumer, and the solutions chosen for the European **DVB** system (Digital Video Broadcasting) based on the international **MPEG-2** compression standard.

The book is intended for readers with a background in electronics and some knowledge of conventional analog television (a reminder of the basic principles of existing television standards is presented for those who require it) and for those with a basic digital background. The main goal is to enable readers to understand the principles of this new technology, to have a relatively global perspective on it, and, if they wish, to investigate further any particular aspect by reading more specialized and more detailed books. At the end, there is a short bibliography and a glossary of abbreviations and expressions which will help readers to access some of these references.

For ease of understanding, after a general presentation of the problem, the order in which the main aspects of digital television broadcast standards are described follows the logical progression of the signal processing steps on the transmitter side—from raw digitization used in TV studios to **source coding** (MPEG-2 compression and multiplexing), and on to **channel coding** (from forward error correction to RF modulation). **JPEG** and **MPEG-1** "predecessor" standards of MPEG-2 are also described, as MPEG-2 uses the same basic principles.

The book ends with a functional description of a digital **IRD** (integrated receiver decoder), or **set-top box**, which the concepts discussed in preceding chapters will help to demystify, and with a discussion of future prospects.

This third edition includes important updates, including discussion of TV-over-IP, also known as IPTV or broadband TV (generally via ADSL); high-definition television (HDTV); as well as TV for handheld devices (DVB-H and its competitors).

This edition also introduces new standards for compression (MPEG-4 part 10 AVC, also known as H.264) and transmission (DVB-S2, DVB-H, DVB-IP, etc.), which are just beginning or will soon be used by these new television applications.

H. Benoit

# Acknowledgments

I would like to thank all those who lent me their support in the realization of this book, especially Philips Semiconductors labs for their training and many of the figures illustrating this book; and also the DVB Project Office, the EBU Technical Publication Service, and the ETSI Infocentre for permission to reproduce the figures of which they are the source.

# Introduction

At the end of the 1980s, the possibility of broadcasting fully digital pictures to the consumer was still seen as a faraway prospect, and one that was definitely not technically or economically realistic before the turn of the century. The main reason for this was the very high bit-rate required for the transmission of digitized 525- or 625-line live video pictures (from 108 to 270 Mb/s without compression). Another reason was that, at that time, it seemed more urgent and important—at least in the eyes of some politicians and technocrats—to improve the quality of the TV picture, and huge amounts of money were invested by the three main world players (first Japan, then Europe, and finally the U.S.A.) in order to develop Improved Definition TeleVision (IDTV) and High Definition TeleVision systems (HDTV), with vertical resolutions from 750 lines for IDTV to 1125 or 1250 lines for HDTV.

Simply digitized, HDTV pictures would have required bit-rates that were four times higher than "conventional" pictures, of the order of up to one gigabit per second! This is why most of the HDTV proposals (MUSE in Japan, HD-MAC in Europe, and the first American HD proposals) were at that time defined as analog systems with a digital assistance which can be seen as a prelude to fully digital compression.

However, by the beginning of the 1990s, the situation had completely changed. Very quick development of efficient compression algorithms, resulting in, among other things, the JPEG standard for fixed images and later the MPEG standard for moving pictures, showed the possibility to drastically reduce the amount of data required for the transmission of digital pictures (bit-rates from 1.5 to 30 Mb/s depending on the resolution chosen and the picture content).

At the same time, continuous progress in IC technology allowed the realization, at an affordable price, of the complex chips and associated memory required for decompression of digital pictures. In addition, it appeared that the price of an HDTV receiver would not quickly reach a level affordable by most consumers, not so much due to the electronics cost, but mainly because of the very high cost of the display, regardless of the technology used (big 16/9 tube, LCD projector, or any other known technology). Furthermore, most consumers seemed more interested in the content and the number of programs offered than in an improvement in the picture quality, and economic crises in most countries resulted in a demand for "brown goods" oriented more toward the cheaper end of the market.

Mainly on the initiative of the U.S. industry, which could take advantage of its traditional predominance in digital data processing to regain influence in the electronic consumer goods market, studies have been reoriented toward the definition of systems allowing diffusion of digital pictures with equivalent or slightly better quality than current analog standards, but with many other features made possible by complete digitization of the signal. The first digital TV broadcasting for the consumer started in mid-1994 with the "DirecTV" project, and its success was immediate, resulting in more than one million subscribers after one year.

However, the Europeans had not gone to sleep—they decided at the end of 1991 to stop working on analog HDTV (HD-MAC), and created the European Launching Group (ELG) in order to define and standardize a digital TV broadcasting system. This gave birth in 1993 to the DVB project (Digital Video Broadcasting), based on the "main profile at main level" (MP@ML) of the international MPEG-2 compression standard.

MPEG-2 is downward-compatible with MPEG-1 and has provisions for a compatible evolution toward HDTV by using higher levels and profiles. This resulted in the standardization of three variants for the various transmission media—satellite (DVB-S), cable (DVB-C), and terrestrial (DVB-T)—which occurred between 1994 and 1996.

In Europe, the first commercial digital broadcasts were started by Canal+ on Astra 1 in 1996, shortly followed by TPS and AB-Sat on Eutelsat's "Hot Birds."

It is, however, the Sky group of bouquets—despite having started digital transmissions on Astra 2 only at the end of 1998 in the United Kingdom—which has by far the biggest number of subscribers in Europe (around 10 million at the end of 2005). In addition to BSkyB in the United Kingdom, the group has included Sky Italia since 2002, thanks to the acquisition and development of the former Canal+ Italia.

In the last years of the twentieth century, other forms of digital television appeared: digital cable television, digital terrestrial television, and, more recently, digital television via the telephone subscriber line (IPTV over ADSL). These developments will bring about the extinction of analog television in Europe around the end of the first decade of the twenty-first century, with the pace of the transition from analog to digital varying by country.

On the other hand, the rapid price decrease of large flat-screen TVs (LCD or Plasma) with a resolution compatible with HDTV requirements makes them now accessible to a relatively large public. This price drop coincides with the availability of more effective compression standards (such as MPEG-4 AVC/H.264), which will, finally, enable real wide-scale development of HDTV in Europe.

Last but not least, the ever-increasing sophistication of mobile phones—most of them equipped with color screens of relatively big size and high resolution—and the development of transmission standards adapted to mobility (DVB-H, T-DMB, ISDB-T, MediaFlo™...) promise the development of a personal television that is transportable virtually everywhere.

# Color television: a review of current standards

**1**

Let us begin with a bit of history . . .

## 1.1 Monochrome TV basics

It should be borne in mind that all current TV standards in use today are derived from the "black and white" TV standards started in the 1940s and 1950s, which have defined their framework.

The first attempts at electromechanical television began at the end of the 1920s, using the Nipkow disk for analysis and reproduction of the scene to be televised, with a definition of 30 lines and 12.5 images per second. This low definition resulted in a video bandwidth of less than 10 kHz, allowing these pictures to be broadcast on an ordinary AM/MW or LW transmitter. The resolution soon improved to 60, 90, and 120 lines and then stabilized for a while on 180 lines (Germany, France) or 240 lines (England, the United States) around 1935. Scanning was progressive, which means that all lines of the pictures were scanned sequentially in one frame, as depicted in Figure 1.1 (numbered here for a 625-line system).

These definitions, used for the first "regular" broadcasts, were the practical limit for the Nipkow disk used for picture analysis; the

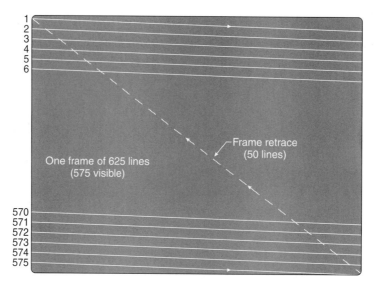

**Figure 1.1** Schematic representation of progressive scanning.

cathode ray tube (CRT) started to be used for display at the receiver side. In order to avoid disturbances due to electromagnetic radiation from transformers or a ripple in the power supply, the picture rate (or frame rate) was derived from the mains frequency. This resulted in refresh rates of 25 pictures/s in Europe and 30 pictures/s in the United States. The bandwidth required was of the order of 1 MHz, which implied the use of VHF frequencies (in the order of 40–50 MHz) for transmission. However, the spatial resolution of these first TV pictures was still insufficient, and they were affected by a very annoying flicker due to the fact that their refresh rate was too low.

During the years just preceding World War II, image analysis had become fully electronic with the invention of the iconoscope, and definitions in use attained 405 lines (England) to 441 lines (the United States, Germany) or 455 lines (France), thanks to the use of interlaced scanning. This ingenious method, invented in 1927, consisted of scanning a first field made of the odd lines of the frame and then a second field made of the even lines (see Fig. 1.2), allowing the picture refresh rate for a given vertical resolution to be doubled

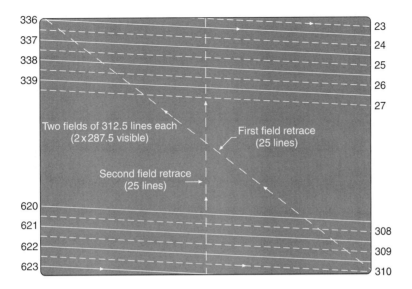

**Figure 1.2** Schematic representation of interlaced scanning (625 lines).

(50 or 60 Hz instead of 25 or 30 Hz) without increasing the bandwidth required for broadcasting.

The need to maintain a link between picture rate and mains frequency, however, inevitably led to different standards on both sides of the Atlantic, even when the number of lines was identical (as in the case of the 441-line U.S. and German systems). Nevertheless, these systems shared the following common features:

- a unique composite picture signal combining video, blanking, and synchronization information (abbreviated to VBS, also described as video baseband signal; see Fig. 1.3);

- an interlaced scanning (order 2), recognized as the best compromise between flicker and the required bandwidth.

Soon afterward, due to the increase in the size of the picture tube, and taking into account the eye's resolution in normal viewing conditions, the spatial resolution of these systems still appeared insufficient, and most experts proposed a vertical definition of between 500 and 700 lines. The following characteristics were finally chosen

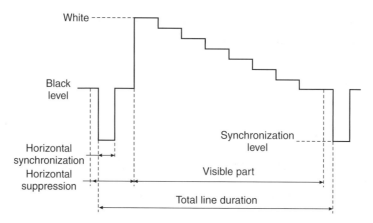

**Figure 1.3**   View of a line of a composite monochrome video signal.

in 1941 for the U.S. monochrome system, which later became NTSC when it was upgraded to color in 1952:

- 525 lines, interlaced scanning (two fields of 262.5 lines);

- field frequency, 60 Hz (changed to 59.94 Hz upon the introduction of color; see Note 1.1);

- line frequency, 15,750 Hz (60 × 262.5); later changed to 15,734 Hz with color (59.94 × 262.5);

- video bandwidth, 4.2 MHz; negative video modulation;

- FM sound with carrier 4.5 MHz above the picture carrier.

After World War II, from 1949 onward, most European countries (except France and Great Britain) adopted the German GERBER standard, also known as **CCIR**. It can be seen as an adaptation of the U.S. system to a 50 Hz field frequency, keeping a line frequency as near as possible to 15,750 Hz; this allowed some advantage to be taken of the American experience with receiver technology. This choice implied an increased number of lines (approximately in the ratio 60/50) and, consequently, a wider bandwidth in order to obtain well-balanced horizontal and vertical resolutions. The following characteristics were defined:

- 625 lines, interlaced scanning (two fields of 312.5 lines);
- field frequency, 50 Hz;
- line frequency, 15,625 Hz (50 × 312.5);
- video bandwidth, 5.0 MHz; negative video modulation;
- FM sound carrier 5.5 MHz above the picture carrier.

This has formed the basis of all the European color standards defined later (PAL, SECAM, D2-MAC, PAL+).

Until the beginning of the 1980s, different systems have been in use in the UK (405 lines, launched in 1937 and restarted after a long interruption during the war) and in France (819 lines, launched in 1949 by Henri de France, who also invented the SECAM system in 1957). These systems were not adapted to color TV for consumer broadcasting due to the near impossibility of color standard conversion with the technical means available at that time, and were finally abandoned after a period of simulcast with the new color standard.

## 1.2   Black and white compatible color systems

As early as the late 1940s, U.S. TV set manufacturers and broadcasting companies competed in order to define the specifications of a color TV system. The proposal officially approved in 1952 by the **FCC** (Federal Communications Commission), known as **NTSC** (National Television Standard Committee), was the RCA proposal. It was the only one built on the basis of bi-directional compatibility with the existing monochrome standard. A monochrome receiver was able to display the new color broadcasts in black and white, and a color receiver could, in the same way, display the existing black and white broadcasts, which comprised the vast majority of transmissions until the mid-1960s.

In Europe, official color broadcasts started more than 10 years later, in 1967, with SECAM (séquentiel couleur à mémoire) and PAL (phase alternating line) systems.

Extensive preliminary studies on color perception and a great deal of ingenuity were required to define these standards which, despite their imperfections, still satisfy most of the end users more than 40 years after the first of them, NTSC, came into being. The triple red/green/blue (RGB) signals delivered by the TV camera had to be transformed into a signal which, on the one hand, could be displayable without major artifacts on current black and white receivers, and on the other hand could be transmitted in the bandwidth of an existing TV channel—definitely not a simple task.

The basic idea was to transform, by a linear combination, the three $(R, G, B)$ signals into three other equivalent components, $Y$, $C_b$, $C_r$ (or $Y$, $U$, $V$):

$Y = 0.587G + 0.299R + 0.1145B$ is called the *luminance* signal

$C_b = 0.564(B - Y)$ or $U = 0.493(B - Y)$ is called the *blue chrominance* or color difference

$C_r = 0.713(R - Y)$ or $V = 0.877(R - Y)$ is called the *red chrominance* or color difference

The combination used for the luminance (or "luma") signal has been chosen to be as similar as possible to the output signal of a monochrome camera, which allows the black and white receiver to treat it as a normal monochrome signal. The two chrominance (or "chroma") signals represent the "coloration" of the monochrome picture carried by the $Y$ signal, and allow, by linear recombination with $Y$, the retrieval of the original RGB signals in the color receiver.

Studies on visual perception have shown that the human eye's resolution is less acute for color than for luminance transients. This means, for natural pictures at least, that chrominance signals can tolerate a strongly reduced bandwidth (one-half to one-quarter of the luminance bandwidth), which will prove very useful for putting the chrominance signals within the existing video spectrum. The Y, $C_b$, $C_r$ combination is the common point to all color TV systems, including the newest digital standards, which seems to prove that the choices of the color TV pioneers were not so bad!

In order to be able to transport these three signals in an existing TV channel (6 MHz in the United States, 7 or 8 MHz in Europe), a subcarrier was added within the video spectrum, modulated by the reduced bandwidth chrominance signals, thus giving a new composite signal called the **CVBS** (Color Video Baseband Signal; see Fig. 1.4).

In order not to disturb the luminance and the black and white receivers, this carrier had to be placed in the highest part of the video spectrum and had to stay within the limits of the existing video bandwidth (4.2 MHz in the United States, 5-6 MHz in Europe; see Fig. 1.5).

Up to this point, no major differences between the three world standards (NTSC, PAL, SECAM) have been highlighted. The differences that do exist mainly concern the way of modulating this subcarrier and its frequency.

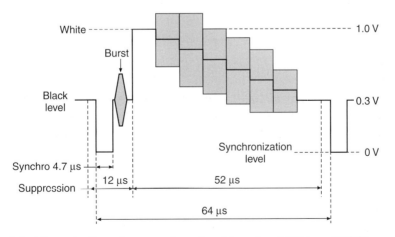

**Figure 1.4** View of a line of composite color video signal (PAL or NTSC).

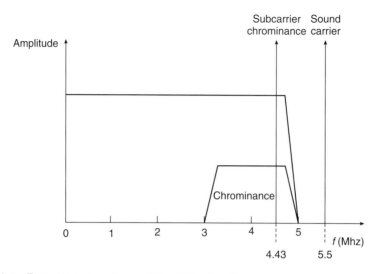

**Figure 1.5** Frequency spectrum of the PAL signal.

## 1.2.1 NTSC

This system uses a line-locked subcarrier at 3.579545 MHz ($= 455 \times F_h/2$), amplitude modulated with a suppressed carrier following two orthogonal axes (quadrature amplitude modulation, or QAM), by two signals, I (in phase) and Q (quadrature), carrying the chrominance information. These signals are two linear combinations of $(R - Y)$ and $(B - Y)$, corresponding to a 33° rotation of the vectors relative to the $(B - Y)$ axis. This process results in a vector (Fig. 1.6), the phase of which represents the tint, and the amplitude of which represents color intensity (saturation).

A reference burst at 3.579545 MHz with a 180° phase relative to the $B - Y$ axis superimposed on the back porch allows the receiver to rebuild the subcarrier required to demodulate I and Q signals. The choice for the subcarrier of an odd multiple of half the line frequency is such that the luminance spectrum (made up of discrete stripes centered on multiples of the line frequency) and the chrominance spectrum (discrete stripes centered on odd multiples of half the line frequency) are interlaced, making an almost perfect separation theoretically possible by the use of comb filters in the receiver.

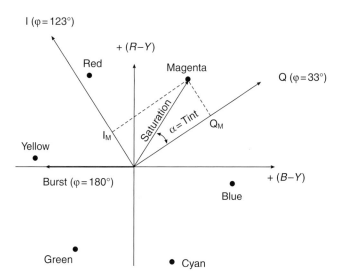

**Figure 1.6**  Color plan of the NTSC system.

Practice, however, soon showed that NTSC was very sensitive to phase rotations introduced by the transmission channel, which resulted in very important tint errors, especially in the region of flesh tones (thus leading to the necessity of a tint correction button accessible to the user on the receivers and to the famous "never twice the same color" expression). This led Europeans to look for solutions to this problem, which resulted in the SECAM and PAL systems.

## 1.2.2  SECAM

This standard eliminates the main drawback of the NTSC system by using frequency modulation for the subcarrier, which is insensitive to phase rotations; however, FM does not allow simultaneous modulation of the subcarrier by two signals, as does QAM.

The clever means of circumventing this problem consisted of considering that the color information of two consecutive lines was sufficiently similar to be considered identical. This reduces chroma resolution by a factor of 2 in the vertical direction, making it more consistent with the horizontal resolution resulting from bandwidth reduction of the chroma signals. Therefore, it is possible to transmit alternately one chrominance component, $D'_b = 1.5(B - Y)$, on one line and the other, $D'_r = -1.9(R - Y)$, on the next line. It is then up to the receiver to recover the two $D'_b$ and $D'_r$ signals simultaneously, which can be done by means of a $64 \, \mu s$ delay line (one line duration) and a permutator circuit. Subcarrier frequencies chosen are 4.250 MHz ($= 272 \times F_h$) for the line carrying $D'_b$ and 4.406250 MHz ($= 282 \times F_h$) for $D'_r$.

This system is very robust, and gives a very accurate tint reproduction, but it has some drawbacks due to the frequency modulation—the subcarrier is always present, even in non-colored parts of the pictures, making it more visible than in NTSC or PAL on black and white, and the continuous nature of the FM spectrum does not allow an efficient comb filtering; rendition of sharp transients between highly saturated colors is not optimum due to the necessary truncation of maximum FM deviation. In addition, direct mixing of two or more SECAM signals is not possible.

### 1.2.3 PAL

This is a close relative of the NTSC system, whose main drawback it corrects. It uses a line-locked subcarrier at 4.433619 MHz ($= 1135/4 + 1/625 \times F_h$), which is QAM modulated by the two color difference signals $U = 0.493 \, (B - Y)$ and $V = 0.877 \, (R - Y)$. In order to avoid drawbacks due to phase rotations, the phase of the $V$ carrier is inverted every second line, which allows cancellation of phase rotations in the receiver by adding the $V$ signal from two consecutive lines by means of a $64 \, \mu s$ delay line (using the same assumption as in SECAM, that two consecutive lines can be considered identical). In order to synchronize the $V$ demodulator, the phase of the reference burst is alternated from line to line between $+135°$ and $-135°$ compared to the $U$ vector ($0°$).

Other features of PAL are very similar to NTSC. In addition to the main PAL standard (sometimes called PAL B/G), there are two other less well-known variants used in South America in order to accommodate the 6 MHz channels taken from NTSC:

- PAL M used in Brazil (525 lines/59.94 Hz, subcarrier at 3.575611 MHz);

- PAL N used in Argentina (625 lines/50 Hz, subcarrier at 3.582056 MHz).

### 1.2.4  MAC (multiplexed analog components)

During the 1980s, Europeans attempted to define a common standard for satellite broadcasts, with the goal of improving picture and sound quality by eliminating drawbacks of composite systems (cross-color, cross-luminance, reduced bandwidth) and by using digital sound. This resulted in the MAC systems, with a compatible extension toward HDTV (called **HD-MAC**).

**D2-MAC** is the most well-known of these hybrid systems, even if it did not achieve its expected success due to its late introduction and an earlier development of digital TV than anticipated. It replaces frequency division multiplexing of luminance, chrominance, and sound (bandwidth sharing) of composite standards by a time division multiplexing (time sharing). It is designed to be compatible with normal (4:3) and wide-screen (16:9) formats and can be considered in some aspects an intermediate step on the route to all-digital TV signal transmission.

On the transmitter side, after sampling (Note 1.2) and analog-to-digital conversion, Y, $C_b$ and $C_r$ signals are time-compressed by a factor of 2/3 for Y and 1/3 for $C_b$ and $C_r$, scrambled if required, and then reconverted into analog form in order to be transmitted sequentially over one line duration (see Fig. 1.7 illustrating one line of a D2-MAC signal). The part of the line usually occupied by synchronization and blanking is replaced by a burst of so-called duobinary data (hence the "D2" in D2-MAC). These data carry the digital sound, synchronization, and other information such as teletext, captioning, and picture format (4:3 or 16:9), and in addition,

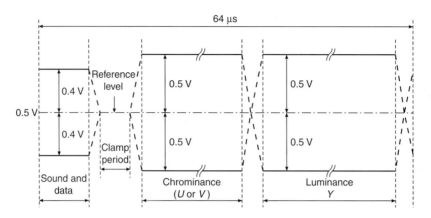

**Figure 1.7** Composition of a line of a D2-MAC signal.

for pay TV programs, they carry the access control messages of the Eurocrypt system used with D2-MAC.

As in SECAM, $C_b$ and $C_r$ chroma components are transmitted alternately from line to line in order to reduce the necessary bandwidth and obtain equivalent resolutions along the two axes of the picture for the chrominance. This resolution corresponds to the so-called 4:2:0 format (see Section 2.2.2, p. 21); it is almost equivalent to the professional 4:2:2 format used in TV studios. Time division multiplexing results in the total elimination of cross-color and cross-luminance effects, and in a luminance bandwidth of 5 MHz, a substantial improvement compared with PAL or SECAM.

## 1.2.5  PAL+

This is a recent development, the primary objective of which was to allow terrestrial transmission of improved definition 16:9 pictures (on appropriate receivers) in a compatible way with existing 4/3 PAL receivers (Note 1.3). To do this, the PAL+ encoder transforms the 576 useful lines of a 16:9 picture into a 4:3 picture in letterbox format (a format often used for the transmission of films on TV, with two horizontal black stripes above and below the picture). The visible part occupies only 432 lines ($576 \times 3/4$) on a 4/3 receiver, and additional information for the PAL+ receiver is encoded in the remaining 144 lines.

The 432-line letterbox picture is obtained by vertical low-pass filtering of the original 576 lines, and the complementary high-pass filtering is transmitted on the 4.43 MHz subcarrier during the 144 black lines, which permits the PAL+ receiver to reconstruct a full-screen 16/9 high resolution picture.

In order to obtain the maximum bandwidth for luminance (5 MHz) and to reduce cross-color and cross-luminance, the phase of the subcarrier of the two interlaced lines of consecutive fields is reversed. This process, known as "colorplus," allows (by means of a frame memory in the receiver) cancellation of cross-luminance by adding the high part of the spectrum of two consecutive frames, and reduction of cross-color by subtracting them.

A movement compensation is required to avoid artifacts introduced by the colorplus process on fast moving objects, which, added to the need for a frame memory, contributes to the relatively high cost of current PAL+ receivers. The PAL+ system results in a subjective quality equivalent to D2-MAC on a 16:9 receiver in good reception conditions (high signal/noise ratio).

In order to inform the receiver of the format of the program being broadcast (4:3 or 16:9), signalling bits (**WSS**: wide screen signalling) and additional information (sound mode, etc.) are added to the first half of line 23 (Fig. 1.8), which permits the receiver to adapt its display format. The WSS signal can also be used by ordinary PAL 16/9 receivers simply to modify the vertical amplitude according to the format, which is sometimes referred to as the "poor man's PAL+."

After this introduction (hopefully not too lengthy), we will now attempt to describe as simply as possible the principles which have allowed the establishment of new all-digital television standards and services.

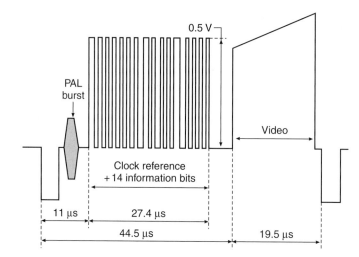

0.5 V

PAL burst

Video

Clock reference
+ 14 information bits

11 μs    27.4 μs

44.5 μs    19.5 μs

**Figure 1.8**  View of line 23 of a PAL+ signal (WSS bits).

## Note 1.1

This slight change in line and field frequencies was introduced in order to minimize the visual effect of beat frequency between sound (4.50 MHz) and color (3.58 MHz) subcarriers in the receiver. This change was done by using the sound intercarrier as a reference for the line frequency

$$(15{,}734 = 4{,}500{,}000/286)$$

## Note 1.2

D2-MAC is based on the 4:2:0 digital format (720 points/line for Y and 360 for $C_b$ and $C_r$), but for practical reasons, these numbers had to be slightly reduced to 700 and 350, respectively. This is due to the fact that the duration of 720 samples at 13.5 MHz (53.33 μs) is more than the useful part of the analog video line (52 μs), which could disturb clamping circuits in the receiver.

**Note 1.3**

PAL+ development took place between 1990 and 1992; after a period of experimental transmissions, official broadcasts started in Germany and other countries after the international 1995 Berlin radio/TV exhibition (IFA). PAL+ is officially adopted by most countries currently using the PAL system. The WSS format signalling information will also be used independently of PAL+ for conventional PAL or SECAM transmissions.

# Digitization of video signals    2

## 2.1   Why digitize video signals?

For a number of years, video professionals at television studios have been using various digital formats, such as D1 (components) and D2 (composite), for recording and editing video signals. In order to ease the interoperability of equipment and international program exchange, the former **CCIR** (Comité Consultatif International des Radiocommunications; Note 2.1) has standardized conditions of digitization (recommendation CCIR-601) and interfacing (recommendation CCIR-656) of digital video signals in component form (Y, $C_r$, $C_b$ in 4:2:2 format).

The main advantages of these digital formats are that they allow multiple copies to be made without any degradation in quality, and the creation of special effects not otherwise possible in analog format, and they simplify editing of all kinds, as well as permitting international exchange independent of the broadcast standard to be used for diffusion (NTSC, PAL, SECAM, D2-MAC, MPEG). However, the drawback is the very important bit-rate, which makes these formats unsuitable for transmission to the end user without prior signal compression.

## 2.2 Digitization formats

If one wants to digitize an analog signal of bandwidth $F_{max}$, it is necessary to sample its value with a sampling frequency $F_s$ of at least twice the maximum frequency of this signal to keep its integrity (Shannon sampling theorem). This is to avoid the negative **aliasing** effects of spectrum fall-back: in effect, sampling a signal creates two parasitic sidebands above and below the sampling frequency, which range from $F_s - F_{max}$ to $F_s + F_{max}$, as well as around harmonics of the sampling frequency (Fig. 2.1).

In order to avoid mixing the input signal spectrum and the lower part of the first parasitic sideband, the necessary and sufficient condition is that $F_s - F_{max} > F_{max}$, which is realized if $F_s > 2F_{max}$. This means that the signal to be digitized needs to be efficiently filtered in order to ensure that its bandwidth does not exceed $F_{max} = F_s/2$.

For component video signals from a studio source, which can have a bandwidth of up to 6 MHz, the CCIR prescribes a sampling frequency of $F_s = 13.5$ MHz locked on the line frequency (Note 2.2). This frequency is independent of the scanning standard, and represents $864 \times F_h$ for 625-line systems and $858 \times F_h$ for 525-line systems. The number of active samples per line is 720 in both cases. In such a line-locked sampling system, samples are at the same fixed place on all lines in a frame, and also from frame to frame, and

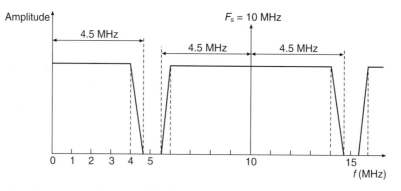

**Figure 2.1** Spectrum of a sampled signal (when $F_s > 2 \times F_{max}$).

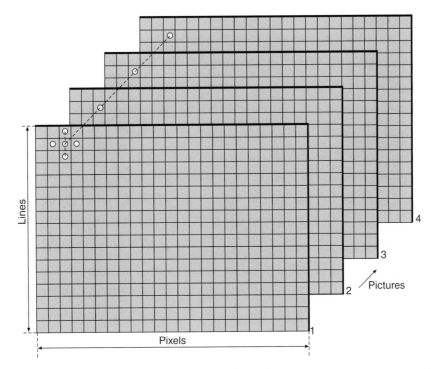

**Figure 2.2** Orthogonal sampling structure of a picture.

so are situated on a rectangular grid. For this reason, this sampling method is called orthogonal sampling (Fig. 2.2), as opposed to other sampling schemes used for composite video sampling ($4 \times F_{sc}$ subcarrier locked sampling for instance).

The most economic method in terms of bit-rate for video signal digitization seems, *a priori*, to be to use the composite signal as a source; however, the quality will be limited by its composite nature. Taking into account the fact that 8 bits (corresponding to 256 quantization steps) is the minimum required for a good signal to quantization noise ratio ($S_v/N_q = {}^*59$ dB; Note 2.3), the bit rate required by this composite digitization is $13.5 \times 8 = 108$ Mb/s, which is already a lot!

However, digitization of a composite signal has little advantage over its analog form for production purposes (practically the only one is the possibility of multiple copies without degradation). Therefore, this is not the preferred method for source signal digitization in broadcast applications, as the composite signal is not very suitable for most signal manipulations (editing, compression) or international exchanges.

## 2.2.1   The 4:2:2 format

Recommendation CCIR-601, established in 1982, defines digitization parameters for video signals in component form based on a Y, $C_b$, $C_r$ signal in 4:2:2 format (four Y samples for two $C_b$ samples and two $C_r$ samples) with 8 bits per sample (with a provision for extension to 10 bits per sample). The sampling frequency is 13.5 MHz for luminance and 6.75 MHz for chrominance, regardless of the standard of the input signal. This results in 720 active video samples per line for luminance, and 360 active samples per line for each chrominance. The position of the chrominance samples corresponds to the odd samples of the luminance (see Fig. 2.3).

Chrominance signals $C_r$ and $C_b$ being simultaneously available at every line, vertical resolution for chrominance is the same

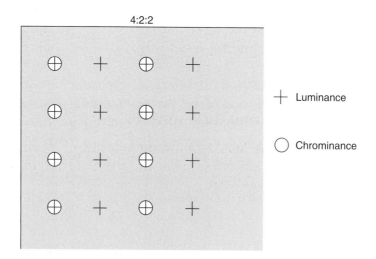

**Figure 2.3**   Position of samples in the 4:2:2 format.

as for luminance (480 lines for 525-line systems, 576 lines for 625-line systems). The total bit-rate resulting from this process is $13.5 \times 8 + 2 \times 6.75 \times 8 = 216\,\text{Mb/s}$. With a quantization of 10 bits, the bit-rate becomes 270 Mb/s! However, if one takes into account the redundancy involved in digitizing the inactive part of the video signal (horizontal and vertical blanking periods), the useful bit-rate goes down to 166 Mb/s with 8 bits per sample. These horizontal and vertical blanking periods can be filled with other useful data, such as digital sound, sync, and other information.

Recommendation CCIR-656 defines standardized electrical interfacing conditions for 4:2:2 signals digitized according to recommendation CCIR-601. This is the format used for interfacing D1 digital video recorders, and is therefore sometimes referred to as the *D1 format*.

The parallel version of this recommendation provides the signal in a multiplexed form $(C_{r1}, Y_1, C_{b1}, Y_2, C_{r3}, Y_3, C_{b3}\ldots)$ on an 8-bit parallel interface, together with a 27 MHz clock (one clock period per sample). Synchronization and other data are included in the data flow. The normalized connector is a DB25 plug.

There is also a serial form of the CCIR-656 interface for transmission on a 75 $\Omega$ coaxial cable with BNC connectors, requiring a slightly higher bit-rate (243 Mb/s) due to the use of 9 bits per sample in this mode.

## 2.2.2   4:2:0, SIF, CIF, and QCIF formats

For applications that are less demanding in terms of resolution, and in view of the bit-rate reduction, a certain number of *byproducts* of the 4:2:2 format have been defined, as follows.

### The 4:2:0 format

This format is obtained from the 4:2:2 format by using the same chroma samples for two successive lines, in order to reduce the amount of memory required in processing circuitry while at the same time giving a vertical resolution of the same order as the horizontal resolution. Luminance and horizontal chrominance resolutions are the same as for the 4:2:2 format, and thus

- luminance resolution: $720 \times 576$ (625 lines) or $720 \times 480$ (525 lines);

- chrominance resolution: $360 \times 288$ (625 lines) or $360 \times 240$ (525 lines).

Figure 2.4 shows the position of chroma samples in the 4:2:0 format.

In order to avoid the chrominance line flickering observed in SECAM at sharp horizontal transients (due to the fact that one chrominance comes from the current line and the second comes from the preceding one), $C_b$ and $C_r$ samples are obtained by interpolating 4:2:2 samples of the two successive lines they will "color-ize" at display time.

This 4:2:0 format is of special importance as it is the input format used for D2-MAC and MPEG-2 (MP@ML) coding.

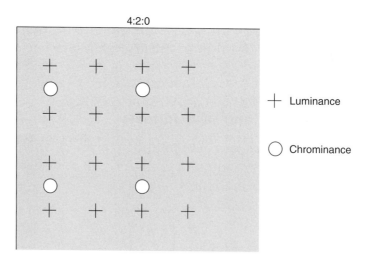

**Figure 2.4**  Position of samples in the 4:2:0 format.

## The SIF (source intermediate format)

This format is obtained by halving the spatial resolution in both directions as well as the temporal resolution, which becomes 25 Hz for 625-line systems and 29.97 Hz for 525-line systems. Depending on the originating standard, the spatial resolutions are then:

- luminance resolution: $360 \times 288$ (625 lines) or $360 \times 240$ (525 lines);

- chrominance resolution: $180 \times 144$ (625 lines) or $180 \times 120$ (525 lines).

Figure 2.5 illustrates the position of the samples in the SIF format. Horizontal resolution is obtained by filtering and subsampling the input signal. The reduction in temporal and vertical resolution is normally obtained by interpolating samples of the odd and even fields, but is sometimes achieved by simply dropping every second field of the interlaced input format. The resolution obtained is the base for MPEG-1 encoding, and is resulting in a so-called "VHS-like" quality in terms of resolution.

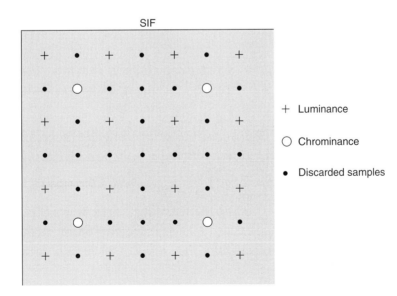

**Figure 2.5** Position of samples in the SIF format.

## The CIF (common intermediate format)

This is a compromise between European and American SIF formats: spatial resolution is taken from the 625-line SIF ($360 \times 288$) and temporal resolution from the 525-line SIF (29.97 Hz). It is the basis used for video conferencing.

## The QCIF (quarter CIF)

Once again, this reduces the spatial resolution by 4 (2 in each direction) and the temporal resolution by 2 or 4 (15 or 7.5 Hz). It is the input format used for ISDN videotelephony using the H261 compression algorithm.

### 2.2.3 High definition formats 720p, 1080i

After a few false starts (MUSE, HD-MAC, ATSC to some degree) the conditions necessary to engender wide-scale adoption of high-definition television (**HDTV**) seem to have finally been met.

Two standard picture formats have been retained for broadcast HDTV applications, each existing in two variants (59.94 Hz or 50 Hz depending on continent):

- The 720p format: this is a progressive scan format with a horizontal resolution of 1280 pixels and a vertical resolution of 720 lines (or pixels).

- The 1280i format: this interlaced format offers a horizontal resolution of 1920 pixels and a vertical resolution of 1080 lines (or pixels).

For these two formats, the horizontal and vertical resolution are equivalent (*square pixels*) because they have the same ratio as the aspect ratio of the picture (16:9).

A quick calculation of the required bit-rate for the digitization in 4:4:4 format of these two HD formats gives bit-rates on the order of

1 to 1.5 Gb/s depending on the frame rate and resolution, which is 4 to 5 times greater than for standard-definition interlaced video.

## 2.3 Transport problems

It is clear that a bit-rate of the order of 200 Mb/s, as required by the 4:2:2 format, cannot be used for direct broadcast to the end user, as it would occupy a bandwidth of the order of 40 MHz with a 64-QAM modulation (6 bits/symbol) used for cable, or 135 MHz with a QPSK modulation (2 bits/symbol) used for satellite. This would represent 5–6 times the bandwidth required for transmission of an analog PAL or SECAM signal, and does not even take into account any error correction algorithm (these concepts will be explained later in Chapters 6 and 7 on channel coding and modulation). It would of course be even more unthinkable with the 4 to 5 times higher bit-rates generated by the digitization of high-definition pictures in 720p or 1080i format.

Compression algorithms, however, have been in use for some years for contribution links in the field of professional video, which reduce this bit-rate to 34 Mb/s, but this is still too high for consumer applications, as it does not give any advantage in terms of capacity over existing analog transmissions. It was the belief that this problem would not be solved economically in the foreseeable future (in large part due to the cost of the memory size required) that gave birth in the 1980s to hybrid standards such as D2-MAC (analog video, digital sound) and delayed the introduction of 100 % digital video. However, the very rapid progress made in compression techniques and IC technology in the second half of the 1980s made these systems obsolete soon after their introduction.

The essential conditions required to start digital television broadcast services were the development of technically and economically viable solutions to problems which can be classified into two main categories:

- *Source coding.* This is the technical term for compression. It encompasses all video and audio compression techniques used

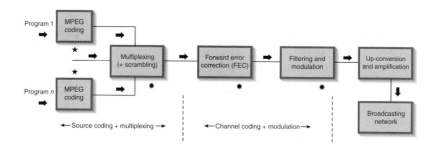

**Figure 2.6** Sequence of main operations on the broadcasting side.

to reduce as much as possible the bit-rate (in terms of Mb/s required to transmit moving pictures of a given resolution and the associated sound) with the lowest perceptible degradation in quality.

- *Channel coding.* This consists of developing powerful error correction algorithms associated with the most spectrally efficient modulation techniques (in terms of Mb/s per MHz), taking into account the available bandwidth and the foreseeable imperfections of the transmission channel.

Taking into account the fact that many programs can be transmitted on one RF channel, the sequence of operations to be performed on the transmitter side is roughly as illustrated in Figure 2.6. We will follow the order of the functional boxes in this figure when we discuss them in the following chapters.

**Note 2.1**

The CCIR was the radiocommunication branch of the former **CCITT** (Comité Consultatif International du Télégraphe et du Téléphone), recently renamed the ITU (International Telecommunications Union). The CCIR is now called the ITU-R.

**Note 2.2**

For some multimedia applications (video in PCs mainly), other sampling frequencies are often used in order to obtain so-called

**square pixels** to ease mixing of live video and computer images without aspect ratio distortion. In fact, the aspect ratio of a standard TV picture and of a computer display is 4/3 (ratio of the width to the height of the picture); in order to have identical resolutions in the horizontal and vertical directions, which is the case for today's computer display formats, it is necessary that the ratio of the number of pixels per line to the number of useful lines be 4/3. This is not the case for CCIR-601 derived formats, either in 625-line standards (720/576 < 4/3) or in 525-line standards (720/480 > 4/3).

For 525-line standards (480 useful lines), square pixels imply $480 \times 4/3 = 640$ pixels/line, which is obtained with a sampling frequency of 12.2727 MHz. This is not an accident since this resolution of $640 \times 480$ corresponds to the basic VGA graphics mode—this mode is, in fact, an *uninterlaced* or progressive variant of the NTSC scanning standard (line frequency = 31,468 Hz, frame frequency = 59.94 Hz). For 625-line standards (576 useful lines), square pixels imply $576 \times 4/3 = 768$ pixels/line, which requires a sampling frequency of 14.75 MHz.

The 720p and 1080i high-definition formats which have the same ratio between their horizontal and vertical pixel numbers as the aspect ratio of the picture (16:9) are *square-pixel* formats.

## Note 2.3
*Dynamic*
The dynamic $D$ of a signal with a maximum peak-to-peak amplitude $F_{PP}$, quantized with $m$ steps (with $m = 2^b$, where $b$ is the number of bits of the quantization), is the ratio between $V_{PP}$ and the maximum peak value of the quantization error, which is equal to the quantization step $Q$.

By definition, $Q$ is equal to the maximum peak-to-peak amplitude $F_{PP}$ divided by the number of quantization steps $m$, i.e., $Q = V_{PP}/m = V_{PP}/2^b$. Hence, the dynamic $D$ (in dB) is equal to

$$D(\text{dB}) = 20 \times \log(V_{\text{PP}}/Q) = 20 \times \log(V_{\text{PP}} \times 2^b/V_{\text{PP}})$$

$$= 20 \times \log 2^b = b \times 20 \times \log 2$$

Hence

$$D \cong b \times 6 \text{ dB}$$

*Example 1 (video). A quantization with 8 bits (b = 8) results in*
$D \cong 48 \, dB.$

*Example 2 (audio). A quantization with 16 bits (b = 16) results in*
$D \cong dB.$

*Signal to quantization noise ratio*

If $Q$ is the quantization step, the **quantization noise** voltage $N_q$ is equal to $Q/\sqrt{12}$.

For a video signal, $V_{\text{PP}}$ is equal to the black-to-white amplitude $V_{\text{BW}}$, and so $Q = V_{\text{BW}}/m = V_{\text{BW}}/2^b$. The signal-to-quantization noise ratio, $S_V/N_q$, is the ratio of the black-to-white signal $F_{\text{BW}}$ to the quantization noise voltage $N_q$:

$$S_V/N_q(\text{dB}) = 20 \times \log(V_{\text{BW}} \times 2^b \times \sqrt{12}/V_{\text{BW}})$$
$$= 20 \times \log(2^b \times \sqrt{12}) \cong b \times 6 + 20 \times \log \sqrt{12}$$

or

$$S_V/N_q \cong D + 10.8 \, \text{dB}$$

Therefore, in the case of Example 1 above (video signal quantized with 8 bits), $D \cong 48 \, \text{dB}$ and $S_V/N_q \cong 58.8 \, \text{dB}$.

For an audio signal, the signal-to-quantization noise ratio, $S_A/N_q$, is the ratio of the root mean square (RMS) signal $V_{\text{RMS}}$ to the quantization noise voltage $N_q$. If we assume a sinusoidal signal of maximum peak-to-peak amplitude $V_{PP}$, the corresponding maximum RMS voltage is $V_{RMS} = V_{PP}/2y/2$. Thus

$$S_A/N_q(\text{dB}) = 20 \times \log(V_{PP} \times 2^b \times \sqrt{12}/V_{PP} \times 2\sqrt{2})$$

$$= 20 \times \log(2^b \times \sqrt{12}/2\sqrt{2}) \text{ or}$$

$$S_A/N_q(dB) \cong b \times 6 + 20(\log \sqrt{12} - \log 2\sqrt{2}) \cong D + 20 \times 0.09$$

$$S_A/N_q \cong D + 1.8 \text{ dB}$$

Thus, in the case of Example 2 (audio signal quantized with 16 bits), $D \cong 96$ dB and $S_A/N_q \cong 97.8$ dB.

# Source coding: compression of video and audio signals

# 3

In the preceding chapter, we explained why compression was an absolute must in order to be able to broadcast TV pictures in a channel of acceptable width. A spectrum bandwidth comparable to conventional analog broadcasts (6–8 MHz for cable or terrestrial broadcasts, 27–36 MHz for satellite) implies in practice maximum bit-rates of the order of 30–40 Mb/s, with the necessary error correction algorithms and modulation schemes, which are explained in Chapters 6 and 7.

We will now examine the principles and various steps of video and audio compression which allow these bit-rates (and in fact much less) to be achieved, and which are currently being used in the various video/audio compression standards. These compression methods use general data compression algorithms applicable to any kind of data, and exploit the spatial redundancy (correlation of neighboring points within an image) and the specificities of visual perception (lack of sensitivity of the eye to fine details) for fixed pictures (JPEG), and the very high temporal redundancy between successive images in the case of moving pictures (MPEG). In the same way, audio compression methods exploit particularities of the human aural perception to reduce bit-rates by eliminating inaudible information (psychoacoustic coding).

## 3.1  Some general data compression principles

### 3.1.1  Run length coding (RLC)

When an information source emits successive message elements which can deliver relatively long series of identical elements (which, as explained later in this chapter, is the case with the DCT after thresholding and quantization), it is advantageous to transmit the code of this element and the number of successive occurrences rather than to repeat the code of the element; this gives a variable compression factor (the longer the series, the bigger the compression factor). This type of coding which does not lose any information is defined as reversible. This method is commonly employed for file compression related to disk storage or transmission by computers (zip, etc.); it is also the method used in fax machines.

### 3.1.2  Variable length coding (VLC) or entropy coding

This bit-rate reduction method is based on the fact that the probability of occurrence of an element generated by a source and coded on $n$ bits is sometimes not the same (i.e., equiprobable) for all elements among the $2^n$ different possibilities. This means that, in order to reduce the bit-rate required to transmit the sequences generated by the source, it is advantageous to encode the most frequent elements with less than $n$ bits and the less frequent elements with more bits, resulting in an average length that is less than a fixed length of $n$ bits.

However, if this is to be done in real time, it implies a previous knowledge of the probability of occurrence of each possible element generated by the source. We have this knowledge, for example, in the case of the letters of the alphabet in a given language, and this allows this method to be used for text compression. This method is also valid for video images compressed by means of DCT, where energy is concentrated on a relatively small number of coefficients, as opposed to the temporal representation of the video signal where all values are almost equiprobable.

One can demonstrate that the information quantity $Q$ transmitted by an element is equal to the logarithm (base 2) of the inverse of its probability of appearance $p$:

$$Q = \log_2(1/p) = -\log_2(p)$$

The sum of the information quantity of all elements generated by a source multiplied by their probability of appearance is called the entropy, $H$, of the source:

$$H = \sum_i pi \log_2(1/pi)$$

The goal of variable length coding (**VLC**), or entropy coding, is to approach, as near as is possible, the entropic bit-rate (corresponding to an averaged number of bits per element as near as possible to the source's entropy). The most well-known method for variable length coding is the Huffmann algorithm (illustrated in Fig. 3.1), which assumes previous knowledge of the probability of each element. It works in the following way:

- Each element is classified in order of decreasing probability, forming an "occurrence table" (left part of Fig. 3.1).

- The two elements of lowest probability are then grouped into one element, the probability of which is the sum of the two probabilities. Bit 0 is attributed to the element of lowest probability and 1 to the other element; this reduces by one the number of elements to be classified.

- The new element is then grouped in the same way with the element having the next highest probability. 0 and 1 are attributed in the same way as above, and the process is continued until all the elements have been coded (sum of the probability of the last two elements = 100%).

- In this way, the Huffmann coding tree is built (central part of Fig. 3.1): the code for each element is obtained by positioning sequentially the bits encountered in moving along the Huffmann tree from left to right.

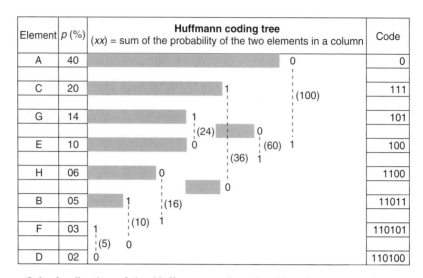

| Element | p (%) | Huffmann coding tree (xx) = sum of the probability of the two elements in a column | Code |
|---|---|---|---|
| A | 40 | 0 | 0 |
| C | 20 | 1 (100) | 111 |
| G | 14 | 1 (24) | 101 |
| E | 10 | 0 (60) 1 (36) 1 | 100 |
| H | 06 | 0 0 | 1100 |
| B | 05 | 1 (16) | 11011 |
| F | 03 | 1 (10) 1 | 110101 |
| D | 02 | (5) 0 0 | 110100 |

**Figure 3.1** Application of the Huffmann coding algorithm (gray zones indicate horizontal links).

To illustrate this method, we have assumed a source generating eight elements with the following probabilities: $p(A) = 40\%$, $p(B) = 50\%$, $p(C) = 20\%$, $p(D) = 2\%$, $p(E) = 10\%$, $p(F) = 3\%$, $p(G) = 14\%$, $p(H) = 6\%$. In this example, the average word length after coding (sum of the products of the number of bits of each element and its probability) is 2.51 bits, while the entropy $H = \sum_i Pi \log_2(1/pi)$ is equal to 2.44 bits; this is only 3% more than the optimum, a very good efficiency for the Huffmann algorithm. In this example with eight elements, a pure binary coding would require 3 bits per element, so the compression factor $\eta$ achieved with the Huffmann coding is

$$\eta = 2.51/3.00 = 83.7\%$$

This type of coding is reversible (it does not lose information) and can be applied to video signals as a complement to other methods which generate elements of non-uniform probability (DCT followed by quantization for instance). The overall gain can then be much more important.

## 3.2  Compression applied to images: the discrete cosine transform (DCT)

The discrete cosine transform is a particular case of the Fourier transform applied to discrete (sampled) signals, which decomposes a periodic signal into a series of sine and cosine harmonic functions. The signal can then be represented by a series of coefficients of each of these functions.

Without developing the mathematical details, we will simply indicate that, under certain conditions, the DCT decomposes the signal into only one series of harmonic cosine functions in phase with the signal, which reduces by half the number of coefficients necessary to describe the signal compared to a Fourier transform.

In the case of pictures, the original signal is a sampled bidimensional signal, and so we will also have a bidimensional DCT (horizontal and vertical directions), which will transform the luminance (or chrominance) discrete values of a block of $N \times N$ pixels into another block (or matrix) of $N \times N$ coefficients representing the amplitude of each of the cosine harmonic functions.

In the transformed block, coefficients on the horizontal axis represent increasing horizontal frequencies from left to right, and on the vertical axis they represent increasing vertical frequencies from top to bottom. The first coefficient in the top left corner (coordinates: 0, 0) represents null horizontal and vertical frequencies, and is therefore called the DC coefficient, and the bottom right coefficient represents the highest spatial frequency component in the two directions.

In order to reduce the complexity of the circuitry and the processing time required, the block size chosen is generally $8 \times 8$ pixels (Fig. 3.2), which the DCT transforms into a matrix of $8 \times 8$ coefficients (Fig. 3.3).

A visual representation of the individual contribution of each coefficient to the appearance of the original block of $8 \times 8$ pixels can be

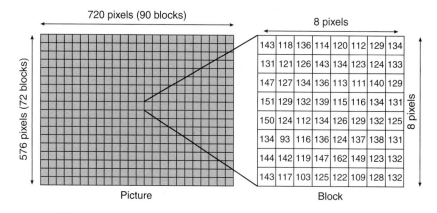

**Figure 3.2** Cutting out blocks of 8 × 8 pixels (values represent the luminance of a pixel).

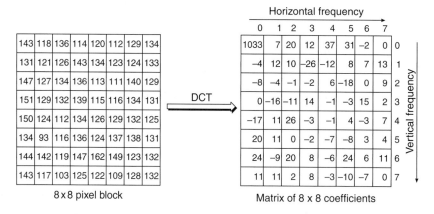

**Figure 3.3** Transformation of a block of 8 × 8 pixels into a matrix of 8 × 8 coefficients using the DCT.

seen in Figure 3.4: the appearance of the original picture block can be obtained by averaging each of the 64 squares in Figure 3.4 by its coefficient and summing the results.

Depending on the number of details contained in the original block, the high frequency coefficients will be bigger or smaller, but generally the amplitude decreases rather quickly with the frequency, due to the smaller energy of high spatial frequencies in most "natural" images. The DCT thus has the remarkable property of concentrating the energy of the block on a relatively low number of coefficients

Horizontal frequency

Vertical frequency

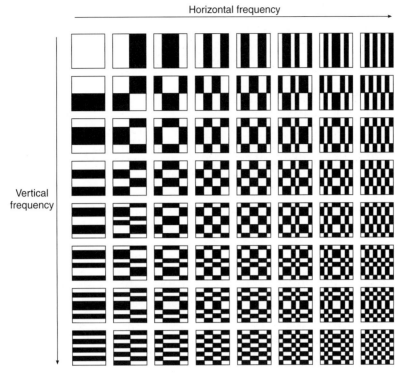

**Figure 3.4** Contribution of each of the DCT coefficients to the appearance of the 8 × 8 pixel block.

situated in the top left corner of the matrix. In addition, these coefficients are decorrelated from each other. These two properties will be used to advantage in the next steps of the compression process.

Up to this point, there is no information loss: the DCT transform process is reversible. However, due to the psychophysiological specificities of human vision (reduced sensitivity to high spatial frequencies), it is possible, without perceptible degradation of the picture quality, to eliminate the values below a certain threshold function of the frequency. The eliminated values are replaced by 0 (an operation known as thresholding); this part of the process is obviously not reversible, as some data are thrown away. The remaining coefficients are then quantized with an accuracy decreasing with the increasing spatial frequencies, which once again reduces the

| 1033 | 7 | 20 | 12 | 37 | 31 | −2 | 0 |
|---|---|---|---|---|---|---|---|
| −4 | 12 | 10 | −26 | −12 | 8 | 7 | 13 |
| −8 | −4 | −1 | −2 | 6 | −18 | 0 | 9 |
| 0 | −16 | −11 | 14 | −1 | −3 | 15 | 2 |
| −17 | 11 | 26 | −3 | −1 | 4 | −3 | 7 |
| 20 | 11 | 0 | −2 | −7 | −8 | 3 | 4 |
| 24 | −9 | 20 | 8 | −6 | 24 | 6 | 11 |
| 11 | 11 | 2 | 8 | −3 | −10 | −7 | 0 |

Thresholding
+ quantization
⟹

| 129 | 1 | 1 | 1 | 2 | 1 | 0 | 0 |
|---|---|---|---|---|---|---|---|
| 0 | 1 | 1 | −1 | −1 | 0 | 0 | 0 |
| 0 | 0 | 0 | 0 | 0 | −1 | 0 | 0 |
| 0 | −1 | 0 | 1 | 0 | 0 | 0 | 0 |
| −1 | 0 | 1 | 0 | 0 | 0 | 0 | 0 |
| 1 | 0 | 0 | 0 | 0 | 0 | 0 | 0 |
| −1 | 0 | 1 | 0 | 0 | 1 | 0 | 0 |
| 0 | 0 | 0 | 0 | 0 | 0 | 0 | 0 |

**Figure 3.5** Result of thresholding and quantization.

quantity of information required to encode a block; here again the process is not reversible, but it has little effect on the perceived picture quality. The thresholding/quantization process is illustrated in Figure 3.5. The thresholding and quantization parameters can be used dynamically to regulate the bit-rate required to transmit moving pictures, as will be explained in Section 3.4.

A serial bitstream is obtained by "zig-zag" reading of the coefficients, as shown in Figure 3.6. This method is one of those allowing a

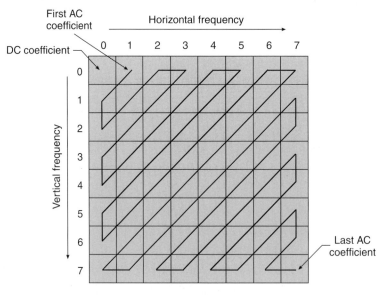

**Figure 3.6** "Zig-zag" reading of the coefficients of the matrix.

relatively long series of null coefficients to be obtained as quickly as possible, in order to increase the efficiency of the following steps—run length coding followed by variable length coding (see Section 3.1).

## 3.3  Compression of fixed pictures

The first applications aimed at reducing the amount of information required for coding fixed pictures appeared in the 1980s, and they had as their primary objective the significant reduction of the size of graphics files and photographs in view of storing or transmitting them. In 1990, the **ISO** (International Standards Organization) created an international working group called **JPEG** (Joint Photographic Experts Group) which had the task of elaborating an international compression standard for fixed pictures of various resolutions in Y, $C_r$, $C_b$, or RGB format. The resulting international standard (widely known as JPEG) was published in 1993 under the reference ISO/IEC 10918, and it can be considered a toolbox for fixed picture compression. We will not describe it in detail because it is not the object of this book, but we will nevertheless go through its main steps, as it has largely inspired the way in which **MPEG** works.

It should be noted that JPEG compression can be either **lossy** or **lossless** (reversible), depending on the application and the desired compression factor. Most common applications use the lossy method, which allows compression factors of more than 10 to be achieved without noticeable picture quality degradation, depending on the picture content. We will only examine the case of lossy JPEG compression, as the coding of **I** (intra) pictures of MPEG uses the same process; lossless JPEG compression uses a different predictive coding which is not based on DCT, so we will not discuss it here.

Lossy JPEG compression can be described in six main steps:

1.  *Decomposition of the picture into blocks.* The picture, generally in Y, $C_b$, $C_r$ format, is divided into elementary blocks of $8 \times 8$ pixels (Fig. 3.2), which represents for a 4:2:2 CCIR-601 picture a total number of 6480 luminance (Y) blocks and 3240

blocks for each $C_r$ and $C_b$ component. Each block is made up of 64 numbers ranging from 0 to 255 (when digitized on 8 bits) for luminance, and $-128$ to $+127$ for chrominance $C_r$ and $C_b$.

2. *Discrete cosine transform.* As explained previously, the DCT applied to each Y, $C_b$, $C_r$ block generates for each one a new $8 \times 8$ matrix made up of the coefficients of increasing spatial frequency as one moves away from the origin (upper left corner) which contains the DC component representing the average luminance or chrominance of the block. The value of these coefficients decreases quickly when going away from the origin of the matrix, and the final values are generally a series of small numbers or even zeros. So, if the block is of uniform luminance or chrominance, only the DC coefficient will not be zero, and only this coefficient will have to be transmitted.

3. *Thresholding and quantization.* This step takes into account the specificities of human vision, particularly the fact that the eye does not distinguish fine details below a certain luminance level. It consists of zeroing the coefficients below a predetermined threshold, and quantizing the remaining ones with decreasing accuracy as the frequency increases. Contrary to the 63 other (AC) coefficients, the DC coefficient is **DPCM** coded (differential pulse code modulation) relative to the DC coefficient of the previous block, which allows a more accurate coding with a given number of bits. This allows the visibility of the blocks on the reconstructed picture to be reduced, as the eye, although not very sensitive to fine details, is nevertheless very sensitive to small luminance differences on uniform zones.

4. *Zig-zag scan.* Except for the DC coefficient, which is treated separately, the 63 AC coefficients are read using a zig-zag scan (Fig. 3.6) in order to transform the matrix into a flow of data best suited for the next coding steps (RLC/VLC).

5. *Run length coding.* In order to make the best possible use of the long series of zeros produced by the quantization and the zig-zag scan, the number of occurrences of zero is coded, followed

by the next non-zero value, which reduces the amount of information to transmit.

6. *Variable length coding (Huffmann coding).* This last step uses a conversion table in order to encode the most frequently occurring values with a short length, and the less frequent values with a longer one. These last two steps (RLC and VLC) alone ensure a compression factor of between 2 and 3.

When the compression/decompression time is not of prime importance, which is often the case for fixed pictures, all the above-described steps can be done entirely using software. There are, however, a number of specialized processors which can speed up this process a great deal. The simplified principle of a JPEG decoder can be seen in the block diagram in Figure 3.7.

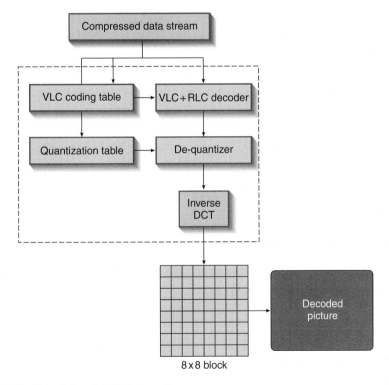

**Figure 3.7** Principle of JPEG decoding.

## 3.4   Compression of moving pictures (MPEG)

In 1990, the need to store and reproduce moving pictures and the associated sound in digital format for multimedia applications on various platforms led the ISO to form an expert group along the same lines as JPEG, with members coming from the numerous branches involved (computer industry, telecoms, consumer electronics, semi-conductors, broadcasters, universities, etc.); this group was called **MPEG** (Motion Pictures Experts Group).

The first outcome of its work was the International Standard ISO/IEC 11172, widely known as MPEG-1. The main goal was to allow the storage on CD-ROM or CD-I (single speed at that time) of live video and stereo sound, which implied a maximum bit-rate of 1.5 Mb/s. In addition to the intrinsic spatial redundancy exploited by JPEG for fixed pictures, coding of moving pictures allows exploitation of the very important temporal redundancy between successive pictures which make up a video sequence.

Given the very high compression rate objective for these applications (more than 100 compared to the original 4:2:2/CCIR 601 picture), the difficulty of the task is reduced from the beginning of the process by sacrificing the resolution. The format chosen for the pictures to be encoded is the SIF format (described in Section 2.2.2—uninterlaced pictures, $360 \times 288 @ 25$ Hz or $360 \times 240 @ 30$ Hz depending on the original video standard), which corresponds roughly to the resolution of a consumer video recorder.

The sound compression algorithm used for the accompanying audio channels is known as **MUSICAM**, also used in the European digital radio system (**DAB**, Digital Audio Broadcasting). We will examine the principles of audio compression in Section 3.5.

The MPEG-1 standard consists of three distinct parts, published in November 1992:

- MPEG-1 system (ISO/IEC 11172-1): defines the MPEG-1 multiplex structure (cf. Chapter 4);

- MPEG-1 video (ISO/IEC 13818-2): defines MPEG-2 video coding;

- MPEG-1 audio (ISO/IEC 13818-3): defines MPEG-2 audio coding.

However, the picture quality of MPEG-1 was not suitable for broadcast applications, since, among other things, it did not take into account the coding of interlaced pictures or evolution toward HDTV. The MPEG group thus worked on the definition of a flexible standard optimized for broadcasting. This international standard is known as MPEG-2.

As its predecessor, MPEG-2 is specified in three distinct parts, published in November 1994:

- MPEG-2 system (ISO/IEC 13818-1): defines the MPEG-2 streams (cf. Chapter 4);

- MPEG-2 video (ISO/IEC 13818-2): defines MPEG-2 video coding;

- MPEG-2 audio (ISO/IEC 13818-3): defines MPEG-2 audio coding.

MPEG-2 is, among other things, the source coding standard used by the European DVB (Digital Video Broadcasting) TV broadcasting system, which is the result of the work started in 1991 by the ELG (European Launching Group), later to become the DVB committee.

### 3.4.1  Principles behind the video coding of MPEG-1 (multimedia applications)

As indicated previously, the main objective for MPEG-1 was to reach a medium quality video with a constant total bit-rate of 1.5 Mb/s for storing video and audio on CD-ROM. The video part uses 1.15 Mb/s, the remaining 350 kb/s being used by audio and additional data required by the system and other information. However, the MPEG-1 specification is very flexible and allows different parameters to be chosen depending on the compromise between encoder complexity, compression rate, and quality.

The video coding uses the same principles as lossy JPEG, to which new techniques are added to form the MPEG-1 "toolbox"; these techniques exploit the strong correlation between successive pictures in order to considerably reduce the amount of information required to transmit or store them. These techniques, known as "prediction with movement compensation," consist of deducing most of the pictures of a sequence from preceding and even subsequent pictures, with a minimum of additional information representing the differences between pictures. This requires the presence in the MPEG encoder of a **movement estimator**, which is the most complex function and greatly determines the encoder's performance; fortunately, this function is not required in the decoder.

As we are talking about moving pictures, decoding has to be accomplished in real time (this means an acceptable and constant processing delay); this implies, for the time being at least, some specialized hardware. The coding, which is much more complex, can be done in more than one pass for applications where real time is not required but where quality is of prime importance (engraving of disks for instance); real time (which does not mean null processing time) will, however, be required for many applications, such as live video transmissions.

The practical realization of the encoder is therefore a trade-off between speed, compression rate, complexity, and picture quality. In addition, synchronization time and random access time to a sequence have to be maintained within an acceptable limit (not exceeding 0.5 s), which restricts the maximum number of pictures that can be dependent on the first picture to between 10 and 12 for a system operating at 25 pictures/s.

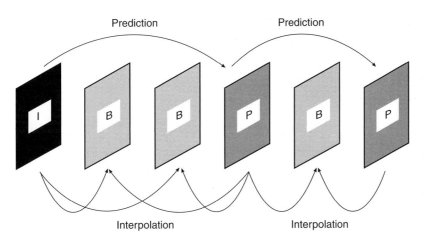

**Figure 3.8** Concatenation of the three types of pictures in MPEG.

## The different types of MPEG pictures

MPEG defines three types of pictures (Note 3.1) which are arranged as shown in Figure 3.8.

- **I (intra) pictures** are coded without reference to other pictures, in a very similar manner to JPEG, which means that they contain all the information necessary for their reconstruction by the decoder; for this reason, they are the essential entry point for access to a video sequence. The compression rate of I pictures is relatively low, and is comparable to a JPEG coded picture of a similar resolution.

- **P (predicted) pictures** are coded from the preceding I or P picture, using the techniques of motion-compensated prediction. P pictures can be used as the basis for next predicted pictures, but since motion compensation is not perfect, it is not possible to extend the number of P pictures between two I pictures a great deal. The compression rate of P pictures is significantly higher than for I pictures.

- **B (bi-directional or bi-directionally predicted) pictures** are coded by bi-directional interpolation between the I or P picture which precedes and follows them. As they are not used for coding subsequent pictures, B pictures do not propagate coding errors. B pictures offer the highest compression rate.

- Depending on the complexity of the encoder used, it is possible to encode I only, I and P, or I, P, and B pictures, with very different results with regard to compression rate and random access resolution, and also with regard to encoding time and perceived quality.

- Two parameters, $M$ and $N$, describe the succession of I, P, and B pictures (Fig. 3.9).

- $M$ is the distance (in number of pictures) between two successive P pictures.

- $N$ is the distance between two successive I pictures, defining a "group of pictures" (**GOP**).

The parameters generally used are $M = 3$ and $N = 12$, in order to obtain a satisfactory video quality with an acceptable random access time ($<0.5$ s) within a bit-rate of $1.15$ Mb/s. With these parameters, a video sequence is made up as follows: $1/12$ of its pictures are I pictures (8.33%), $1/4$ are P pictures (25%), and $2/3$ are B pictures (66%); the global compression rate is maximized by the fact that the most frequent pictures have the highest compression rate.

### Re-ordering of the pictures

It is obvious that the sequence of the pictures after decoding has to be in the same order as the original sequence before encoding. With

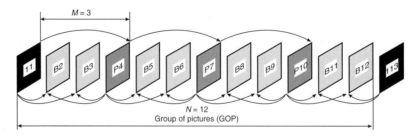
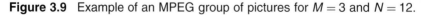

**Figure 3.9**   Example of an MPEG group of pictures for $M = 3$ and $N = 12$.

the above parameters ($M = 3$, $N = 12$), the correspondence between the original picture number and its coded type is as follows:

  1(I) 2(B) 3(B) 4(P) 5(B) 6(B) 7(P) 8(B) 9(B) 10(P) 11(B) 12(B) 13(I)...

However, in order to encode or decode a B (bi-directional) picture, both the encoder and the decoder will need the I or P preceding picture and the I or P subsequent picture. This requires re-ordering of the original picture sequence such that the decoder and the encoder have at their disposal the required I and/or P pictures before the B pictures are processed. The re-ordering thus gives the following sequence:

  1(I) 4(P) 2(B) 3(B) 7(P) 5(B) 6(B) 10(P) 8(B) 9(B) 13(I) 11(B) 12(B)...

The increase in compression rate permitted by the B pictures has to be paid for by an increase in encoding delay (two extra picture durations) and in the memory size required for both encoding and decoding (one extra picture to store).

## Decomposition of an MPEG video sequence in layers

MPEG defines a hierarchy of **layers** within a video sequence, as illustrated in Figure 3.10. Each of these layers has specific function(s) in the MPEG process. Starting from the top level, the successive layers are:

- **Sequence.** This is the highest layer which defines the context valid for the whole sequence (basic video parameters, etc.).

- **Group of pictures (GOP).** This is the layer determining the random access to the sequence, which always starts with an I picture. In the above example ($M = 3$, $N = 12$), the GOP is made up of 12 pictures.

- **Picture.** This is the elementary display unit, which can be of one of the three types (I, P, or B).

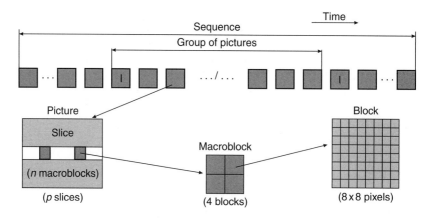

**Figure 3.10**  Hierarchy of the MPEG video layers.

- **Slice.** This is the layer for intra frame addressing and (re)synchronization, for instance for error recovery. It is defined as a suite of contiguous macroblocks. The ensemble of the slices covers the whole picture without any overlap between different slices. The size of a slice can theoretically range from one macroblock to the whole picture, but it is often a complete row of macroblocks.

- **Macroblock.** This is the layer used for movement estimation/compensation. A macroblock has a size of $16 \times 16$ pixels and is made up of four blocks of luminance and two blocks of chrominance (one $C_r$ and one $C_b$) covering the same area (Fig. 3.11).

- **Block.** As in JPEG, a picture is divided into blocks of $8 \times 8$ pixels. The block is the layer where the DCT takes place.

Owing to the division of the picture into an integer number of macroblocks, the horizontal resolution of MPEG-1/SIF is reduced to 352 pixels for luminance (22 macroblocks) from the 360 pixels of the original SIF picture, since 360 is not a multiple of 16. The effective resolution is then $352 \times 288$@25 Hz ($22 \times 18 = 396$ macroblocks) for pictures originating from 625-line systems, and $352 \times 240$@30 Hz ($22 \times 15 = 330$ macroblocks) for pictures originating from 525-line systems.

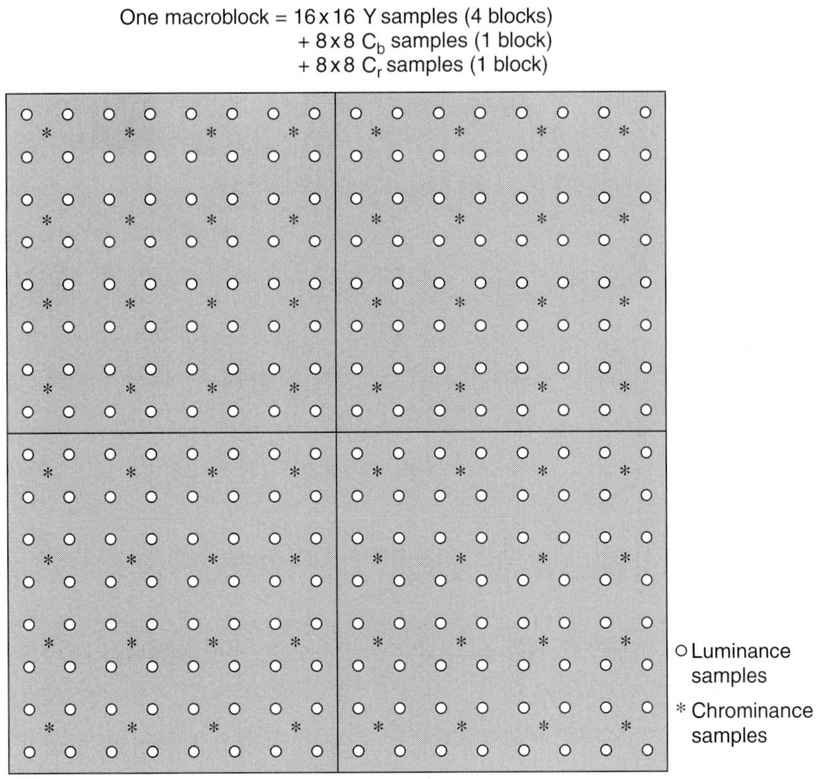

One macroblock = 16 x 16 Y samples (4 blocks)
+ 8 x 8 C$_b$ samples (1 block)
+ 8 x 8 C$_r$ samples (1 block)

○ Luminance samples

* Chrominance samples

**Figure 3.11** Composition of a 4:2:0 macroblock (Y samples, * = C$_b$ and C$_r$ samples).

## Prediction, motion estimation, and compensation

We have indicated before that P and B pictures were "predicted" from preceding and/or subsequent pictures. We will now see how.

In a sequence of moving pictures, moving objects lead to differences between corresponding zones of consecutive pictures, so that there is no obvious correlation between these two zones. *Motion estimation* consists of defining a *motion vector* which ensures the correlation between an arrival zone on the second picture and a departure zone on the first picture, using a technique known as *block matching*. This is done at the macroblock level (16 × 16 pixels) by moving a macroblock of the current picture within a small search window from the previous picture, and comparing it to all possible macroblocks

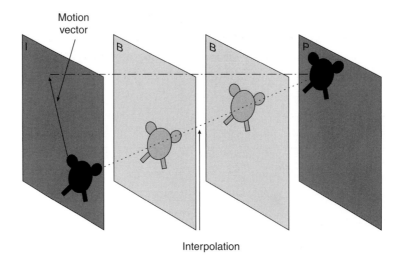

**Figure 3.12** Simplified illustration of motion compensation.

of the window in order to find the one that is most similar. The difference in position of the two matching macroblocks gives a motion vector (Fig. 3.12) which will be applied to all three components of the macroblock (Y, $C_b$, $C_r$).

In comparing a P picture and an I picture, or two P pictures, due to the temporal distance between these pictures (three pictures in the case of $M = 3$, $N = 12$), block matching will generally not be perfect and motion vectors can be of relatively high amplitude. That is why the difference (or *prediction error*) between the actual block to be encoded and the matching block is calculated and encoded in a similar way to the blocks of the I pictures (DCT, quantization, RLC/VLC). This process is called *motion compensation*.

For B pictures, motion vectors are calculated by temporal interpolation of the vectors of the next P picture in three different ways (forward, backward, and bi-directional); the result giving the smallest prediction error is retained, and the error is encoded in the same way as for P pictures. Only the macroblocks differing from the picture(s) used for prediction will need to be encoded, which substantially reduces the amount of information required for coding B and P pictures. As the size of the moving objects is generally bigger than a macroblock, there is a strong correlation between the motion vectors of consecutive blocks, and a differential coding method (DPCM) is used to encode the vectors, thus reducing the number of bits required. When the prediction does not give a usable result (for instance in the case of a moving camera where completely new zones appear in the picture), the corresponding parts of the picture are "intra" coded, in the same way as for I pictures.

## Output bit-rate control

The bitstream generated by the video (or audio) encoder is called the elementary stream (**ES**). In order to fulfill the constraints of the channel (transmission or recording/playback) and of the specified input buffer for the reference MPEG decoder, the bit-rate of this elementary stream must generally be kept constant (Note 3.2). This is not guaranteed by the coding process described above, taking into account the exceedingly differing amounts of detail and movement in the pictures to be encoded.

In order to control the bit-rate at the output of the encoder, the encoder output is equipped with a **FIFO** buffer; the amount of information held in this buffer is monitored and maintained within predetermined limits by means of a feedback loop modifying the quantization parameters, which have a major influence on the bit-rate of the encoded bitstream. In this way, it is possible to obtain a constant bit-rate, with a resolution that depends on the picture content and amount of movement in the picture (the more move-ment, the lower the resolution). A schematic block diagram of an MPEG encoder, which gives only a poor idea of its real complexity, is shown in Figure 3.13.

The decoder (Fig. 3.14) does not have to perform motion estimation and so is much simpler, which was one of the main objectives of the standard, as there will be many more decoders than encoders, the application of MPEG being mostly asymmetric.

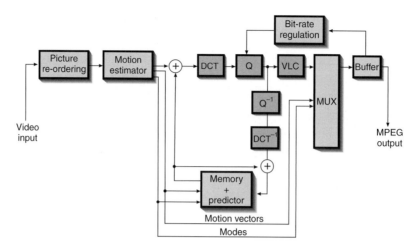

**Figure 3.13**  Schematic diagram of the MPEG encoder.

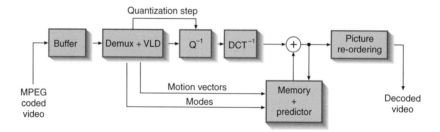

**Figure 3.14**  Schematic diagram of the MPEG decoder.

## 3.4.2  Video coding of MPEG-2 (broadcast applications)

MPEG-2 can be described as a "compression toolbox." It is more complex than MPEG-1, to which it can be considered a super-set, since it uses all the MPEG-1 tools and adds some new ones. MPEG-2 is also upward compatible with MPEG-1, which means that an MPEG-2 decoder can decode all MPEG-1–compliant elementary streams.

### MPEG-2 levels and profiles

The MPEG-2 standard has four levels which define the resolution of the picture, ranging from SIF to HDTV, and five profiles which

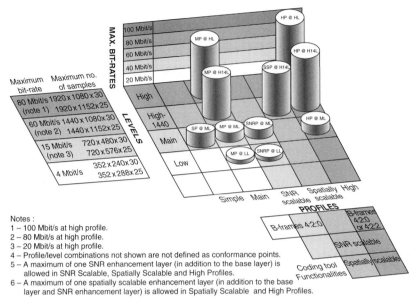

**Figure 3.15** MPEG-2 levels and profiles (Source: *Going Ahead with Digital Television*. © DVB Project Office 1995).

determine the set of compression tools used; hence, there is a compromise between compression rate and the cost of the decoder. Certain combinations of levels and profiles of little interest are not used. Figure 3.15 illustrates the main characteristics of the different levels and profiles of MPEG-2.

The four levels can be described as follows:

- the *low level* corresponds to the SIF resolution used in MPEG-1 (up to 360 × 288);

- the *main level* corresponds to standard 4:2:0 resolution (up to 720 × 576);

- the *high-1440 level* is aimed at HDTV (resolution up to 1440 × 1152);

- the *high level* is optimized for wide screen HDTV (resolution up to 1920 × 1152).

In the case of profiles, it is a little more complicated:

- The *simple profile* is defined in order to simplify the encoder and the decoder, at the expense of a higher bit-rate, as it does not use bi-directional prediction (B pictures).

- The *main profile* is the best compromise between compression rate and cost today, as it uses all three image types (I, P, B) but leads to a more complex encoder and decoder.

- The *scalable profiles* (hierarchy coding) are intended for future use. They will allow transmission of a basic quality picture (*base layer*) in terms of spatial resolution (spatially scalable profile) or quantization accuracy (SNR scalable profile), and of supplementary information (*enhanced layer*) allowing the picture characteristics to be enhanced. This could be used, for instance, to transmit in a compatible way the same program in basic resolution on standard decoders and in higher resolution on special HD decoders, or alternatively to allow a basic quality reception in the case of difficult receiving conditions and enhanced quality in good receiving conditions (terrestrial TV).

- The *high profile* is intended for HDTV broadcast applications in 4:2:0 or 4:2:2 format.

There is an ascending compatibility between profiles, and a decoder of a given profile will be able to decode all lower profiles (left part of Fig. 3.15).

The most important combination in the short term, as it is the one retained for consumer broadcast applications in Europe, is known as *main profile at main level* (MP@ML). It corresponds to MPEG-2 encoding of interlaced pictures in 4:2:0 format with a resolution of $720 \times 480@30\,\text{Hz}$ or $720 \times 576@25\,\text{Hz}$, with a toolbox including coding of I, P, and B pictures. Depending on the compromise struck between bit-rate and picture quality and the nature of the pictures to be transmitted, the bit-rate will generally be between 4 Mb/s (giving a quality similar to PAL or SECAM) and 9 Mb/s (near CCIR-601 studio quality).

Apart from the resolution of the original picture and the processing of interlaced pictures, which we will discuss later, the complete process described in Section 3.4.1 for MPEG-1 is valid for MPEG-2 (MP@ML) encoding and decoding, and in particular the layer hierarchy (from block to sequence) shown in Figure 3.10. There is a small difference, however, in the definition of the slices, as they do not necessarily cover the whole picture and are only made up of contiguous blocks of the same horizontal row (Fig. 3.16).

If we exclude the levels and profiles, the main new feature of MPEG-2 compared to MPEG-1 is the processing of interlaced pictures, which introduces some complexity and certain specific modes. For best results, interlaced pictures will have to be processed in different ways depending on the importance of movements between the two fields of a picture: the extreme cases are, on the one hand, pictures originating from cinema films, where the two fields come from the same cinema picture (at least in 50 Hz systems), and on the other, TV pictures from sporting events where differences due to motion between the two fields of a picture can be important.

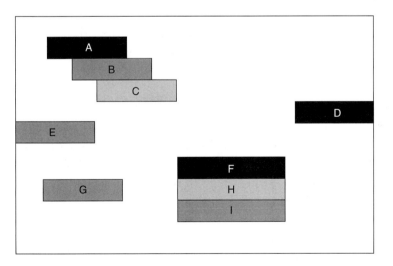

**Figure 3.16** The MPEG-2 slices in the most general case.

## MPEG-2 specific prediction modes (interlaced pictures)

The temporal sequence of the vertical position of the lines belonging to successive fields in an interlaced system is shown in Figure 3.17. For the intra coding of interlaced pictures, MPEG-2 permits one to choose between two image structures, a frame and a field:

- The frame structure (also called progressive) is best suited for cases where there is little movement between two successive fields. Macroblocks and blocks are then cut out of the complete frame (Fig. 3.18), and so the DCT is applied to consecutive vertical points separated from each other by a period of 20 ms (duration of a field in 50 Hz systems), which is no problem for the parts of the picture with little movement. In this mode, however, it is possible to code the most animated blocks in the interfield mode, which means positioning the blocks in one field only.

- The field structure (also called interlaced) is preferable when there are important movements between successive fields; in this case, in order to avoid an important high vertical frequency content which would reduce the efficiency of the compression steps following the DCT, macroblocks are cut out of one field (Fig. 3.19), which is then considered an independent picture. In the case of motion estimation, different modes are also possible; a macroblock can be predicted in frame, field, or mixed modes.

- In the frame mode, a macroblock taken from an odd field is used to predict a corresponding macroblock in the next odd field, and the same holds for even fields. The motion vectors correspond in this case to the duration of two fields (40 ms).

- In the field mode, the prediction of a macroblock is made using the preceding field, and motion vectors correspond to the duration of one field (20 ms).

- In the mixed mode, prediction is made from macroblocks belonging to two frames.

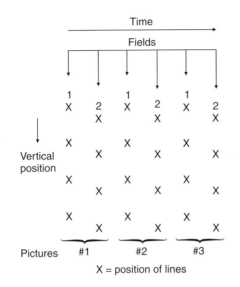

Figure 3.17   Position of lines of successive fields in an interlaced system.

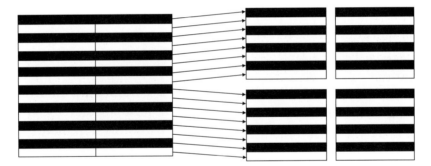

**Figure 3.18**   Cutting blocks out of macroblocks (frame mode).

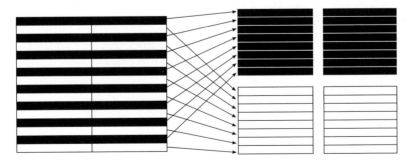

**Figure 3.19**   Cutting blocks out of macroblocks (field mode).

The diagrams of the MPEG encoder and decoder of Figures 3.13 and 3.14 also apply to MPEG-2, given the very limited level of detail which they show.

### 3.4.3   The MPEG-4.10 video compression standard (H.264/AVC)

The new MPEG-4.10 video compression standard is the result of the efforts of a Joint Video Team (JVT) that includes members of the Video Coding Expert Group (VCEG) of the l'ITU-T and of the Motion Pictures Expert Group (MPEG) of the ISO-IEC, which is the reason for its double naming (H.264 and MPEG-4.10). The standard is also often referred to as H.264/AVC (Advanced Video Coding).

This standard, registered under the number ISO-IEC 14496-10, provides a considerable increase in compression efficiency over MPEG-2 (a gain of at least 50%). This efficiency is of particular importance in view of high-definition television (HDTV), which in MPEG-2 requires a bit-rate of at least 15 to 18 Mb/s.

This is why in September 2004 the DVB consortium allowed the standard's use as an alternative to MPEG-2 for television by satellite, cable, terrestrial, or any other broadband transmission means (such as ADSL).

The H264/AVC standard consists of two layers: a video coding layer (VCL), which represents, in the most compact form possible, the video content; and a network abstraction layer (NAL), which formats the VCL representation in the form most appropriate to its destination (transport or storage).

- The *NAL layer* formats the data produced by the VCL coding into *NAL units*, which contain an integral number of bytes. Depending on the destination of the generated stream (transport stream or pure bitstream), the NAL units are preceded or not by a start prefix.

- The *VCL part* represents the proper H.264 coding. Like MPEG-1 and 2, it is a hybrid of *inter* frame compression, which exploits the temporal statistical dependencies between successive pictures and *intra* frame compression, which exploits the spatial dependencies by means of a coding method based on a transform of the prediction residual. In the mixed mode, prediction is made from macroblocks belonging to two frames.

Like MPEG-2, H.264 supports the coding of interlaced or progressive pictures in 4:2:0 format, but in the case of H.264, a sequence can include both types of pictures.

The last extensions to the H.264 standard (FRExt) allow coding of pictures in 4:2:2 and 4:4:4 formats with different color spaces (YcbCr, RGB, YCgCo) and allow a precision higher than 8 bits (10 or 12) for the video samples.

The very important efficiency improvement of H.264 relative to MPEG-2 does not result from a revolutionary algorithm, but from an addition of multiple, relatively small improvements if taken separately.

This result has been obtained by the combined use of the following:

- more sophisticated prediction modes, which can vary within a picture and refer to a larger number of successive pictures.

- an integer transform, instead of the DCT, using blocks of 4*4 and 8*8.

- a more efficient adaptive entropy coding (CAVLC and CABAC).

The entropy coding is *context-adaptive* and can use two modes, CABAC (Context-Adaptive Binary Arithmetic Coding) and CAVLC (Context-Adaptive Variable-Length Coding). CABAC allows on its own a reduction of approximately 10 to 15% of the bit-rate required of a picture at equivalent quality compared to CAVLC, which is itself significantly more efficient than the usual VLC of MPEG-2.

The use of new tools, PicAFF (Picture Adaptive Frame Field) and MBAFF (MacroBlock Adaptive Frame Field) enables optimization of the processing of interlaced pictures.

Finally, a *deblocking* filter allows a reduction in the visibilty of the blocks and macroblocks—a common drawback of most video compression systems—and, as a consequence, can provide an additional 5 to 10% reduction of the bit-rate at equivalent subjective picture quality.

Like MPEG-2, H264/AVC comprises many profiles and levels summarized by Table 3.1. The profiles define the complexity of the chosen set of coding tools.

The *high profile* is a relatively late addition to the standard, which had only three originally. It is an extension of the *main profile*, of which it increases the efficiency by means of the *Fidelity Range Extensions* (FRExt). The high profile is made of four subprofiles, of which only the first one is shown in this table since it is the only one intended for consumer broadcast applications. Regarding levels, they correspond to the resolution of the picture and scale 1

**Table 3.1**  Coding tools of the various profiles of the H.264 standard.

| Coding tools | Baseline | Main | Extended | High (1) |
|---|---|---|---|---|
| I and P slices | × | × | × | × |
| CAVLC | × | × | × | × |
| CABAC | | × | | × |
| B slices | | × | × | × |
| Interlaced pictures (PicAFF, MBAFF) | | × | × | × |
| Error resilience (FMO, ASO, RS) | × | | × | |
| Enhanced error resilience (DP) | | | × | |
| SP and SI slices | | | × | |
| Transform on 8 × 8 or 4 × 4 blocks | | | | × |
| Quantification adaptation matrices | | | | × |
| Separated QP control for Cb and Cr | | | | × |
| Monochrome video format | | | | × |

**Table 3.2** Levels of the H.264 standard.

| H.264 level | Picture size | Pictures/second | Max. bit-rate (b/s) | Max. ref. frames |
|---|---|---|---|---|
| 1 | QCIF | 15 | 64 k | 4 |
| 1b | QCIF | 15 | 128 k | 4 |
| 1.1 | CIF or QCIF | 7.5 (CIF)/30 (QCIF) | 192 k | 2 (CIF)/9 (QCIF) |
| 1.2 | CIF | 15 | 384 k | 6 |
| 1.3 | CIF | 30 | 768 k | 6 |
| 2 | CIF | 30 | 2 M | 6 |
| 2.1 | HHR (480i/576i) | 30 or 25 | 4 M | 6 |
| 2.2 | SD (720*480i/576i) | 15 | 4 M | 5 |
| 3 | SD (720*480i/576i) | 30 or 25 | 10 M | 5 |
| 3.1 | $1280 \times 720p$ | 30 | 14 M | 5 |
| 3.2 | $1280 \times 720p$ | 60 | 20 M | 4 |
| 4 | 720p/1080i | 60 or 50/30 or 25 | 20 M | 4 |
| 4.1 | 720p/1080i | 60 or 50/30 or 25 | 50 M | 4 |
| 4.2 | $1920 \times 1080p$ | 60 | 50 M | 4 |
| 5 | 2k*1k | 72 | 135 M | 5 |
| 5.1 | 2k*1k or 4k*2k | 120/30 | 240 M | 5 |

(QCIF) to 5 (1k*2k), with many intermediate levels. The consumer High Definition (1080i or 720p) corresponds to the levels 4 and 4.1. Table 3.2 details the various levels.

## 3.5   Compression of audio signals

A total of 14 proposals were on the table at the beginning of the MPEG audio works, of which only two (MUSICAM for layers I and II, and ASPEC for layer III) have been used as a basis for the final MPEG audio specification.

### 3.5.1   Principles of MPEG audio

Here again, the limitations of the human ear will be exploited in order to reduce the amount of information required to encode audio signals without deteriorating in a perceptible way the quality of the sound to be reproduced.

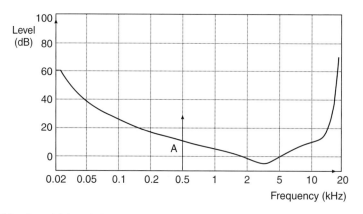

**Figure 3.20**  Sensitivity of the ear as a function of frequency (signal A is audible).

For a long time, it has been known that the human ear has a maximum sensitivity for audio frequencies ranging from 1 to 5 kHz. The sensitivity curve, which represents the audibility or perception threshold as a function of frequency in the absence of any "disturbing" signal, is shown in Figure 3.20, where it can be seen that signal A is audible, since it exceeds the audibility threshold.

More recently, however, it has been suggested that this curve is modified in the presence of multiple signals; for instance, in the case of two signals of relatively near frequencies, the strongest signal has the effect of increasing the perception threshold in the vicinity of its frequency, which makes the ear less sensitive in this frequency region. This effect is illustrated in Figure 3.21, where it can be seen that signal A, previously audible, is now masked by signal B which is more powerful than A. This effect is known as *frequency masking.*

There is also another effect called *temporal masking:* a sound of strong amplitude also masks sounds immediately preceding it or following it in time, as illustrated in Figure 3.22.

In order to quantify these effects as precisely as possible, a lot of experiments have been conducted which have led to the definition of a **psychoacoustic model** of human hearing. This model was used as the basis for the conception of a *perceptual encoder*, characterized

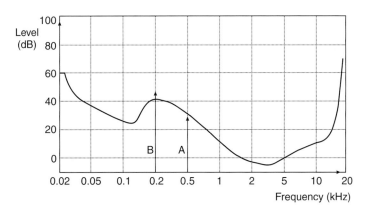

**Figure 3.21** Frequency masking effect (signal A is masked by signal B).

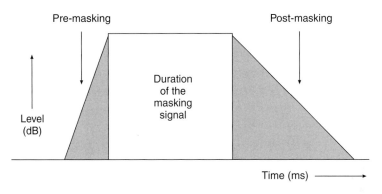

**Figure 3.22** Temporal masking effect.

by a masking curve and a quantization of signals that vary as a function of the signals to be encoded.

The principle of the coding process consists of first dividing the audio frequency band into 32 sub-bands of equal width by means of a *polyphase* filter bank. The output signal from a sub-band filter corresponding to a duration of 32 **PCM** samples is called a **sub-band sample**. The principle of perceptual coding is illustrated in Figure 3.23.

The psychoacoustical model allows elimination of all sub-band signals below their perception threshold, as they would not be heard

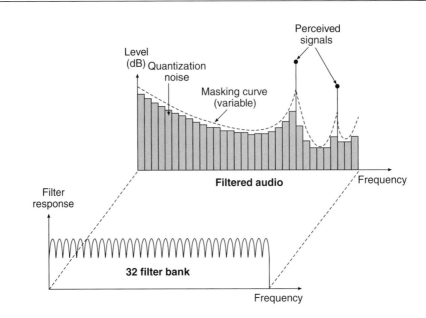

**Figure 3.23** Principle of perceptual audio coding.

by the listener, and defines the required quantization accuracy for each sub-band in order that the quantization noise stay below the audibility threshold for this sub-band.

In this way, frequency regions where the ear is more sensitive can be quantified with more accuracy than other regions. Simplified diagrams of the MPEG audio encoder and decoder are shown in Figures 3.24 and 3.25, respectively.

Analysis of the signal to determine the masking curve and quantization accuracy is not carried out for each PCM sample, being carried out instead in a time interval called a frame, which corresponds to the duration of $12 \times 32$ PCM samples (MPEG-1 layer 1) or $12 \times 96$ PCM samples (MPEG-1 layer 2). In this interval, the encoder has to evaluate the maximum amplitude of the signal in order to define a **scaling factor**, which is coded on 6 bits, covering a dynamic range of 128 dB in 64 steps of 2 dB. All information necessary for sound

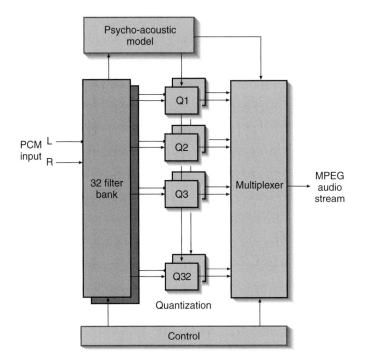

**Figure 3.24** Principle behind the MPEG audio encoder.

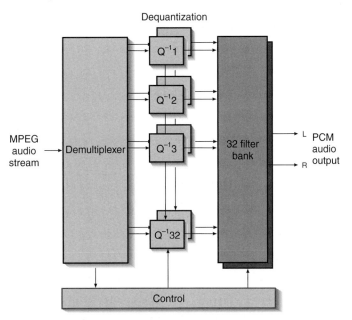

**Figure 3.25** Principle behind the MPEG audio decoder.

decoding is supplied at the frame level, which is the smallest unit for random access to the sequence (comparable to the group of pictures for video).

### 3.5.2 The MPEG audio layers

The MPEG audio standard defines three coding **layers** which offer very different compression rates for a given perceived audio quality.

- **Layer I** or "pre-MUSICAM." This uses the PASC algorithm (precision adaptive sub-band coding) developed by Philips for its DCC digital audio cassette. It uses one fixed bit-rate chosen among 14 possibles ranging from 32 to 448 kb/s; subjective hi-fi quality requires 192 kb/s per audio channel, and therefore 384 kb/s in stereo. The main advantage of layer I is the relative simplicity of the encoder and decoder.

The psychoacoustical model used is known as model 1. Quantization accuracy of the sub-band coefficients is defined for the whole duration of the frame by a 4-bit number which allows a coding from 0 to 15 bits for each sub-band, and the 6-bit scaling factor is also defined for the whole frame.

- **Layer II**. This is the main mode used in the DVB system and uses the algorithm known as MUSICAM which was developed for the European digital radio (DAB, digital audio broadcasting). For an equivalent audio quality, layer II requires a 30–50% smaller bit-rate than layer I, at the expense of a moderate increase in complexity for the encoder and the decoder. The bit-rate is fixed and chosen from 32 to 192 kb/s per channel, the hi-fi quality being obtained from 128 kb/s per channel (256 kb/s in stereo).

The psychoacoustical model used is the same as for layer I (model 1), but the frame duration is three times longer. In order to reduce the bit-rate, the quantization accuracy of the sub-band coefficients decreases with the frequency (quantization defined on 4 bits for low bands, 3 bits for medium bands and 2 bits for high bands) instead of the fixed format used in layer I. In addition, two or three consecutive sub-band samples can be grouped and coded with the same coefficient.

- **Layer III.** This is the now-famous **MP3** format, which is a development using a different psychoacoustical model (model 2), a Huffmann coding, and a DCT based signal analysis instead of the sub-band coding used in layers I and II. For a given quality, the compression rate achievable with layer III is approximately twice as high as with layer II, but the encoder and decoder are substantially more complex and the encoding/decoding time is much longer. Hi-fi quality requires only 64 kb/s per channel (128 kb/s for stereo).

Layer III is mainly intended for unidirectional applications on low bit-rate media (ISDN for instance), and its use is not foreseen for consumer digital TV broadcasting, so we will not discuss it further.

As is the case for MPEG-2 video levels and profiles, MPEG audio layers are upward compatible, which means that a layer III decoder will be able to decode also layers I and II, and a layer II decoder will also decode layer I.

The DVB digital TV standard allows the use of layers I and II of MPEG-1 audio (Note 3.3). Four main audio modes are possible:

- stereo—in this mode, the left and right channels are coded completely independently;

- **joint_stereo**—exploits the redundancy between left and right channels in order to reduce the audio bit-rate (two codings are possible: intensity_stereo or MS_stereo, see Note 3.4);

- dual_channel—two independent channels carrying uncorrelated sounds (e.g., bilingual);

- mono—only one audio channel.

### 3.5.3 Format of the MPEG audio frame

The audio frame is the elementary access unit to an MPEG audio sequence. It is made up of four main parts:

- a header of 32 bits,

- parity (CRC) over 16 bits,

- audio data of variable length,

- ancillary data (AD) of variable length.

### Format of the layer I frame

The MPEG audio layer I frame (see Fig. 3.26) represents 384 PCM samples of the audio signal, and contains 12 successive sub-band samples. As the number of samples is independent of the sampling frequency, the frame duration is inversely proportional to the sampling frequency. This duration is 12 ms at 32 kHz, 8.7 ms at 44.1 kHz, and 8 ms at 48 kHz.

| Header | CRC | AUDIO data | | | | AD |
|---|---|---|---|---|---|---|
| System 32 bits | Parity 16 bits | Allocation bits/SBS | Scaling factors | Sub-band samples (SBS) (12×32 sub-band samples) | | Ancillary data |

- The header carries the synchronization and system information (see Table 3.1).
- The use of the parity (CRC) is optional.
- The "bit allocation per SBS" field contains 32 integers coded on 4 bits, each of them defining the resolution for coding the samples of one of the 32 sub-bands.
- The "scaling factors" field contains 32 integers coded on 6 bits, each of them giving the multiplication factor of the samples of one sub-band.

**Figure 3.26** Simplified representation of the MPEG audio layer I frame.

| Header | CRC | AUDIO data | | | | | AD |
|--------|-----|-----------|---|---|---|---|-----|
| System 32 bits | Parity 16 bits | Allocation bits/SBS | Selection SCFSI | Scaling factors | Sub-band samples (SBS) (three portions of 12 sub-band samples each) | | Ancillary data |

- The header carries the synchronization and system information (see Table 3.1).
- The use of the parity (CRC) is optional.
- The "bit allocation per SBS" field contains 32 integers coded on 2–4 bits depending on the sub-band, each of them defining the resolution for coding the samples of one of the 32 sub-bands and whether or not these sub-band samples are grouped in threes.
- The SCFSI (scale factor selection information) field indicates whether the scale factor is valid for the whole frame duration or whether there are two or three different scale factors.
- The "scaling factors" field contains 32 integers coded on 6 bits, each of them giving the multiplication factor of the samples of one sub-band for the portion of the frame defined by the SCFSI.

**Figure 3.27** Simplified representation of the MPEG audio layer II frame.

## Format of the Layer II frame

In this case (see Fig. 3.27), the frame is made up of 12 **granules**, each representing 96 ($3 \times 32$) PCM audio samples, and so there are 1152 samples in total. The duration is thus three times the duration of the layer I frame (i.e., 36 ms at 32 kHz, 26.1 ms at 44.1 kHz, 24 ms at 48 kHz). The audio part of the layer II frame differs from that of layer I, and its bit allocation is more complex due to the numerous coding options.

## 3.5.4  Other audio coding systems: Dolby Digital (AC-3), DTS

As multichannel sound has become more and more important with the wide availability of home theater systems, the DVB has added the ability to transmit a 5.1 audio (Note 3.5) using the Dolby Digital system (AC-3) or DTS (Note 3.6). The inclusion of these additional formats is a direct result of the failure of MPEG-2 audio with multichannel extensions to meet its expected success, even in Europe.

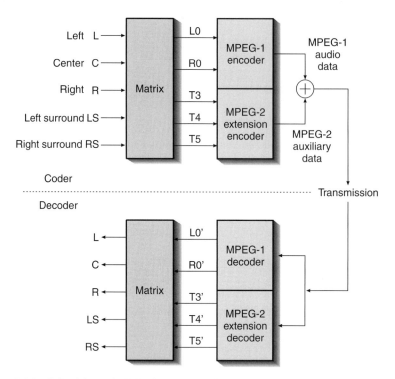

**Figure 3.28** Principle of MPEG-2 (MPEG-1-compatible) "surround" encoding/decoding.

AC-3 (see Fig. 3.28) and DTS multichannel sound are Packetized Elementary Streams (PES) transmitted as private data and must be signalized if present. Public DVB descriptors (AC-3 descriptor and DTS descriptor) have been defined for this purpose.

MPEG-1 Layer 2 (ISO/IEC11172-3) or MPEG-2 multichannel (ISO/IEC13818-3) audio must nevertheless always be transmitted in order that the majority of existing receivers can receive in stereo or mono the sound of programs using multichannel audio. AC-3 and DTS decoders are generally not included in the receivers in order not to have to pay twice the license costs of these systems (these decoders being integrated in most recent home theater amplifiers). See Figure 3.29 for a schematic diagram of the AC-3 decoder. Consequently, the multichannel stream is generally transmitted *as is* to

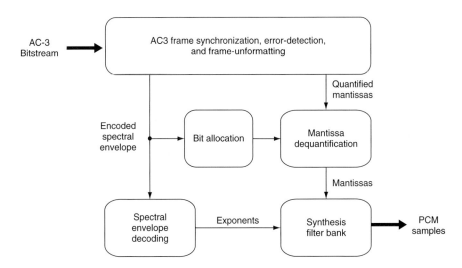

**Figure 3.29** Schematic diagram of the AC-3 decoder.

the multichannel amplifier by means of an SP-DIF interface (Sony Philips Digital Interface) in electrical or optical form.

The Dolby Digital system uses perceptual coding based on the same broad principles as MPEG audio. It offers the advantage over MPEG-2 multichannel of having been used in movie theaters for many years, and more recently having been adopted as the de facto standard for DVD-Video.

Dolby Digital supports sampling frequencies of 32, 44.1, and 48 kHz and audio bit-rates from 32 to 640 kb/s, and it can represent the audio in mono, stereo, or 5.1 multichannel. It is also the audio coding system used by the American DTV systems ATSC (terrestrial) DSS (satellite). Its frame format can schematically be represented as follows:

| Sync | CRC1 | Sy. info | BSI | Audio 1 | Audio 2 | Audio 3 | Audio 4 | Audio 5 | Audio 6 | Aux | CRC2 |
|------|------|----------|-----|---------|---------|---------|---------|---------|---------|-----|------|
|      |      |          |     |         |         |         |         |         |         |     |      |

The frame contains two CRC fields (Cyclic Redundancy Check), allowing detection of errors within a frame. The BSI field indicates the sampling frequency, the bit-rate, the number of audio channels, and the available services (dynamic range control, karaoke mode, etc.).

The payload is made of six audio blocks of 256 samples each, or 1536 audio samples per frame. The effective duration of the frame depends on the sampling frequency and the allocated bit-rate.

## Note 3.1
A fourth type of image (D type) is foreseen by MPEG-1, which is very rough and simple to decode as it only uses the DC coefficient for coding. D pictures are mainly intended for browsing quickly inside a video sequence (e.g., for a picture search).

## Note 3.2
In case of TV broadcasting, many programs are transmitted in one channel (see next chapter, "Source Multiplexing"). In this case, constant bit-rate coding (CBR) is replaced advantageously by a variable bit-rate coding (VBR) in which the instantaneous bit-rate allocated to a program can vary according to the needs (movements in the image).

The instantaneous bit-rate allocation to each of the programs of the multiplex must of course take into account the bit-rate needs of the other programs at the same moment. Since the probability that all programs require simultaneously a maximum bit-rate is low, this allows most of the time to allocate a higher bit-rate to a program during phases of important movements in the scene without quality alteration of the other programs. This type of coding is known as **statistical multiplexing**.

## Note 3.3
The MPEG-2 audio standard includes all the features of MPEG-1, but adds some new extensions such as an MPEG-1 compatible multichannel sound mode (5 channel surround sound for

instance), which is also foreseen in the DVB specifications. This compatibility is ensured by transmitting two main left and right channels compatible with the MPEG-1 standard and adding supplementary information in the "ancillary_data" field which indicates in which extension packets (with different PID) the multichannel information can be found. These extension data are simply ignored by a standard MPEG-1 decoder and processed only by an appropriate extension in the MPEG-2 decoder. The principle of compatible surround encoding and decoding is illustrated in Figure 3.28.

The MPEG-2 standard includes also the possibility of using sampling frequencies of half the standard values (16 kHz/22.05 kHz/24 kHz), which divide the required bit-rate by a factor of 2, but which also reduce the audio bandwidth in the same ratio.

### Note 3.4
With layers I and II, only the "intensity_stereo" mode of joint_stereo is allowed; layer III allows intensity_stereo and MS_stereo, and even a combination of both.

### Note 3.5
5.1 means 5-channel sound with full audio bandwidth (20 Hz to 20 kHz): front left, front right, center, rear left, and rear right, plus a channel with reduced bandwidth (subwoofer, bandwidth 3 Hz to 120 Hz) represented by the .1 figure.

### Note 3.6
DTS is not currently used for broadcast due to the very high bit-rates it requires.

# Source multiplexing

# 4

## 4.1 Organization of the MPEG-1 multiplex: system layer

Audio and video encoders deliver as their output elementary streams (ES) which are the constituents of the so-called **compression layer**. Each elementary stream carries access units (**AU**) which are the coded representations of presentation units (**PU**), i.e., decoded pictures or audio frames, depending on the nature of the elementary stream.

These bitstreams, as well as other streams carrying other *private data*, have to be combined in an organized manner and supplemented with additional information to allow their separation by the decoder, synchronization of picture and sound, and selection by the user of the particular components of interest. Part I (system) of ISO/IEC 11172 International Standard (MPEG-1) defines the rules governing the constitution of a **system layer** grouping *video*, *audio*, and *private* data elementary streams into a single bitstream, as well as the constraints on the elementary streams necessary to allow their combination (optional *padding* streams are also foreseen, for instance, to obtain a constant rate).

The main basic functions of the system layer which surrounds (or "packetizes") the compression layer are as follows:

- packetization and combination of multiple streams into one single bitstream,

- addition of time stamps on elementary streams for synchronization at playback,

- initialization and management of the buffers required to decode the elementary streams.

A complete MPEG-1 system encoding device therefore has to effect video and audio encoding, the multiplexing of these data, private data, and the necessary information to synchronize the audio and video parts of the decoder, and to indicate the necessary resources required for decoding the MPEG-1 bitstream (such as the size of the buffers required for decoding individual elementary streams with a theoretical reference decoder known as system target decoder—**STD**).

Each elementary stream is cut into packets to form a packetized elementary stream (**PES**); a packet starts with a *packet header* followed by the elementary stream's data. Table 4.1 details the different fields of an MPEG-1 packet.

The packet header starts with a start code on 32 bits, the last eight of which indicate the type (audio, video, private) and the identification number of the elementary stream from which it comes. The header then indicates the packet length (in bytes, on 16 bits; hence a maximum length of 64 kbytes) and the buffer size required by the STD for decoding. It may also contain optional time stamps: a decoding time stamp (**DTS**) indicating the decoding time of the first AU of the packet, and/or a presentation time stamp (**PTS**), indicating the time at which the corresponding PU should be presented (displayed or made audible, depending on its nature). These time stamps are used for audio and video synchronization and are sent frequently (the standard specifies a maximum interval of 0.7 s between consecutive

**Table 4.1**  Structure of the MPEG-1 packet

| Field | Definition (comment) | No. of bits |
|---|---|---|
| Start_code_prefix | Start code (00 00 01 hex) | 24 |
| Stream_id | PES type (4 MSB) and number (4 LSB) | 8 |
| Packet_length | Length of the packet (number of bytes to follow these two) | 16 |
| Stuffing_bytes | Optional stuffing (value FF hex) | 0 to 16 × 8 |
| Bits '01' | Beginning of STD_buffer field | 2 |
| STD_buffer_scale | Buffer size unit (0 = 128 bytes, 1 = 1024 bytes) | 1 |
| STD_buffer_size | Buffer size (in multiples of 128 or 1024 bytes) | 13 |
| PTS (optional) | Presentation time stamp (4 code bits + 33 bits + 3 marker bits) | 40 |
| DTS (optional) | Decoding time stamp (same structure as PTS) | 40 |
| Packet_data_byte | Data ($N$ = packet_length less the six following fields) | $N \times 8$ |

stamps of a PES). Time stamps are coded on 33 bits, which represent an absolute time expressed in periods of a 90 kHz reference clock (see also SCR and STC below).

A packet can carry a variable number of data bytes (within the 16-bit length limit), depending on the characteristics of the transmission or digital storage medium (**DSM**) for which it is destined. The standard also foresees the possibility of adding stuffing bytes to the packet (up to 16 bytes per packet), for instance to align on the physical sectors of a storage medium.

Packets are grouped in *packs*, the header of which contains timing and bit-rate information by means of the system clock reference (**SCR**) and mux_rate fields. The SCR field is used in the decoder to synchronize a 90 kHz system time clock (**STC**) common to all elementary streams, and which is used as a time base and measuring unit for the DTS and PTS time stamps sent in the packets. The pack header, which is detailed in Table 4.2, starts with a start code on 32 bits.

The first pack of an MPEG-1 system stream always starts with a pack header. The system header, detailed in Table 4.3, starts with

**Table 4.2** Structure of the MPEG-1 pack header

| Field | Definition (comment) | No. of bits |
|---|---|---|
| Pack_start_code | Start code (00 00 01 BA hex) | 32 |
| Bits '0010' | Beginning of SCR field | 4 |
| SCR [32...30] | System clock reference (4 MSB) | 3 |
| Marker_bit | Always 1 | 1 |
| SCR [29...15] | System clock reference (15 intermediate bits) | 15 |
| Marker_bit | Always 1 | 1 |
| SCR [14...0] | System clock reference (15 LSB) | 15 |
| Marker_bit | Always 1 | 1 |
| Marker_bit | Always 1 | 1 |
| Mux_rate | MPEG multiplex bit-rate (in multiples of 50 bytes/s) | 22 |
| Marker_bit | Always 1 | 1 |

**Table 4.3** Structure of the MPEG-1 system header

| Field | Definition (comment) | No. of bits |
|---|---|---|
| System_header_start_code | Start code | 32 |
| Header_length | (Number of bytes to follow) | 16 |
| Marker_bit | Always 1 | 1 |
| Rate_bound | Maximum bit-rate (mux_rate) in the sequence | 22 |
| Marker_bit | Always 1 | 1 |
| Audio_bound | Number of audio PES in the bitstream (0–32) | 6 |
| Fixed_flag | Indicates fixed ('1') or variable ('0') bit-rate | 1 |
| CSPS_flag | '1' = bitstream uses the constrained parameter set | 1 |
| System_audio_lock_flag | '1' = harmonic relation between STC and audio $F_{sampling}$ | 1 |
| System_video_lock_flag | '1' = harmonic relation between STC and frame frequency | 1 |
| Marker bit | Always 1 | 1 |
| Video_bound | Number of video PES in the bitstream (0–16) | 5 |
| Reserved_byte | Reserved for future extension | 8 |

**Table 4.3** (Continued)

| Field | Definition (comment) | No. of bits |
|---|---|---|
| Stream_ID$_1$ | Identification of first PES (type and number) | 8 |
| Bits '11' | Beginning of STD_buffer field | 2 |
| STD_buffer_bound_scale$_1$ | Buffer size unit (0 = 128 bytes, 1 = 1024 bytes) | 1 |
| STD_buffer_size_bound$_1$ | Buffer size (in multiples of 128 or 1024 bytes) | 13 |
| Stream_ID$_2$ | Identification of second PES (type and number) | 8 |
| Bits '11' | Beginning of STD_buffer field | 2 |
| STD_buffer_bound_scale$_2$ | Buffer size unit (0 = 128 bytes, 1 = 1024 bytes) | 1 |
| STD_buffer_size_bound$_2$ | Buffer size (in multiples of 128 or 1024 bytes) | 13 |
| etc.... for $(n-2)$ other PES | Idem for all PES (max: 16 video, 32 audio, 2 private) | $(n-2) \times 24$ |

a start code on 32 bits. It is a special packet which delivers all the system parameters used during this stream (maximum bit-rate, identification of audio, video private data, minimum size of the input buffers, etc.). The system header can optionally be repeated at any new pack in the MPEG-1 stream in order to ease the access to a random point in the sequence.

The number of elementary streams in an MPEG-1 elementary stream is specified as follows:

- video, 0–16,
- audio, 0–32,
- private data, 0–2.

The MPEG-1 system stream ends with an "end" code on 32 bits (00 00 01 B9 hex). Figure 4.1 illustrates the content of a complete MPEG-1 stream.

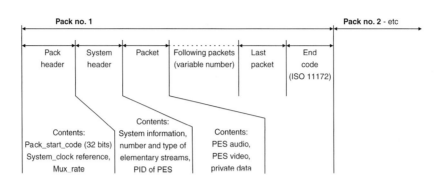

**Figure 4.1** Composition of the packs of an MPEG-1 bitstream.

## 4.2 Organization of the MPEG-2 multiplex: program and transport streams

In the same way as for MPEG-1, MPEG-2 ESs are packetized in order to form the video, audio, and private data PESs. As in the case of MPEG-1, packets from PES start with a packet header, the format of which is illustrated in Figure 4.2 and detailed in Table 4.4.

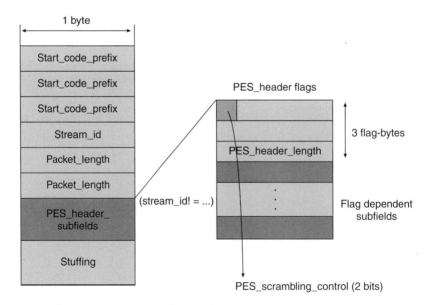

**Figure 4.2** Structure of the MPEG-2 PES header.

**Table 4.4** Structure of the MPEG-2 PES header

| Field | Definition | No. of bits |
|---|---|---|
| Start_code_prefix | Start code (00 00 01 hex) | 24 |
| Stream_id | PES identification | 8 |
| Packet_length | Length of the packet (in bytes after these two) | 16 |
| PES_scrambling_control | Indicates whether PES is scrambled and control word number | 2 |
| Flags | Various flags | 14 |
| PES_header_length | Length of the remaining part of the PES ($x + y$) | 8 |
| PES_header_subfields | Variable field depending on flags | $x$ bytes |
| Stuffing | Optional stuffing | $y$ bytes |

The system part of MPEG-2 (ISO/IEC 13818-1), which defines the organization of the multiplex, foresees two different ways of multiplexing these PESs in order to form two different kinds of bitstreams depending on the application. Figure 4.3 illustrates schematically the way in which these two types of bitstreams are constructed.

## Program stream

The MPEG-2 program stream is made up of one or more PESs (video, audio, private) which must necessarily share the same STC. This type of stream is suitable for applications where the transmission channel or storage medium is supposed to introduce only a very low number of errors (bit error rate, BER $< 10^{-10}$). This type of medium is usually called *quasi error-free* (**QEF**). This is generally the case in multimedia applications based on CD-ROM or hard disk. In these cases, packets can be relatively long (e.g., 2048 bytes), and as the stream organization is similar to the MPEG-1 system stream, we will not discuss it here (see Section 4.1). This kind of multiplex will most probably be used for storage of MPEG-2 video on the digital versatile disk (**DVD**), which will soon be available.

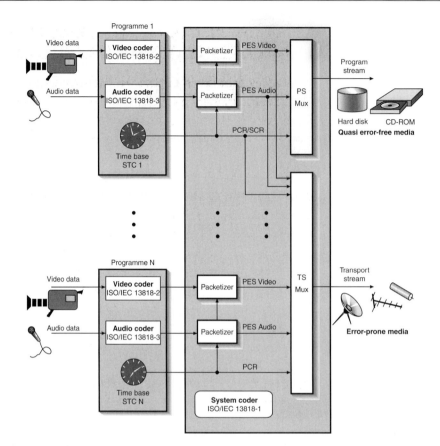

**Figure 4.3** Conceptual diagram of the generation of MPEG-2 transport and program streams.

## Transport stream

As its name implies, the MPEG-2 transport stream is primarily intended for the transport of TV programs over long distances via transmission supports or in environments susceptible to the introduction of relatively high error rates (BER higher than $10^{-4}$). These types of media are defined as *error-prone*.

In these cases, the packet length should be relatively short, in order to allow implementation of efficient correction algorithms, which will be detailed in Chapter 6. The length of the MPEG-2 transport packet therefore has been fixed to 188 bytes for the transmission of TV

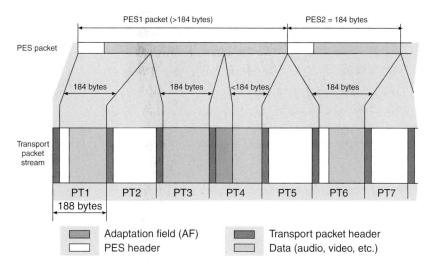

**Figure 4.4** Arrangement of the PESs that make up an MPEG-2 transport stream (PES1 is split between the transports packets PT1, PT3, and PT4; PES2 fits exactly into the transport packets PT6).

programs via satellite, cable, or terrestrial transmitters following the European DVB standard.

This type of stream can combine in the same multiplex many programs which do not need to share a common STC. However, the different PESs which make up a given program have to use the same clock in order for the decoder to synchronize them. Figure 4.4 illustrates the way in which the PESs that make up a transport stream are organized.

## 4.2.1 Composition of the MPEG-2 transport packet

A transport packet of 188 bytes is made up of a packet header of 4 bytes and a **payload** of up to 184 bytes, preceded by an optional adaptation field (see Fig. 4.5).

In this context, the payload means the data from the PES composing the TV programs, to which are added a certain number of data allowing the decoder to find its way in the MPEG-2 transport stream.

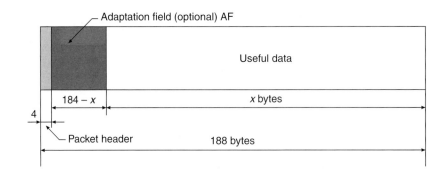

**Figure 4.5** Composition of the transport packet.

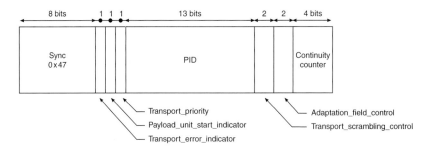

**Figure 4.6** Detail of the transport packet header.

The format of the transport packet header is illustrated in Figure 4.6 and detailed in Table 4.5.

The ISO/IEC 13818-1 prescribes that a transport packet should carry only data coming from one PES packet, and that a PES packet should always start at the beginning of the payload part of a transport packet and end at the end of a transport packet (as shown in Fig. 4.4).

As transport packets (188 bytes including 4-byte header) are generally (much) shorter than PES packets (e.g., 2048 bytes), PES packets will have to be divided into data blocks of 184 bytes. Since the length of PES packets is not generally an exact multiple of 184 bytes, the last transport packet carrying a PES packet will have to start with

**Table 4.5**  Structure of the MPEG-2 transport packet header

| Field | Definition (comment) | No. of bits |
|---|---|---|
| Sync_byte | Synchronization byte (10000111 = 47hex) | 8 |
| EI | Transport_error_indicator (indicates error from previous stages) | 1 |
| PUSI | Payload_unit_start_indicator (start of PES in the packet) | 1 |
| TPR | Transport_priority (priority indicator) | 1 |
| PID | Packet identifier (identifies the content of the packet) | 13 |
| SCR_flags | Transport_scrambling_flags (transport scrambling type) | 2 |
| AF | Adaptation_field_flag (presence of adaptation field in packet) | 1 |
| PF | Payload_flag (presence of payload data in the packet) | 1 |
| CC | Continuity_counter (between truncated PES portions) | 4 |

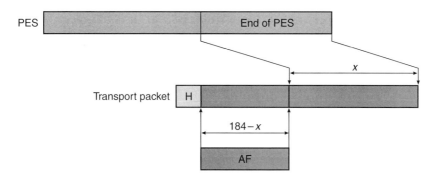

**Figure 4.7**  Composition of the packet containing the end of a PES.

an adaptation field, the length of which will be equal to 184 bytes less the number of bytes remaining in the PES packet (Fig. 4.7).

In addition to this "stuffing" function, the adaptation field will be used to carry various optional data and the program clock reference (**PCR**), which has the same role in an MPEG-2 program as the SCR has in an MPEG-1 system stream. The minimum repetition rate

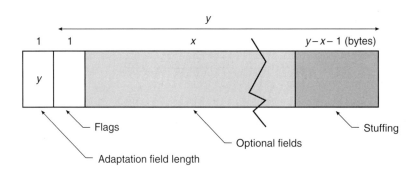

**Figure 4.8** Detail of the adaptation field.

**Table 4.6** Composition of the MPEG-2 adaptation field

| Field | Definition | No. of bits |
|---|---|---|
| Adaptation_field_length flags | Total length $(y - 1)$ bytes | 8 |
| | Information on the next field | 8 |
| Optional_fields | Optional data field ($x$ bytes) | $x^* \times 8$ |
| Stuffing | Value FFh | $(y - 1 - x) \times 8$ |

of the PCR is 10 times a second. In some cases, the payload of a transport packet can be solely composed of an adaptation field of 184 bytes (e.g., for the transport of private data). Figure 4.8 illustrates the general format of the adaptation field, the content of which is detailed in Table 4.6.

## 4.2.2 Organization of the transport multiplex: MPEG-2 and DVB-SI tables

As we have seen, the MPEG-2 transport multiplex can transport more than one program, each of them being composed of one or more PESs. In order that the receiver be able to find its way in this jungle, MPEG-2 has defined four types of tables, which together make up the MPEG-2 Program Specific Information (**PSI**). Each table, depending on its importance, is made up of one or more *sections* (maximum 256 sections, each of which has a maximum 1024 bytes, except for the private sections which can be of up to 4096 bytes in length).

## The MPEG-2 tables

### *Program allocation table (PAT)*

The presence of this table is mandatory, and it is carried by the packets of PID equal to zero (PID $= 0 \times 0000$). Its purpose is to indicate, for each program carried by the transport multiplex, the link between the program number (from 0 to 65535) and the PID of packets carrying a "map" of the program (Program Map Table—**PMT**). The PAT is always broadcast "in the clear," even if all programs of the multiplex are scrambled.

### *Conditional access table (CAT)*

This table must be present as soon as at least one program in the multiplex has conditional access. It is transported by the packets of PID $= 0 \times 0001$ and indicates the PID of packets carrying the EMM for one (or more) conditional access systems. (The EMM is one of the two pieces of information required for descrambling conditional access programs; see Chapter 5.)

### *Program map table (PMT)*

There is one PMT for each program present in the multiplex. It indicates (in the clear) the PID of the elementary streams making up the program and, optionally, other private information relating to the program, which can eventually be scrambled (e.g., the ECM, which is one of the two pieces of information necessary for unscrambling programs with conditional access, the other being the EMM carried by the CAT; see below and Chapter 5). The PMT can be transported by packets of arbitrary PID defined by the broadcaster and indicated in the PAT (except $0 \times 0000$ and $0 \times 0001$, which are reserved for PAT and CAT, respectively).

### *Transport stream description table (TDST)*

As its name implies, this table describes the contents of the multiplex. It is transported by packets of PID $= 0 \times 0002$.

## Private tables

These tables carry private data, which are either in free format (see Table 4.10) or in a format similar to the CAT, except for the section length, which can be as much as 4096 bytes, compared with 1024 for the other tables.

The DVB standard adds complementary tables to the MPEG-2 tables, of which only a part is mandatory. Called **DVB-SI** (Service Information), this data enables the receiver to configure itself automatically and allow the user to navigate the numerous programs and services available. This information is made up of four mandatory tables and three optional ones.

## Mandatory tables of DVB-SI

These tables apply to the current multiplex (actual transport stream).

### Network information table (NIT)

This table, as its name implies, carries information specific to a network made up of more than one RF channel (and hence more than one transport stream), such as frequencies or channel numbers used by the network, which the receiver can use to configure itself, for instance. This table is carried by packets with $PID = 0 \times 0010$.

### Service description table (SDT)

This table lists the names and other parameters associated with each service in the multiplex. It is transported by packets with $PID = 0 \times 0011$.

### Event information table (EIT), present/following

This table is used to transmit information relating to events occurring or going to occur in the current transport multiplex. It is transported by packets with $PID = 0 \times 0012$.

## Time and date table (TDT)
This table is used to update the internal real-time clock of the set-top box. It is transported by packets with PID $= 0 \times 0014$.

## Optional tables of DVB-SI
These tables apply to the current multiplex (actual transport stream).

## Bouquet association table (BAT)
This table (present in all multiplexes making up the bouquet) is used as a tool for grouping services that the set-top box may use to present the various services to the user (e.g., by way of the EPG). A given service or program can be part of more than one bouquet. It is transported by packets with PID $= 0 \times 0011$.

## Event information table (EIT), schedule
This table is used to transmit information relative to events occurring or going to occur in the current transport multiplex. It is transported by packets with PID $= 0 \times 0012$.

## Running status table (RST)
This table is transmitted only once for a quick update of the status of one or more events at the time that this status changes, and not repeatedly as with the other tables. It is transported by packets with PID $= 0 \times 0013$.

## Time offset table (TOT)
This table indicates the time offset to the GMT. It is transported by packets with PID $= 0 \times 0014$.

## Stuffing tables (ST)
These tables are used, for example, to replace previously used tables which have become invalid. They are transported by packets with PID $= 0 \times 0010$ to $0 \times 0014$.

## Tables concerning other multiplexes (other transport streams)

These have the same format and use the same PID as the corresponding tables for the actual transport streams.

*Network information table (NIT)*

*Service description table (SDT)*

*Event information table (EIT), present/following and schedules*

The repetition frequency of the tables must be high enough to allow the decoder to access the wanted program quickly in case of physical channel change and to speed up the installation process. The document ETSI TR 101 290 defines the minimum and maximum repetition frequencies of the tables depending on their type.

Each table consists, depending on its importance, of one or more sections (maximum 256) of a maximum size of 1024 bytes, except for private tables which can be up to 4096 bytes long.

Tables 4.7 to 4.10 show the structure and various fields of the sections of the four categories of tables (PAT, PMT, CAT/TSDT, and private) defined by the MPEG-2 standard. The additional DVB tables have a similar format simply adapted to their contents.

**Table 4.7** Section of the program allocation table (PAT)

| Field (PAT) | Comment | No. of bits |
|---|---|---|
| Table_id (00) | Always 00 for the PAT | 8 |
| Section_syntax_indicator 0 | Always 1 | 1 |
| | Always 0 | 1 |
| Reserved | | 2 |
| Section_length | Max. value 1021 (2 MSB = 0) | 12 |
| Transport_stream_id | Stream identification (in a network) | 16 |
| Reserved | | 2 |
| Version_number | Incremented at every PAT modification | 5 |

**Table 4.7** (Continued)

| Field (PAT) | Comment | No. of bits |
|---|---|---|
| Current_next_indicator | 1 = current PAT, 0 = next | 1 |
| Section_number | Number of current section (1st = 00) | 8 |
| Last_section_number | Number of last section ($JV_{tot} - 1$) | 8 |
| Program number 0[a] | 0 = network information table (NIT) | 16 |
| Reserved | | 3 |
| Network_PID | PID of the NIT | 13 |
| Program_number 1 | Program number (1 = 1st prog.) | 16 |
| Reserved | | 3 |
| Program_map_PID | PID of the PMT | 13 |
| ... etc. | 4 bytes per additional programme | ... |
| CRC_32 | CRC on 32 bits | 32 |

**Table 4.8** A section of the program map table (PMT)

| Field (PMT) | Comment | No. of bits |
|---|---|---|
| Table id (02) | Always 02 for the PMT | 8 |
| Section_syntax_indicator | Always 1 | 1 |
| 0 | Always 0 | 1 |
| Reserved | | 2 |
| Section_length | Maximum value 1021 (2 MSB = 0) | 12 |
| Program_number | Prog. number (1 to 65536) | 16 |
| Reserved | | 2 |
| Version_number | Incremented at every PMT change | 5 |
| Current_next_indicator | 1 = current PAT, 0 = next | 1 |
| Section_number | Always 00 (only one section) | 8 |
| Last_section_number | | 8 |
| Reserved | | 3 |
| PCR_PID | PID of elementary stream no. 1 | 13 |
| Reserved | | 4 |
| Program_info_length | Length of the useful data (bytes) | 12 |

*(continued)*

**Table 4.8**  (Continued)

| Field (PMT) | Comment | No. of bits |
|---|---|---|
| Stream_type$_1$ | Nature of elementary stream no. 1 | 8 |
| Reserved | | 3 |
| Elementary_PID$_1$ | PID of elementary stream no. 1 | 13 |
| Reserved | | 4 |
| ES info length$_1$ | $N_1$ = length of descriptors$_1$ field | 12 |
| Descriptors$_1$ | Additional data | $N_1$ bytes |
| Stream_type$_2$ | Nature of elementary stream no. 2 | 8 |
| Reserved | | 3 |
| Elementary_PID$_2$ | PID of elementary stream no. 2 | 13 |
| Reserved | | 4 |
| ES info length$_2$ | $N_2$ = length of descriptors$_2$ field | 12 |
| Descriptors$_2$ | Additional data | $N_2$ bytes |
| ... etc. | (ES no. $x$) | ... |
| CRC_32 | CRC on 32 bits | 32 |

**Table 4.9**  A section of the conditional access table (CAT)

| Field (CAT)/(TSDT) | Comment | No. of bits |
|---|---|---|
| Table_id (01)/(03) | 01 for CAT, 03 for TSDT | 8 |
| Section_syntax_indicator | Always 1 | 1 |
| 0 | Always 0 | 1 |
| Reserved | | 2 |
| Section_length | Max. value 1021 (2 MSB = 0) | 12 |
| Reserved | | 16 |
| Reserved | | 2 |
| Version_number | Incremented at every CAT change | 5 |
| Current_next_indicator | 1 = current, 0 = next | 1 |
| Section_number | Number of current section (1 = 00) | 8 |
| Last_section_number | Number of last section ($N_{tot} - 1$) | 8 |
| Descriptors | Access control data/TS description data | Maximum 1012 bytes |
| CRC_32 | CRC on 32 bits | 32 |

**Table 4.10** A private data section

| Field (private) | Comment | No. of bits |
|---|---|---|
| Table_id | Any (except 00h to 3Fh and FFh) | 8 |
| Section_syntax_indicator | 0 = free format, 1 = standard | 1 |
| Private_indicator | User-defined flag | 1 |
| Reserved | | 2 |
| Private_section_length | Max. value 4093 (2MSB = 1) | 12 |
| Private_data_byte[a] | Private user data | Maximum 4093 bytes |

[a]The private data byte part is assumed here to be in free format (syntax_indicator = 0). If the syntax_indicator = 1, the format of this part is similar to the CAT (except length).

## Insertion of sections into the transport packets

Contrary to the PES, sections do not necessarily start at the beginning nor finish at the end of a transport packet. Whenever a section or a PES starts in a transport packet, the PUSI indicator (payload_unit_start_indicator) is set to 1. In the case of a section, the packet can start with the end of another section, whether or not it is preceded by an adaptation field (**AF**). In order to know where the new section starts, the first byte or the payload is a pointer field giving the offset of the beginning of the new section. This case is illustrated by Figure 4.9, where a new section starts in a transport packet after an adaptation field and the end of a preceding section. Note that the PUSI bit is set at 1 when there is at least one section start in the transport packet. Note as well that if the sections are not aligned on the packet start, the first byte of the payload (pointer_field) gives the offset of the section start.

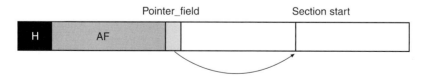

**Figure 4.9** Section start in a transport packet (general case).

### 4.2.3   Navigating an MPEG-2 multiplex

At installation time, during channel search, the receiver builds a list of available services by means of PAT and PMT tables (and/or optional NIT tables) which can count up to many thousands in the case of multi-satellite reception.

An Electronic Program Guide (**EPG**) can be built by using the EIT schedule information. This guide shows the content of present and future transmissions up to one week in advance, depending on the broadcaster.

In order to access the most often viewed programs more quickly and easily, the non-proprietary receivers allow the creation of favorite-channel lists which users can group by theme, language, or any criteria they choose.

In case of a proprietary receiver (for pay TV), the stored channels can be limited to those belonging to or associated with the bouquet by using the BAT tables. They are generally numbered according to an order determined by the operator, modifiable or not by the user.

The lists established in this way store the PIDs of the elements of each program or service, allowing users to access them without consulting the PAT or PMT, assuming no change in the multiplex happened in between.

These changes can be taken into account by regularly consulting the NIT tables. This option is now, however, very easy to put in practice for a non-proprietary (satellite) set-top box receiving many multiplexes from various origins and belonging to one or more bouquets.

In the case of Digital Terrestrial TV, the number of programs is much smaller, and all the multiplexes of a given country most of the time make up a single network with a common NIT containing, among other data, a Logical Channel Number indicating program numbering defined by a regulatory authority.

If a function allowing a regular watch of the network is activated, the DTT receiver will be in the position to automatically update the channel list when changes occur in a multiplex.

# Scrambling and conditional access

## 5

The proportion of free access programs among analog TV transmissions by cable or satellite is decreasing continuously, at the same time as their number increases; hence, it is almost certain that the vast majority of digital TV programs will be pay-TV services, in order to recover as quickly as possible the high investments required to launch these services. Billing forms will be much more diversified (conventional subscription, pay per view, near video on demand) than what we know today, made easier by the high available bit-rate of the system and a "return channel" (to the broadcaster or a bank) provided by a modem.

The DVB standard, as explained in the previous chapter, envisages the transmission of access control data carried by the conditional access table (**CAT**) and other private data packets indicated by the program map table (**PMT**). The standard also defines a common scrambling algorithm (**CSA**) for which the trade-off between cost and complexity has been chosen in order that piracy can be resisted for an appropriate length of time (of the same order as the expected lifetime of the system).

The conditional access (**CA**) itself is not defined by the standard, as most operators did not want a common system, everyone guarding jealously their own system for both commercial (management of the subscribers' data base) and security reasons (the more open the system, the more likely it is to be cracked quickly). However, in order to avoid the problem of the subscriber who wishes to access networks using different conditional access systems having a stack of boxes (one set-top box per network), the DVB standard envisages the following two options:

1. **Simulcrypt.** This technique, which requires an agreement between networks using different conditional access systems but the same scrambling algorithm (for instance, the CSA of the DVB), allows access to a given service or program by any of the conditional access systems which are part of the agreement. In this case, the transport multiplex will have to carry the conditional access packets for each of the systems that can be used to access this program.

2. **Multicrypt.** In this case, all the functions required for conditional access and descrambling are contained in a detachable module in a **PCMCIA** form factor which is inserted into the transport stream data path. This is done by means of a standardized interface (common interface, **DVB-CI**) which also includes the processor bus for information exchange between the module and the set-top box. The set-top box can have more than one DVB-CI slot, to allow connection of many conditional access modules. For each different conditional access and/or scrambling system required, the user can connect a module generally containing a smart card interface and a suitable descrambler.

The multicrypt approach has the advantage that it does not require agreements between networks, but it is more expensive to implement (cost of the connectors, housing of the modules, etc.). The DVB-CI connector may also be used for other purposes (data transfers for instance). Only the future will tell us which of these options will be used in practice, and how it will be used.

# 5.1 Principles of the scrambling system in the DVB standard

Given the very delicate nature of this part of the standard, it is understandable that only its very general principles are available; implementation details only being accessible to network operators and equipment manufacturers under non-disclosure agreements.

The scrambling algorithm envisaged to resist attacks from hackers for as long as possible consists of a cipher with two layers, each palliating the weaknesses of the other:

- a *block layer* using blocks of 8 bytes (reverse cipher block chaining mode),

- a *stream layer* (pseudo-random byte generator).

The scrambling algorithm uses two control words (even and odd) alternating with a frequency of the order of 2 s in order to make the pirate's task more difficult. One of the two encrypted control words is transmitted in the entitlement control messages (**ECM**) during the period that the other one is in use, so that the control words have to be stored temporarily in the registers of the descrambling device. There is also a default control word (which could be used for free access scrambled transmission) but it is of little interest.

The DVB standard foresees the possibility of scrambling at two different levels (transport level and PES level) which cannot be used simultaneously.

**Scrambling at the transport level**

We have seen in the preceding chapter (Fig. 4.6) that the transport packet header includes a 2-bit field called "transport_scrambling_ flags." These bits are used to indicate whether the transport packet is scrambled and with which control word, according to Table 5.1.

**Table 5.1** Meaning of transport_scrambling_flag bits

| Transport_scrambling_flags | Meaning |
| --- | --- |
| 00 | No scrambling |
| 01 | Scrambling with the DEFAULT control word |
| 10 | Scrambling with the EVEN control word |
| 11 | Scrambling with the ODD control word |

Scrambling at transport level is performed after multiplexing the whole payload of the transport packet, the PES at the input of the multiplexer being "in the clear." As a transport packet may only contain data coming from one PES, it is therefore possible to scramble at transport level all or only a part of the PES forming part of a program of the multiplex.

## Scrambling at the PES level

In this case, scrambling generally takes place at the source, before multiplexing, and its presence and control word are indicated by the 2-bit PES_scrambling_control in the PES packet header, the format of which is indicated in Figure 4.4. Table 5.2 indicates the possible options. The following limitations apply to scrambling at the PES level:

- the header itself is, of course, not scrambled; the descrambling device knows where to start descrambling due to information contained in the PES_header length field, and where to stop due to the packet_length field;

- scrambling should be applied to 184-byte portions, and only the last transport packet may include an adaptation field;

- the PES packet header should not exceed 184 bytes, so that it will fit into one transport packet;

- the default scrambling word is not allowed in scrambling at the PES level.

**Table 5.2** Meaning of PES_scrambling_control bits

| PES_scrambling_control | Meaning |
| --- | --- |
| 00 | No scrambling |
| 01 | No scrambling |
| 10 | Scrambling with the EVEN control word |
| 11 | Scrambling with the ODD control word |

## 5.2 Conditional access mechanisms

The information required for descrambling is transmitted in specific conditional access messages (**CAM**), which are of two types: entitlement control messages (**ECM**) and entitlement management messages (**EMM**). These messages are generated from three different types of input data:

- a *control_word*, which is used to initialize the descrambling sequence;

- a *service_key*, used to scramble the control word for a group of one or more users;

- a *user_key*, used for scrambling the service key.

ECM are a function of the control_word and the service_key, and are transmitted approximately every 2 s. EMM are a function of the service_key and the user_key, and are transmitted approximately every 10 s. The process for generating ECM and EMM is illustrated in Figure 5.1.

In the set-top box, the principle of decryption consists of recovering the service_key from the EMM and the user_key, contained, for instance, in a smart card. The service_key is then used to decrypt the ECM in order to recover the control_word allowing initialization of the descrambling device. Figure 5.2 illustrates schematically the process for recovering control_words from the ECM and the EMM.

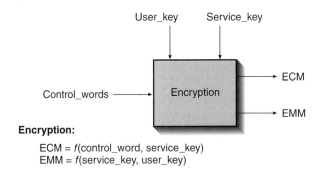

**Encryption:**

ECM = $f$(control_word, service_key)
EMM = $f$(service_key, user_key)

**Figure 5.1** Schematic illustration of the ECM and EMM generation process.

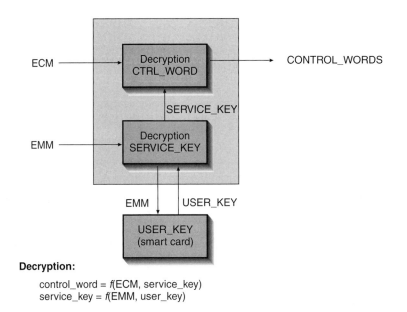

**Decryption:**

control_word = $f$(ECM, service_key)
service_key = $f$(EMM, user_key)

**Figure 5.2** Principle of decryption of the control words from the ECM and the EMM.

Figure 5.3 illustrates the process followed to find the ECM and EMM required to descramble a given program (here program no. 3):

1. the program allocation table (**PAT**), rebuilt from sections in packets with PID $= 0 \times 0000$, indicates the PID (M) of the packets carrying the program map table (**PMT**) sections;

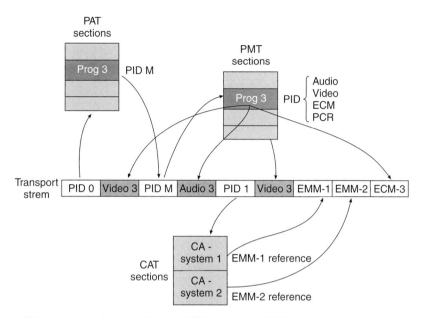

**Figure 5.3** Process by which the ECM and the EMM are found in the transport stream.

2. the PMT indicates, in addition to the PID of the packets carrying the video and audio PESs and the PCR, the PID of packets carrying the ECM;

3. the conditional access table (**CAT**), rebuilt from sections in packets with PID $= 0 \times 0001$, indicates which packets carry the EMM for one (or more) access control system(s);

4. from this information and the user_key contained in the smart card, the descrambling system can calculate the control_word required to descramble the next series of packets (PES or transport depending on the scrambling mode).

The above-described process is indeed very schematic; the support containing the user_key and the real implementation of the system can vary from one operator to another. The details of these systems are, of course, not in the public domain, but their principles are similar.

## 5.3 Main conditional access systems

Table 5.3 indicates the main conditional access systems used by European digital pay TV service providers.

Most of these systems use the DVB-CSA scrambling standard specified by the DVB. The receiver has an internal descrambler controlled by an embedded conditional access software which calculates the descrambler control words from the ECM messages and keys contained in a subscriber smart card with valid access rights updated by the EMM.

Systems allowing pay-per-view often have a second card reader slot for a banking card as well as a modem to order the programs as well as charge the bank account.

**Table 5.3** Main conditional access systems

| System | Origin | Service providers (examples) |
|---|---|---|
| Betacrypt | Betaresearch (obsolete) | Premiere World, German cable |
| Conax | Conax AS (Norway) | Scandinavian operators |
| CryptoWorks | Philips | Viacom, MTV Networks |
| IrDETO | Nethold | Multichoice |
| Mediaguard 1 & 2 | SECA (now Kudelski S.A.) | Canal+, Canal Satellite, Top Up TV |
| Nagravision 1 & 2 | Kudelski S.A. | Dish Network, Premiere, German cable |
| Viaccess 1 & 2 | France Telecom | TPS, AB-Sat, SSR/SRG, Noos |
| Videoguard/ICAM | News Datacom (NDS) | BskyB, Sky Italia |

# Channel coding (forward error correction)

## 6

Once the source coding operations have been performed (including multiplexing and eventually scrambling), a transport stream made of 188 byte packets is available for transmission to the end users via a radio frequency link (satellite, cable, terrestrial network).

We previously indicated that these transmission channels are, unfortunately, not error-free, but rather error-prone due to a lot of disturbances which can combine with the useful signal (noise, interference, echoes). However, a digital TV signal, especially when almost all its redundancy has been removed, requires a very low bit error rate (**BER**) for good performance (BER of the order of $10^{-10}$–$10^{-12}$, corresponding to 0.1–10 erroneous bits in 1 hour for a bit-rate of 30 Mb/s). A channel with such a low BER is called *quasi-error-free* (**QEF**).

It is therefore necessary to take preventive measures before modulation in order to allow detection and, as far as possible, correction in the receiver of most errors introduced by the physical transmission channel. These measures, the majority of which consist of reintroducing a *calculated* redundancy into the signal (which obviously reduces the efficiency of the source coding), are grouped under the terms forward error correction (**FEC**) or channel coding (this term often includes the modulation process). Such measures will of course depend on specificities of the physical transmission medium.

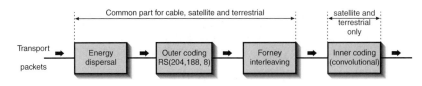

**Figure 6.1**  The main steps of forward error correction on the transmitter side.

The *virtual channel* thus created between the input of the FEC encoder on the transmission side and the output of the FEC decoder on the receiver side is quasi-error-free and is sometimes referred to as a *super channel.*

Figure 6.1 illustrates the successive steps of the forward error correction encoding process in the DVB standard. The terms inner coding and outer coding are seen from the point of view of the above-mentioned virtual channel. These steps are described in the following paragraphs, without going too deeply into the arcane world of the sophisticated error correction codes used, as this would require complex mathematical deviation. However, Appendix A explains the principle by describing some simpler codes, and the reader who is interested in more detail will find some references in the short bibliography at the end of the book.

## 6.1  Energy dispersal (randomizing)

Strictly speaking, this step is not part of the error correction process. However, the DVB requires that it should be undertaken before the correction process in order to obtain an evenly distributed energy within the RF channel.

Transport packets have a length of 188 bytes (see Fig. 6.2), the first of which is a synchronization byte of value $47_{hex}(01000111_{bin})$, the **MSB** being transmitted first. In order to avoid long series of 0's or 1's, which would bring a DC content to the signal, the signal has to be randomized in order to ensure the energy dispersal in the channel. This is obtained by scrambling the signal by means of a

| Sync. 47 h | 187 bytes |
|---|---|

**Figure 6.2**  The transport packet before error correction.

Initialization sequence

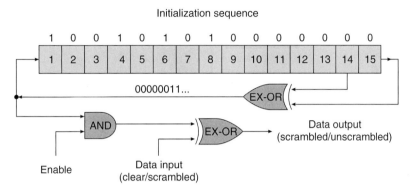

**Figure 6.3**  Diagram of the energy dispersal scrambler/descrambler (Source: prETS 300 421. © ETSI 1995. All rights reserved.)

pseudo-random binary sequency (**PRBS**) with the generator poly-nome $1 + X^{14} - X^{15}$.

The diagram of the pseudo-random generator, which is the same for scrambling and descrambling, is quite simple and is shown in Figure 6.3.

The generator is re-initialized every eight transport packets by loading its register with the sequence 100101010000000. In order that the de-randomizer in the receiver can locate the beginning of the sequence, the synchronizing byte of the first packet of the sequence is inverted ($47_{\text{hex}}$ becomes $B8_{\text{hex}}$), the seven others remaining unchanged. In order that the synchronization bytes are not scrambled, the enable input remains inactive during that time, but the pseudo-random sequence is not interrupted. The energy dispersal device remains active even in the absence of a signal or with a non-MPEG-2 compliant stream as the input. Figure 6.4 shows the transport packet sequence at the output of the energy dispersal circuit.

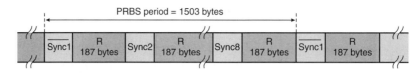

**Figure 6.4** Concatenation of packets after energy dispersal (Source: prETS 300 421. © ETSI 1995. All rights reserved.)

## 6.2 Reed–Solomon coding (outer coding)

In order to be able to correct most errors introduced by the physical transmission channel, it is necessary to introduce some form of redundancy allowing the detection and (up to a certain limit) correction of transmission errors to obtain a QEF channel.

The first error correction coding layer, called outer coding, is used with all DVB-specified transmission media; a second complementary layer, called inner coding, is used only in satellite and terrestrial transmissions (here "inner" and "outer" are relative to the virtual QEF channel formed by the physical medium and the FEC coder and decoder).

The outer coding is a **Reed–Solomon** code **RS(204, 188, T = 8)** which is a shortened version of the code RS(255, 239, T = 8); see Appendix A for a basic explanation on correction codes. This code, in combination with the Forney convolutional interleaving which follows it, allows the correction of burst errors introduced by the transmission channel. It is applied individually to all the packets in Figure 6.4, including the synchronization bytes.

The RS(204, 188, T = 8) coding adds 16 parity bytes after the information bytes of the transport packets, which therefore become 204 bytes long; it can correct up to 8 erroneous bytes per packet. If there are more than 8 erroneous bytes in the packet, it will be indicated as erroneous and not correctible, and it is up to the rest of the circuitry to decide what to do with it. The overhead introduced by this efficient code is rather low (slightly more than 8% = 16/188). Figure 6.5 indicates the format of the protected transport packets.

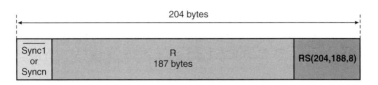

**Figure 6.5** A transport packet after Reed–Solomon coding.

## 6.3 Forney convolutional interleaving (temporal spreading of errors)

The purpose of this step is to increase the efficiency of the Reed–Solomon coding by spreading over a longer time the burst errors introduced by the channel, which could otherwise exceed the correction capacity of the RS coding (8 bytes per packet). This process, known as Forney convolutional interleaving, is illustrated in Figure 6.6.

$L$ is the length of the packet to be protected (204 bytes) and $I$ is the number of branches (here 12) of the interleaving and de-interleaving devices, called the *interleaving depth*. Hence $I = 12$ and $L = 204$. The interleaving device (in the transmitter) consists of a switched bank of 12 FIFOs (indexes $j = 0 - 11$) of length $M \times j$ (where $M = L/I = 204/12 = 17$), and the de-interleaving device (in the receiver) consists of the same switched bank, but with FIFO lengths of $M \times (11 - j)$. Thus, 12 successive bytes of index $j = 0 - 11$ will pass

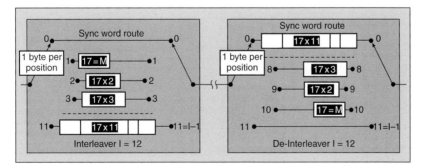

**Figure 6.6** Forney convolutional interleaving/de-interleaving (Source: prETS 300 421. © ETSI 1995. All rights reserved.)

through the branch of the corresponding index, and each byte will be delayed, depending on its index, by $0, 17, 34, \dots, 187$ positions (one position = one byte period) before transmission.

In the receiver, the same process happens simultaneously, and the byte delayed by $j \times 17$ positions at transmission will be delayed by $(11-j) \times 17$ positions, so that the delay is the same for all bytes, i.e., equal to $(j+11-j) \times 17 = 11 \times 17 = 187$ positions, and the initial order is recovered. However, a burst of errors affecting successive bytes in the physical channel will be spread by the de-interleaver over two successive packets, which will improve the efficiency of the RS coding and in most cases allow its correction. The synchronization byte always follows the branch of index $j = 0$.

Up to this point, the forward error correction (**FEC**) process has been the same for all RF transmission media envisaged by the DVB standard (satellite, cable, terrestrial). In the case of cable, the only remaining step before filtering and modulation (64-QAM, see Chapter 7) will be the conversion of the serial bitstream into two I and Q signals of 3 bits each, representing symbols of 6 bits. This purely logical operation is called *symbol mapping*. Figure 6.7 represents this process schematically (the real process is more complex due to the differential modulation of the 2 MSBs of the 6-bit symbols; see Chapter 7).

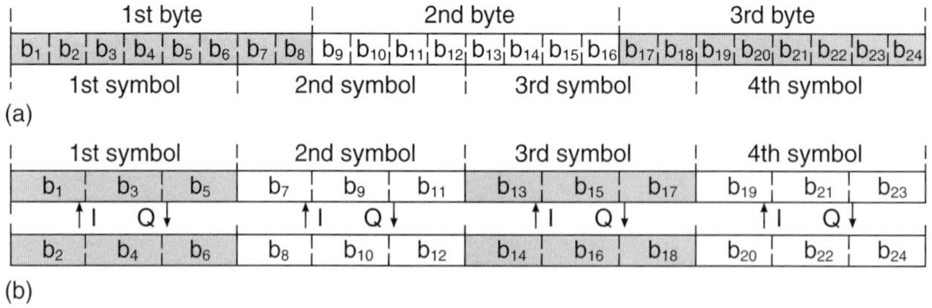

**Figure 6.7** Example of a possible mapping operation, first converting bytes to symbols and then converting symbols to I/Q signals (in the case of 64-QAM). (a) Three successive bytes form four successive 6-bit symbols (64-QAM); (b) 6-bit symbols are converted into I and Q signals (3 bits each).

For satellite and terrestrial transmissions, channel coding requires an additional step which aims mainly to reduce random error due to noise.

## 6.4 Convolutional coding (inner coding)

The *inner coding* is a **convolutional coding** (see explanation in Appendix A) and is an efficient complement to the Reed–Solomon coding and Forney interleaving, as it corrects other kinds of errors. In the case of the DVB standard, the schematic diagram of the convolutional coder is illustrated in Figure 6.8, and the basic parameters of the code are indicated in Table 6.1.

The strong redundancy introduced by the basic convolutional coding (100%, as the convolutional encoder produces two output bitstreams, each with the same bit-rate as the input stream) allows a very powerful error correction. This can be necessary with a very low signal-to-noise ratio (**SNR**) at the input to the receiver, but it reduces by a factor of 2 the spectral efficiency of the channel. In this

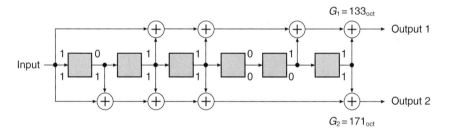

**Figure 6.8**  Principle diagram of the DVB-S convolutional coder.

**Table 6.1**  Basic parameters of the DVB convolutional code.

| Parameter | Abbreviation | Value |
|---|---|---|
| Code rate | $R_c$ | 1/2 |
| Constraint length | $K$ | 7 |
| First polynomial generator | $G_1$ | $171_{oct}$ |
| Second polynomial generator | $G_2$ | $133_{oct}$ |
| Free distance | $d_{free}$ | 10 |

case, the $X$ and $Y$ output streams from the convolutional encoder are applied directly (after filtering) to the I and Q inputs of the QPSK modulator for a satellite transmission (see Chapter 7), and the useful bit-rate of the channel is half the transmitted bit-rate (which is what is meant by $R_c = 1/2$).

In this case, *symbol mapping* (2 bits/symbol for QPSK) is mixed with convolutional coding. However, this type of convolutional coding allows this redundancy to be lowered by means of **puncturing** the output of the convolutional encoder. This involves not taking all successive bits of the two $X$ and $Y$ output bitstreams, but only one of the two simultaneous bits with a certain *puncturing ratio*. The I and Q streams used for modulation are obtained by appropriately alternating the $X$ and $Y$ outputs in order to obtain two balanced bitstreams. In this way, it is possible to obtain the punctured code rates specified by the DVB standard ($R_c = 2/3, 3/4, 5/6$, or $7/8$), which represent the ratio between the useful (input) and transmitted (output) bit-rates. These $R_c$ figures are obtained by multiplying the pure convolutional rate (1/2) by the inverse of the puncturing ratio (input bits/output bits). For instance, the code rate $R_c = 2/3$ is obtained with a puncturing ratio of 3/4 ($2/3 = 1/2 \times 4/3$).

**Table 6.2**  DVB inner coding characteristics (derived from prETS 300 421).

| $R_c$ | 1/2 | 2/3 | 3/4 | 5/6 | 7/8 |
|---|---|---|---|---|---|
| $d_{free}$ | 10 | 6 | 5 | 4 | 3 |
| $X$ | 1 | 10 10 | 101 | 10101 | 1000101 |
| $Y$ | 1 | 11 11 | 110 | 11010 | 1111010 |
| I | $X_1$ | $X_1 Y_2 Y_3$ | $X_1 Y_2$ | $X_1 Y_2 Y_4$ | $X_1 Y_2 Y_4 Y_6$ |
| Q | $Y_1$ | $Y_1 X_3 Y_4$ | $Y_1 X_3$ | $Y_1 X_3 X_5$ | $Y_1 Y_3 X_5 X_7$ |
| $S_{OFDM}$ | $X_1 Y_1$ | $X_1 Y_1 Y_2 X_3 Y_3 Y_4$ | $X_1 Y_1 Y_2 X_3$ | $X_1 Y_1 Y_2 X_3 Y_4 X_5$ | $X_1 Y_1 Y_2 Y_3 Y_4 X_5 Y_6 X_7$ |

*Notes*:
On lines $X$ and $Y$, '0' denotes a suppressed bit, '1' denotes a transmitted bit. For terrestrial transmissions based on OFMD modulation, additional steps are required after the inner coding: serialization of the bitstream, inner interleaving and symbol mapping to adapt the bitstream format to the high number of carriers used (see Chapter 7). The last line of the table. $S_{OFDM}$, represents the serialized bitstream (obtained by alternating I and Q lines) applied to the inner interleaving circuit used in the case of terrestrial OFDM transmission.

Puncturing increases the capacity of the transmission channel at the expense of a reduction of the free distance ($d_{free}$), which is a measure of the correction efficiency of the convolutional code. Given the power of the transponder and the size of the receiving antenna, the code rate chosen by the broadcaster will therefore be a trade-off between a useful bit-rate and the service area. Table 6.2 gives the free distance $d_{free}$, the puncturing scheme of $X$ and $Y$ outputs, and the sequence forming the bitstreams applied to the I and Q inputs of the QPSK modulator (in the case of satellite transmission) for the five code rates ($R_c$) specified by the DVB standard.

# Modulation by digital signals

**7**

Once the source coding operations (MPEG audio and video coding, data insertion, multiplexing, and eventually scrambling) and the channel coding (energy dispersal, outer RS coding, interleaving, inner convolutional coding) have been carried out, we have a data stream ready to be used for modulation of a carrier for transmission to the end users.

Depending on the medium (satellite, cable, terrestrial network), the bandwidth available for transmission depends on technical and administrative considerations, the latter largely depending on the former. In fact, technical conditions—particularly signal-to-noise ratio and echoes—vary considerably between signals coming from a satellite (weak but rather stable since they originate from a low power transmitter located more than 36,000 km away), those from a cable network (where signals are generally strong and stable at the subscriber plug) and those from a terrestrial transmitter where conditions can vary a great deal (especially in the case of mobile reception). As a result:

- for a *satellite* reception, the signal-to-noise ratio (carrier-to-noise ratio C/N or CNR) can be very small (10 dB or less) but the signal hardly suffers from echoes;

- by contrast, for *cable* reception, the SNR is quite strong (generally more than 30 dB), but the signal can be affected by echoes due to impedance mismatches in the network;

- in the case of *terrestrial* reception, conditions are more difficult, especially if mobile reception with very simple antennas is required (variable echoes due to multipath, interference, important signal level variations).

This is why modulation techniques have to be different, so that they can be optimized for the specific constraints of the transmission channel and for compatibility with existing analog transmissions:

- on satellite, the channel width is generally between 27 and 36 MHz, because of the need to use frequency modulation (FM) for transmission of an analog TV program (bandwidth 6–8 MHz with associated sound carriers), due to the low CNR previously described;

- on cable or terrestrial networks, the channel width varies from 6 (United States) to 7 or 8 MHz (Europe) due to the use of AM with a vestigial sideband (**VSB**) for video and one or more audio carriers.

Digital transmissions will inherit this situation and will therefore generally have to use the same channel width as their analog counterparts, so that, among other things, they can coexist with them on the same satellite, cable, or terrestrial network and be compatible with existing transmission and distribution equipment.

## 7.1  General discussion on the modulation of a carrier by digital signals

Digital signals are streams of rectangular pulses representing 0's and 1's. Depending on the channel characteristics, many bits can be combined to form symbols in order to increase the spectral efficiency of the modulation. However, without filtering, the frequency spectrum of digital signals is theoretically infinite, which would imply an infinite bandwidth for their transmission; this is, of course, not possible. As a result, appropriate filtering will be required to limit the required bandwidth; this filtering will have to be chosen in order to optimize the performance of the global transmission chain. Bandwidth limiting of a signal results in a theoretically infinite increase of its temporal response, which, without special precautions, would result in overlapping between successive symbols: this is called inter-symbol interference (**ISI**).

In order to avoid this problem, filtering should satisfy the first Nyquist criterion, in order that the temporal response presents zeros at times which are multiples of the symbol period $T$. The most commonly used filter is called a *raised cosine filter* or, more simply, a Nyquist filter. In order to optimize the bandwidth occupation and the signal-to-noise ratio, filtering is shared equally between the transmitter and the receiver, each of which comprises a half-Nyquist filter (square-root-raised cosine filter). This filtering is characterized by its **roll-off factor**, $\alpha$, which defines its steepness. Its frequency response is described in Table 7.1 (see also Fig. 7.1).

For a signal with a symbol period $T$ (symbol frequency or **symbol rate** $1/T$) the bandwidth $B$ occupied after Nyquist filtering with a roll-off $a$ is given by the relation:

$$B = (1+\alpha) \times 1/2T$$

Figure 7.1 shows the response curve of the Nyquist filtering (normalized to the symbol rate $1/T$) for three values of the roll-off factor (0.2, 0.35, 0.5), and Figure 7.2 shows the corresponding temporal response (normalized to the symbol period $T$). The temporal response shows the presence of zeros at instants that are multiples of the symbol period: in order to reduce the ISI to a minimum, the signal will have to be sampled at these instants with increasing accuracy as the roll-off decreases.

**Table 7.1** Frequency response of the Nyquist filtering

| Frequency | $0 < f < 0.5(1-\alpha)$ | $0.5(1-\alpha) < f < 0.5(1+\alpha)$ | $0.5(1+\alpha) < f < \infty$ |
|---|---|---|---|
| Response | 1 | $0.5\{1 + \sin[\pi T(0.5-f)/aT]\}$ | 0 |

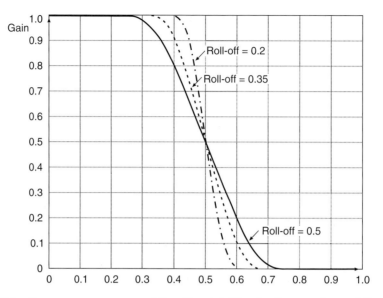

**Figure 7.1** Frequency response of the Nyquist filter for three values of the roll-off factor.

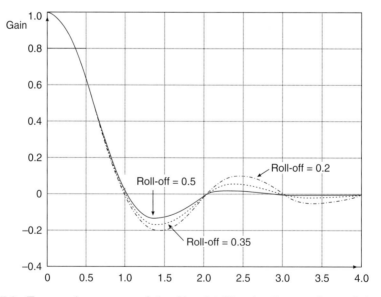

**Figure 7.2** Temporal response of the Nyquist filter for three values of the roll-off ($\alpha = 0.2, 0.35, 0.5$).

## 7.2  Quadrature modulations

In the simplest digital modulation schemes, the carrier is directly modulated by the bitstream representing the information to be transmitted, either in amplitude (**ASK**, amplitude shift keying) or in frequency (**FSK**, frequency shift keying). However, the low spectral efficiency of these modulations makes them inappropriate for the transmission of high bit-rates on channels with a bandwidth which is as small as possible.

In order to increase the spectral efficiency of the modulation process, different kinds of quadrature amplitude modulations (**QAM**) are used. These modulations were initially developed to transmit two independent analog signals on one carrier (the first widely known application, developed at the end of the 1940s, is the modulation of the color subcarrier of the NTSC system by the two color difference signals).

Figure 7.3 represents schematically the process of quadrature modulation and demodulation. Input symbols coded on $n$ bits are converted into two signals I (in-phase) and Q (quadrature), each coded on $n/2$ bits, corresponding to $2^{n/2}$ states for each of the two signals.

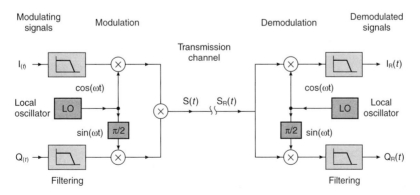

**Figure 7.3**  The basic quadrature modulation/demodulation process.

**Table 7.2**  Main characteristics of quadrature modulations

| I/Q coding (bits) | Bits/symbol | No. of states | Abbreviation |
|---|---|---|---|
| 1 | 2 | 4 | QPSK (= 4-QAM) |
| 2 | 4 | 16 | 16-QAM |
| 3 | 6 | 64 | 64-QAM |
| 4 | 8 | 256 | 256-QAM |

After digital-to-analog conversion (**DAC**), the I signal modulates an output of the local oscillator and the Q signal modulates another output in quadrature with the first (out of phase by $\pi/2$). The result of this process can be represented as a **constellation** of points in the I, Q space, which represents the various values that I and Q can take. Table 7.2 gives the main characteristics and denomination of some quadrature modulation schemes as a function of the number of bits for each of the I and Q signals.

Figures 7.4 and 7.5 show, respectively, the constellations of **QPSK** modulation (quadrature phase shift keying or 4-QAM) and 64-QAM. These figures represent the situation at the output of the modulator, where each point is well distinguished from its neighbors, so that there is no ambiguity concerning the symbol value at this level.

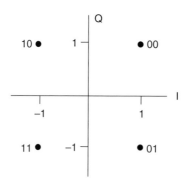

**Figure 7.4**  Constellation of a QPSK signal.

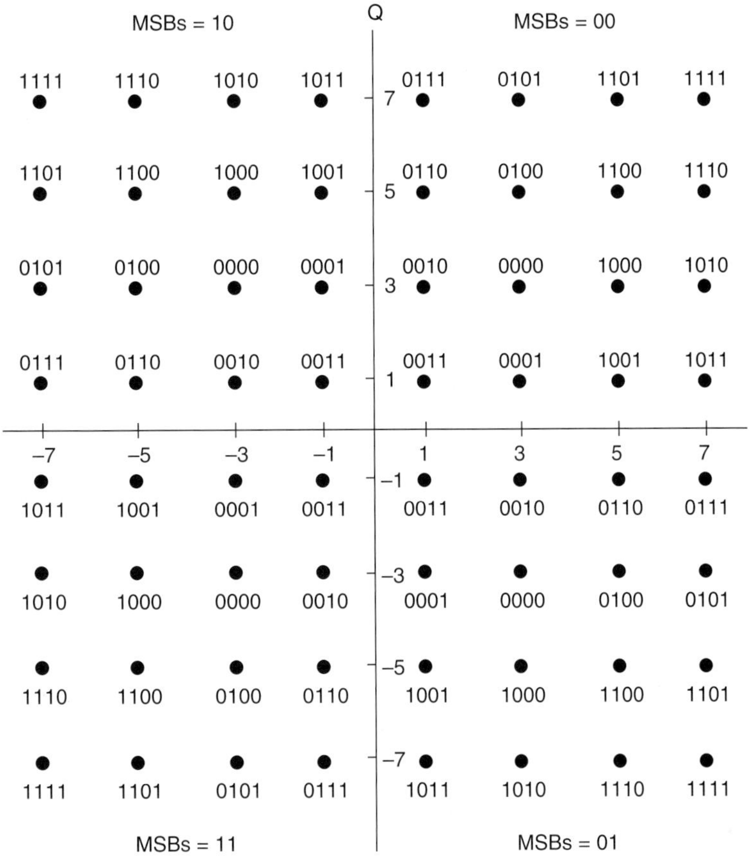

MSBs = 10                    Q                    MSBs = 00

| 1111 | 1110 | 1010 | 1011 | 0111 | 0101 | 1101 | 1111 |
| • | • | • | • | 7 • | • | • | • |

| 1101 | 1100 | 1000 | 1001 | 0110 | 0100 | 1100 | 1110 |
| • | • | • | • | 5 • | • | • | • |

| 0101 | 0100 | 0000 | 0001 | 0010 | 0000 | 1000 | 1010 |
| • | • | • | • | 3 • | • | • | • |

| 0111 | 0110 | 0010 | 0011 | 0011 | 0001 | 1001 | 1011 |
| • | • | • | • | 1 • | • | • | • |

−7   −5   −3   −1        1    3    5    7

| 1011 | 1001 | 0001 | 0011 | 0011 | 0010 | 0110 | 0111 |
| • | • | • | • | −1 • | • | • | • |

| • | • | • | • | −3 • | • | • | • |
| 1010 | 1000 | 0000 | 0010 | 0001 | 0000 | 0100 | 0101 |

| • | • | • | • | −5 • | • | • | • |
| 1110 | 1100 | 0100 | 0110 | 1001 | 1000 | 1100 | 1101 |

| • | • | • | • | −7 • | • | • | • |
| 1111 | 1101 | 0101 | 0111 | 1011 | 1010 | 1110 | 1111 |

MSBs = 11                         MSBs = 01

**Figure 7.5**  Constellation of a 64-QAM signal.

## 7.3  Modulation characteristics for cable and satellite digital TV broadcasting (DVB-C and DVB-S)

In order to make the best possible choice for these modulations, a number of theoretical studies and practical tests have been performed for cable as well as for satellite. Figure 7.6 shows the theoretical bit error rate (BER) in ideal conditions for quadrature modulations from 4-QAM (QPSK) to 64-QAM as a function of the SNR ratio (see Note 7.1). One can see that, for a given BER, QPSK has an advantage over 64-QAM of up to 12 dB.

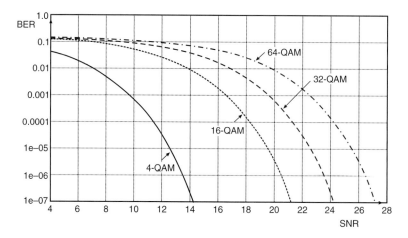

**Figure 7.6** Bit error rate as a function of signal-to-noise ratio for various quadrature modulations.

Taking into account the signal-to-noise ratio obtained on the receiving side, 2 bits/symbol (QPSK modulation) has been found to be the practical maximum, and therefore the best spectral efficiency, for satellite transmissions. In the case of cable, the signal-to-noise ratio is much higher, and a 64-QAM modulation (6 bits/symbol), roughly three times more efficient in spectral terms, can be used; American standards even use 256-QAM (8 bits/symbol).

Figure 7.7 illustrates the effect of noise on the QPSK constellation recovered at the output of the receiver's demodulator in the case of a noisy satellite reception.

Figure 7.8 shows the case of a cable reception of a 64-QAM signal with a low signal-to-noise ratio (of the order of 23 dB). It is conceivable that, above a certain noise level, the demodulator will be unable to distinguish, with certainty, a point in the constellation from its neighbors; there will be ambiguity surrounding the symbol being received and thus a potential error. The greater the number of points in the constellation, the lower the acceptable noise level will be, as the points are nearer to each other.

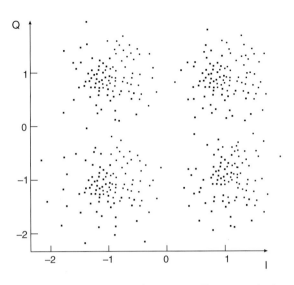

**Figure 7.7** A noisy QPSK constellation (weak satellite reception).

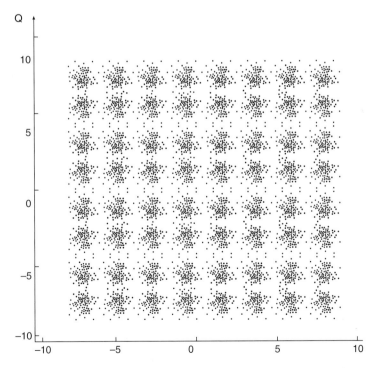

**Figure 7.8** A 64-QAM constellation with a signal-to-noise ratio of 23 dB.

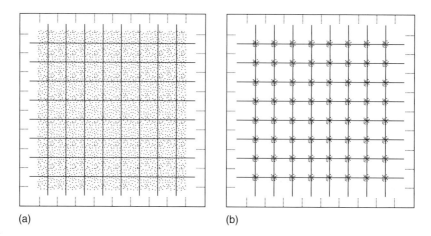

(a)                                        (b)

**Figure 7.9**   (a) A 64-QAM constellation with significant echoes before echo equalizing. (b) The same constellation after echo equalizing.

We stated earlier in this chapter that the cable reception was generally characterized by a high signal-to-noise ratio, but that it could, nevertheless, suffer from important echoes. Figure 7.9(a) shows the effect of echoes on the constellation, where the different points cannot be distinguished because of a very high inter-symbol interference. The use of an appropriate echo equalizer in the receiver allows the recovery of an almost perfect constellation (Fig. 7.9(b)).

Other types of transmission disturbances or imperfections in the transmitting and receiving devices (imperfect frequency response, interference, intermodulation, etc.) increase the inter-symbol interference and appear as noise on the constellation, reinforcing the need for the error correction systems described in Chapter 6.

Another problem which the receiver has to cope with in the case of digital QAM modulations is that it does not have an absolute phase reference to demodulate the constellation (in contrast with NTSC or PAL subcarrier demodulation, where a reference burst is sent at the beginning of each line). For this reason, there is a phase ambiguity of 90° (the carrier recovery system can lock in four different phase

**Table 7.3** Truth table of the differential coding of the two MSBs in DVB-C

| Symbol MSBs | | MSB of I and Q | | Phase change (°) |
|---|---|---|---|---|
| $B_{1T}$ | $B_{2T}$ | $I_T$ | $Q_T$ | |
| 0 | 0 | $I_{T-1}$ | $Q_{T-1}$ | 0 |
| 0 | 1 | $\overline{Q_{T-1}}$ | $I_{T-1}$ | +90 |
| 1 | 0 | $Q_{T-1}$ | $\overline{I_{T-1}}$ | −90 |
| 1 | 1 | $\overline{I_{T-1}}$ | $\overline{Q_{T-1}}$ | 180 |

$B_{1T}$ and $B_{2T}$ are the two MSBs of the transmitted symbol; $I_T$ and $Q_T$ are, respectively, the differentially encoded MSBs of I and Q for this symbol; $I_{T-1}$ and $Q_{T-1}$ are the MSBs of I and Q of the preceding symbol.

states), which will prevent the receiver from synchronizing itself as long as the demodulation phase is incorrect.

In the case of the QAM modulation used for cable, this problem is avoided by using a differential modulation for the two MSBs of the symbol: the state of the MSB of I and Q corresponds to a phase change and not to an absolute phase state, which allows the receiver to operate in any of the four possible lock conditions (the constellation of the LSBs being identical in the four quadrants). Table 7.3 represents the truth table for differential coding of the MSB of the I and Q modulating signals used to generate the QAM employed in DVB-C.

In the case of the (non-differential) QPSK modulation used for satellite, the "out of synchronization" information can be used to modify (up to three times) the phase relation between the recovered carrier and the received signal until synchronization is obtained.

## 7.3.1 Modulations for DVB-C and DVB-S

Taking into account all the above-mentioned considerations (and many others), the main characteristics retained for the DVB-compliant digital TV transmissions are detailed in Table 7.4. Table 7.5 gives the maximum possible bit-rates on a DVB-compliant satellite channel as a function of the channel width and the code rate for a QPSK modulation with $\alpha = 0.35$.

**Table 7.4** Main characteristics retained for DVB compliant digital TV transmissions

| Parameter | Satellite (DVB-S) | Cable (DVB-C) |
|---|---|---|
| Channel width | 26–54 MHz | 8 MHz (7 MHz possible) |
| Modulation type | QPSK (= 4-QAM) | 64, 32 or 16-QAM |
| Roll-off factor ($\alpha$) | 0.35 | 0.15 |

**Table 7.5** Maximum bit-rates as a function of the channel width and the code rate (DVB-S) (derived from prETS 300 421, © European Telecommunication Standards Institute 1995. All rights reserved)

| Channel width (MHz) | Maximum symbol rate (MHz) | Maximum useful bit-rate (Mb/s) | | | | |
|---|---|---|---|---|---|---|
| | | $R_c = 1/2$ | $R_c = 2/3$ | $R_c = 3/4$ | $R_c = 5/6$ | $R_c = 7/8$ |
| 54 | 42.2 | 38.9 | 51.8 | 58.3 | 64.8 | 68.0 |
| 46 | 35.9 | 33.1 | 44.2 | 49.7 | 55.2 | 58.0 |
| 40 | 31.2 | 28.8 | 38.4 | 43.2 | 48.0 | 50.4 |
| 36 | 28.1 | 25.9 | 34.6 | 38.9 | 43.2 | 45.4 |
| 33 | 25.8 | 23.8 | 31.7 | 35.6 | 39.6 | 41.6 |
| 30 | 23.4 | 21.6 | 28.8 | 32.4 | 36.0 | 37.8 |
| 27 | 21.1 | 19.4 | 25.0 | 29.2 | 32.4 | 34.0 |
| 26 | 20.3 | 18.7 | 25.0 | 28.1 | 31.2 | 32.8 |

Gray areas in Table 7.5 indicate the cases which can be transported transparently (without transport stream modification) on a DVB-compliant cable channel of 8 MHz with 64-QAM. In this case, the processing at the cable head-end will be limited to QPSK demodulation, forward error correction (Viterbi decoding, de-interleaving, Reed–Solomon decoding, de-randomizing) in order to recover corrected 188-byte transport packets and to reapply a cable FEC (randomizing, Reed–Solomon coding, interleaving) before modulation (16- to 64-QAM).

A sample calculation of the spectral efficiency with parameters of DVB-S and DVB-C can be found in Appendix B.

## 7.3.2 The second-generation satellite transmission standard DVB-S2 (EN 302307)

DVB-S2 is a second-generation transmission standard, standardized by ETSI under the number EN302307. It can be considered as an extension of both the DVB-S standard (EN300421) for consumer applications and the DVB-DSNG standard (EN301210) intended for point-to-point ad hoc satellite links (Digital Satellite News Gathering). DVB-S2 is destined to progressively replace them both as it improves their efficiency and flexibility.

Unlike the two previous standards mentioned above, DVB-S2 is not limited to the MPEG-2 transport stream format. Like DVB-T, it includes the option of hierarchical modes allowing to carry streams with different priorities corresponding to different degrees of robustness.

This allows for example transmissions in 8-PSK with a non-uniform constellation modulated by two combined synchronous streams. The first one, high priority (HP), could be retro-compatible with the DVB-S standard and would require a relatively small C/N. The second one, low priority (LP), would require a DVB-S2-compliant receiver and a higher C/N.

The DVB-S2 standard covers a much broader range of applications than DVB-S, on one end toward very high bit-rates by using modulation constellations with up to 32 states (32 APSK with 5 bits per symbol), and on the other end with applications requiring an increased robustness by using QPSK modulation and very low code rates.

A spectral efficiency of about 4 bit/Hz can be reached (APSK32, code rate 9/10), which corresponds to a theoretical bit-rate of 135 Mb/s in a 33 MHz channel, if a C/N of 16 dB or more can be guaranteed.

If robustness is the main concern, use of QPSK modulation (2 bits per symbol) and a low code rate of 1/4 makes it possible to maintain the link with a C/N as low as −3dB (i.e., with a noise level which is twice as strong as the signal to be received). It is, of course, at the expense of the signal efficiency, which in this case is less than 0.5 bit/Hz, which corresponds to a bit-rate of about 15 Mb/s in a 33 MHz channel.

A very large number of intermediate combinations is possible, for example, by using the 8-PSK and 16-APSK modulations (3 and 4 bits per symbol respectively) with code rates which can be as low as 1/4 to as high as 9/10.

For consumer broadcast applications, only QPSK (already used in DVB-S) and 8-PSK have to be supported and the code rate range is limited (from 1/2 to 9/10), as shown in Figure 7.10.

The roll-off factor, fixed at 0.35 for DVB-S, can be 0.20, 0.25, or 0.35 in DVB-S2, which makes it possible to better exploit the bandwidth characteristics of the transponder. For broadcast applications, the combined use of these innovations can bring at least a 30% increase of the spectral efficiency over DVB-S for a given C/N. This is visible in Figure 7.11 when comparing, for example, DVB-S2 (8-PSK, code rate 1/2 to DVB-S; QPSK, code rate 3/4 for a C/N level of roughly 7 dB).

This allows either an increase in the bit-rate at identical coverage in the same receiving conditions (for example, to introduce HDTV), or an improvement in coverage at identical bit-rate.

Combined to the efficiency gain of H264 compression, DVB-S2 will allow finding more easily the required bandwidth to the introduction

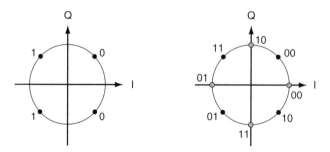

**Figure 7.10**  QPSK and 8-PSK constellations of DVB-S2 (broadcast applications).

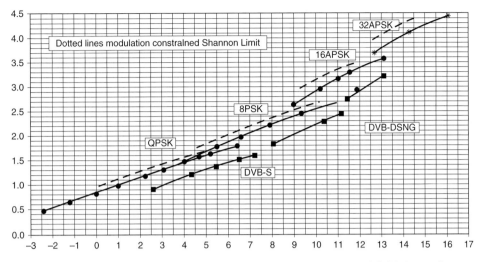

**Figure 7.11** Spectral efficiency (bits per symbol) as a function of C/N depending on modulation and code rate. The dotted line represents the theoretical Shannon limit. (Source: © ETSI/EN, 302307.)

of HDTV by satellite and will contribute to speed up its start. New receivers will obviously be required to receive these HD transmissions, which will only show all their advantages on a high resolution, HD Ready, screen.

One can thus affirm that satellite TV is poised to evolve significantly in the coming months and years, and that high definition TV should result in a regain of interest for this broadcast medium with unrivalled transmission capacity.

## 7.4 OFDM modulation for terrestrial digital TV (DVB-T)

The European Digital Video Broadcasting – Terrestrial system (**DVB-T**) defined by the DVB is based on 2 K/8 K OFDM. It has been released by ETSI and published under the reference ETSI/EBU 300,744. The principle behind this type of modulation involves the distribution of a high rate bitstream over a high number of **orthogonal** carriers (from a few hundred up to a few thousand), each carrying a low bit-rate; the same principle was previously retained for the European digital radio system (Digital Audio Broadcast, **DAB**) which uses 2 K OFDM. Its main advantage is its excellent behavior in the case of multipath reception, which is common in terrestrial mobile or portable reception: in this case the delay of the indirect paths becomes much smaller than the symbol period.

**OFDM** modulation (orthogonal frequency division multiplexing) consists of modulating with symbols of duration $T_s$ (in QPSK or QAM depending on the trade-off between bit-rate and robustness) a high number $N$, of carriers with a spacing of $1/T_s$ between two consecutive carriers. This determines the condition of orthogonality between the carriers, the spectrum of which can be seen in Figure 7.12; for the central frequency of a given carrier, the spectrum of the carriers which surround it presents a zero crossing.

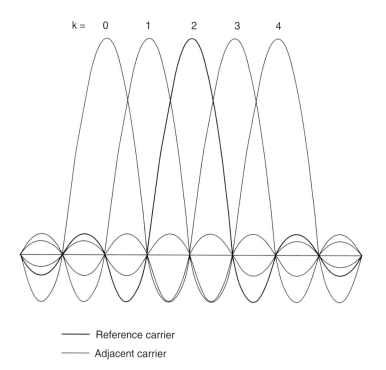

———— Reference carrier

———— Adjacent carrier

**Figure 7.12** Spectrum of adjacent carriers with OFDM modulation (Source: *Revue de l'UER,* no. 224. © EBU/UER (August 1987)).

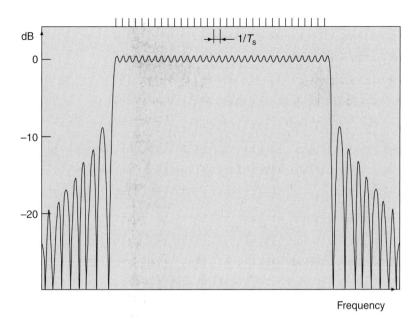

**Figure 7.13** Spectrum of an OFDM signal with 32 carriers (Source: *Revue de l'UER,* no. 224. © EBU/UER (August 1987)).

The relationship between the frequency $f_0$ of the lowest carrier and that of carrier $k(0 < k < N - 1)$, $f_k$, is given by $f_k = f_0 + k/T_s$. The frequency spectrum of such a set of carriers shows secondary parasitic lobes of width $1/T_s$, which can be seen in Figure 7.13 (for $N = 32$ carriers).

However, in real terrestrial receiving conditions, signals coming from multiple indirect paths added to the direct path mean that the condition of orthogonality between carriers is no longer fulfilled, which results in inter-symbol interference. This problem can be circumvented by adding a guard interval $\Delta$ before the symbol period $T_s$ in order to obtain a new symbol period $N'_s = \Delta + T_s$. This guard interval is generally equal to or less than $T_s/4$; it is occupied by a copy of the end of the useful symbol (Fig. 7.14).

In order to simplify filtering and to avoid any aliasing due to sampling, the bandwidth has to be less than half the sampling frequency, which requires suppression of a certain number of carriers at the two extremities of the band (e.g., $N' = 28$ instead of $N' = 32$).

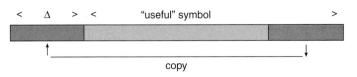

Figure 7.14 Elaboration of the guard interval.

In general $N$ is much greater than 32, and the relative importance of the secondary lobes is much smaller than in Figure 7.13.

### 7.4.1 Residential digital terrestrial television (DVB-T)

For terrestrial digital television, the DVB technical module has retained an OFDM modulation with 2048 carriers (2 K) or 8192 carriers (8 K), for which the spectrum can be considered as virtually rectangular (Fig. 7.15).

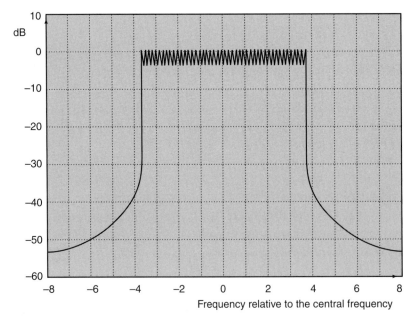

Figure 7.15 Spectrum of a DVB-T channel with a guard interval of $T_s/4$ (8 or 2K OFDM).

**Table 7.6** Main parameters of the DVB-T terrestrial system (OFDM 2 K or 8 K modulation)

| Parameter | 8 K/8 MHz | 8 K/7 MHz | 2 K/8 MHz | 2 K/7 MHz |
|---|---|---|---|---|
| Total number of carriers ($N'$) | 6817 (0 to 6816) | | 1705 (0 to 1704) | |
| "Useful" carriers (data) | 6048 | | 1512 | |
| Scattered pilot carriers | 524 | | 131 | |
| Continual pilot carriers | 177 | | 45 | |
| Signalling carriers (TPS) | 68 | | 17 | |
| "Useful" symbol duration ($T_s$) | 896 μs | 1024 μs | 224 μs | 256 μs |
| Carrier spacing ($1/T_s$) | 1116.07 Hz | 976.65 Hz | 4464.28 Hz | 3906.25 Hz |
| Distance between extreme carriers | 7.61 MHz | 6.66 MHz | 7.61 MHz | 6.66 MHz |
| Guard interval ($\Delta$) | $T_s = 4; T_s = 8; T_s = 16$ or $T_s = 32$ | | | |
| Individual carrier modulation | QPSK, 16-QAM or 64-QAM | | | |
| Hierarchical modes | $\alpha = 1$ or $\alpha = 2$ or $\alpha = 4$ | | | |

The DVB-T standard has been designed to be compatible with all existing TV channellization systems in the world (channel widths of 6, 7 or 8 MHz). It is, however, mainly used with channel widths of 7 (Europe VHF, Australia) and 8 MHz (Europe UHF).

It has also been designed in order to be able to coexist with analog television transmissions thanks to good protection against adjacent channel interference (**ACI**) and against interference from within the channel itself (co-channel interference or **CCI**).

Table 7.6 summarizes the main parameters of DVB-T for European channels of 7 or 8 MHz.

In order to adapt the bitstream to the OFDM modulation and in order to further increase the robustness of the system, after an identical channel coding to the DVB-S satellite system, data follow a complex process of interleaving, which happens in two steps:

- A first interleaving process at the "bit" level is applied and forms matrices of 126 words of 2, 4, or 6 bits depending on the modulation chosen for the individual (QPSK, 16-QAM, or 64-QAM).

- These matrices are then grouped by 12 (2 K mode) or 48 (8 K mode) in order to form OFDM symbols of $1512 \times 2$ bits (2 K mode in QPSK) up to $6048 \times 6$ bits (8 K mode in 64-QAM) which will be used to modulate the 1512 or 6048 useful carriers.

Given their very high number, these carriers are of course not modulated individually; this is done by means of an inverse Fast Fourier Transform (iFFT) on 2048 points (2 K mode) or 8192 points (8 K mode), which converts the complex input data from the time domain to the frequency domain.

In 8 K mode, the long symbol duration (896 ms in the case of 8 MHz channels), combined with the maximum guard interval ($\Delta = 1/4$, corresponding to 224 $\mu$s), allows satisfactory reception even in the presence of very long echoes (difference between path lengths of up to many tens of kilometers), which allows the creation of wide area coverage networks using the same channel everywhere (they are called single frequency networks or **SFN**), made of transmitters which may be many tens of kilometers from each other.

The 2 K mode (Note 7.2) is in principle simpler to implement at the demodulator side, but this simplification is balanced by a division by four of the maximum acceptable echo distances, which makes it unsuitable for single frequency networks, as well as by a weaker immunity against impulsive noise interferences, such as those generated by the ignition of older car engines or some electrical domestic appliances.

However, the carrier spacing in 2 K mode, which is four times bigger than in 8 K mode, divides by four the Döppler effect which happens in case of mobile reception, thus allowing reception at high speed (up to 250 km/h at the upper end of the UHF band in 2 K mode; the maximum allowed speed is four times less in 8 K mode). The maximum speed is also inversely proportional to the channel frequency, so that use of VHF would allow high speeds even with the 8 K mode.

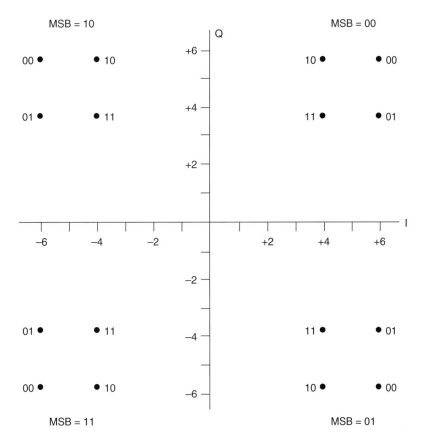

**Figure 7.16** Example of a non-uniform 16-QAM constellation.

The DVB-T standard includes a possibility of hierarchical coding by means of a non-uniform QAM modulation of the carriers, which features on the constellation a greater distance between adjacent states located in different quadrants than between adjacent states belonging to the same quadrant. Non-uniform constellations are defined by a parameter that can take three values ($\alpha = 1$, 2, or 4), which define the distance between the sub-constellations of each quadrant. Figure 7.16 represents the constellation of an example of non-uniform QAM modulation.

This allows the simultaneous transmission of a high priority (HP) bitstream which modulates the two MSBs of a 16- or 64-QAM transmission, thus enabling the receiver to consider it a noisy QPSK signal, and a second low priority (LP) bitstream modulating the remaining LSBs which requires a better C/N at the receiver side for error-free reception. The high priority bitstream is very robust, but at a relatively low bit-rate, whereas the low priority bitstream can have a higher bit-rate, but with less robustness.

Applications of hierarchical coding can be either broadcasting on the same RF channel of programs which can be received in different conditions, or the same program which can be received with different resolution characteristics (e.g., SD or HD) depending on receiving conditions.

Simultaneous broadcasting in the same RF channel of a very robust QPSK bitstream allowing satisfactory mobile reception of a standard definition transmission and of a QAM bitstream at higher bit-rate allowing transmission of one high definition or many standard definition programs, intended for fixed reception with a good antenna, is thus possible.

The DVB-T signal is organized in successive **frames** made of 68 symbols. Four successive frames compose a superframe of 272 symbols which allow the transmission of an integer number of RS-protected packets of 204 bytes, avoiding the need to insert stuffing bytes, whichever parameters allowed by the standard are used.

In order to help the receiver to acquire the signal and to inform it of the modulation and channel coding parameters, the OFDM signal includes carriers which are not modulated by the "useful" bitstream (see Table 7.6).

There are continual pilot carriers which have a fixed position, scattered pilot carriers which shift by three positions at each new symbol and transmission parameter signalling (**TPS**) carriers. Continual pilot carriers are transmitted at a higher power level than other carriers and are modulated by a pseudo-random binary sequence (**PRBS**) with $X^{11}+X^2+1$ as the generating polynom. They allow the receiver

| 1 bit | 16 bits | 37 bits | 14 bits |
|---|---|---|---|
| Ref | Synchronization | TPS parameters | Parity |

**Figure 7.17**  Structure of the TPS frame.

to synchronize and to make a channel estimation (evaluation of the channel alteration due to multiple trajects, etc.) in view of its correction.

TPS carriers transmit at very low rate all the parameters of the transmission by means of a very robust differential bi-phase shift-keying (**BPSK**) modulation (1 bit/symbol). They allow an accelerated acquisition of the signal as well as a quick response to an eventual change in the parameters to the receiver. All TPS carriers transmit simultaneously the same information bit. This very high redundancy makes decoding of the TPS information possible even when the signal is totally unusable for satisfactory reception. The TPS information is transmitted once per frame (68 symbols), thus its length is 68 bits (Fig. 7.17). Table 7.7 shows the detailed TPS bit allocation.

**Table 7.7**  Detailed bit allocation of the TPS information

| Bits | Allocation |
|---|---|
| b0 | Initialization of the BPSK modulator (derived from the reference PRBS) |
| b1-b16 | Synchronization sequence (0011010111101110 inverted at each frame) |
| b17-b22 | Number of useful TPS bits (currently 010111 = 23 decimal) |
| b23-b24 | Current frame number (00 = 1, 01 = 2, 10 = 3, 11 = 4) |
| b25-b26 | Carrier modulation (00 = QPSK, 01 = 16 QAM, 10 = 64 QAM, 11 = reserved) |
| b27-b29 | $\alpha$ value (000 = non-hierarchical, 001 = 1 010 = 2 011 = 4, 1, 1xx = reserved) |
| b30-b32 | Code rate of unique or HP bitstream ⎱ (000 = 1/2, 001 = 2/3, 010 = 3/4, 011 = 5/6) |
| b33-b35 | Code rate of LP bitstream (hierarchical) ⎰ 100 = 7/8, 101...111 = (reserved) |
| b36-b37 | Guard interval (00 = 1/32, 01 = 1/16, 10 = 1/8, 11 = 1/4) |
| b38-b39 | OFDM mode (00 = 2K, 01 = 8K, 10 and 11 = reserved) |
| b40-b53 | Reserved (all bits at 0) |
| b54-b67 | Parity (calculated on the whole TPS message with code BCH 127, 113, $t = 2$) |

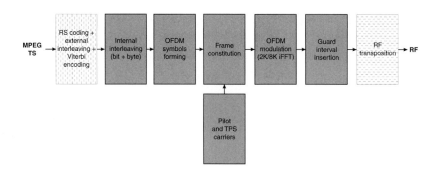

**Figure 7.18** The main steps of channel coding and modulation of DVB-T.

Figure 7.18 represents a block diagram of the DVB-T channel coding and modulation process (specific blocks to DVB-T are in dark gray). This diagram, although very simplified, shows that this process is much more complex than that of cable or satellite. The DVB-T specification was finalized in 1997 and filed by ETSI under the reference ETS 300, 744.

**Exercise:** Calculation of the useful bit-rate in a common DVB-T transmission example (UK case):

- 8 MHz channel;
- 2 K mode (8 K or 2 K is unimportant for the bit-rate);
- modulation: 64-QAM;
- guard interval: 1/32;
- puncturing rate: 2/3.

We have 1512 useful carriers modulated in 64-QAM (6 bits/symbol) with a symbol frequency of 4464.286 Hz, which gives a brutto bit-rate of:

$$1512 \times 6 \times 4464.286 = 40500 \text{ Mb/s}$$

The bit-rate calculation must take into account the guard interval (i.e., 32/33 with $\Delta = 1/32$) and the channel coding overheads (i.e., 2/3 for puncturing and 188/204 for RS coding), therefore the useful bit-rate:

$$40,500 \times 32/33 \times 2/3 \times 188/204 = \mathbf{24,128\ Mb/s}$$

This bit-rate, depending on the trade-off between picture quality and number of programs per channel chosen by the broadcaster, allows transmission of four to six TV programs.

Depending on the trade-off between robustness and bit-rate chosen by the broadcaster (or the broadcasting regulation authority), the DVB-T system can carry the following minimum and maximum bit-rates in an 8 MHz channel:

**Minimum bit-rate: 4.98 Mb/s** (QPSK modulation, guard interval 1/4, code rate 1/2)

**Maximum bit-rate: 31.67 Mb/s** (64-QAM, guard interval 1/32, code rate 7/8)

One can see that the bit-rate can vary in a ratio from 1 to more than 6!

### 7.4.2 Digital terrestrial television for mobile and handheld devices (DVB-H)

The DVB-H standard is an extension of the DVB-T standard. It is intended to bring reception of television programs to mobile and hand-held receivers (the H of DVB-H stands for "handheld," which indicates its main type of target devices). In most cases, it will be a mobile phone. DVB-H principles are described in Chapter 10, Section 10.6.

## 7.5 Summary of DVB transmission characteristics (cable, satellite, terrestrial)

Table 7.8 summarizes the main characteristics of the transmissions following the DVB standard for the three transmission media.

**Table 7.8** Main characteristics of DVB-compliant digital TV signals

| Parameter | Cable (DVB-C) | Satellite (DVB-S) | Sat. (DVB-S2) | Terr. (DVB-T) | Mobile (DVB-H) |
|---|---|---|---|---|---|
| Video coding | MPEG-2 or MPEG-4 AVC (H264) | | | H264, H263 … | |
| Audio coding | MPEG-1 (layer II), Dolby Digital or AAC | | | G7xx, AAC | |
| Scrambling | DVB-CSA (Common Scrambling Algorithm) | | | tbd | |
| Link layer FEC | N.A. | N.A. | N.A. | N.A. | MPE-FEC (optional) |
| Transport packet | 188 bytes | 188 bytes | 188 bytes (1) | 188 bytes | 188 bytes |
| External channel coding | Reed-Solomon (204,188, $T = 8$) | Reed-Solomon (204,188, $T = 8$) | BCH | Reed-Solomon (204,188, $T = 8$) | Reed-Solomon (204,188, $T = 8$) |
| Byte interleaving | Forney, depth = 12 | Forney, depth = 12 | N.A. | Forney, depth = 12 | Forney, depth = 12 |
| Internal channel coding none | Convolutive, $R_c = $ 1/2, 2/3, 3/4, 5/6, or 7/8 | LDPC | 1/4 to 9/10 | Convolutive, $R_c = $ 1/2, 2/3, 3/4, 5/6, or 7/8 | Convolutive, $R_c = $ 1/2, 2/3, 3/4, 5/6, or 7/8 |
| Bit interleaving | N.A. | N.A. | By blocks (8PSK, 16 and 32 APSK) | N.A. | N.A. |
| Roll-off factor | 15% | 35% | 20, 25, or 35% | N.A. | N.A. |
| Modulation | 16 to 256 QAM | QPSK | QPSK to 32 APSK | OFDM 2K/8K | OFDM 2K/4K/8K |
| Channel width | 6, 7, or 8 MHz | 27 ~ 36 MHz | 27 ~ 36 MHz | 6, 7, or 8 MHz | 5, 6, 7, or 8 MHz |

One can remark that source coding is common to all three media and that channel coding is simpler for cable transmissions, and that all media use different, optimized modulations.

**Note 7.1**

The $E_b/N_o$ ratio (average bit energy/noise density) is preferred over the C/N ratio (or CNR) for digital modulations, as it takes into account the number of states of the modulation. In fact, these two ratios, which describe the same physical reality, are related. $E_b/N_o$ is related to $E_s/N_o$ (average symbol energy/noise density) as follows:

$$E_b/N_o = E_s/N_o \log_2 M$$

where $M$ represents the number of states of the modulation (e.g., 4 for 4-QPSK, 64 for 64-QAM). $E_s/N_o$ is itself related to C/N by the equation:

$$E_s/N_o = (C/N) \times B_{eq} \times T$$

where $B_{eq}$ is the equivalent noise band ($\approx$ channel width $BW$) and $T$ is the symbol period. From this comes the relationship between $E_b/N_o$ and C/N (without FEC):

$$E_b/N_o \approx (C/N) \times BW \times T/\log_2 M$$

C/N and $E_b/N_o$ are usually expressed in dB; this relation becomes then:

$$E_b/N_o(\text{dB}) = C/N(\text{dB}) + 10\log[BW \times T/\log_2(\text{M})].$$

In addition, it is referred to the symbol rate $R_s = 1/T$, so:

$$E_b/N_o(\text{dB}) = C/N(\text{dB}) + 10\log[BW/R_s \times \log_2(\text{M})]$$
$$C/N(\text{dB}) = E_b/N_o(\text{dB}) + 10\log[R_s \times \log_2(\text{M})/BW]$$

141

In the case of satellite, $M = 4$ (QPSK); if $BW = 33\,\text{MHz}$ and $R_s = 27.5\,\text{Ms/s}$, then:

$$C/N = E_b/N_o + 2.2(\text{dB})$$

## Note 7.2

The United Kingdom started the first digital terrestrial TV service based on the DVB-T standard at the end of 1998.

It was decided then to use the 2 K version of DVB-T because the first circuits available at that time were only supporting this mode, resulting in a significant cost reduction of the receiver, which, however, disappeared rapidly, since all demodulators soon supported all possible combinations of the DVB-T standard.

# Reception of digital TV signals 8

## 8.1 Global view of the transmission/reception process

As a summary of the various concepts explained in the previous chapters, and as an introduction to the description of an integrated receiver decoder (IRD or more commonly set-top box), we will briefly and in simple terms review the various processing steps the TV signal has to follow from the source to the display on the end user's screen.

The upper portion of Figure 8.1 (similar to Fig. 2.6) illustrates the steps on the transmission side, which has to deliver a multiplex of MPEG-2 programs on one RF channel:

1. Video and audio signals of the programs to be broadcast are each put through an MPEG-2 encoder which delivers the video and audio PESs to the multiplexer (about four to eight programs per RF channel depending on the parameters chosen for the encoding).

2. These PESs are used by the multiplexer to form 188 byte transport packets, which are eventually scrambled (CAT tables carrying conditional access information ECM/EMM are inserted in this case), as well as the PAT, PMT, PSI, and DVB-SI tables for the electronic program guide (**EPG**).

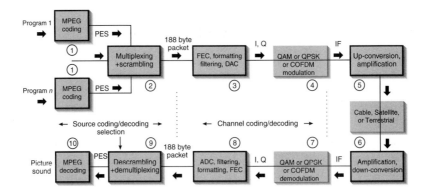

**Figure 8.1** Simplified view of the complete DVB transmission/reception chain.

3. The RS error correction increases the packet length to 204 bytes; in the case of satellite, the convolutional coding further multiplies the bit-rate by a factor of between $1.14$ ($R_c = 7/8$) and $2$ ($R_c = 1/2$); formatting of the data (*symbol mapping*) followed by filtering and D/A conversion produce the I and Q analog signals.

4. The I and Q signals modulate in QPSK (satellite) and QAM (cable) or COFDM (terrestrial) an IF carrier (intermediate frequency of the order of 70 MHz).

5. This IF is up-converted into the appropriate frequency band (depending on the medium) for transmission to the end users.

In the case of satellite, the frequency change will bring it to the required value for the **uplink** to the satellite **transponder**, where it will again be frequency converted for diffusion to the end users in the KU band (from 10.7 to 12.75 GHz).

Direct diffusion by cable is relatively rare in Europe, and most of the time the process involves a satellite and a head-end station which ensures QPSK demodulation/QAM remodulation and transposition on the appropriate VHF or UHF channel.

The lower portion of Figure 8.1 shows the complementary steps which take place on the receiver side; these are, in fact, the reverse of those on the transmission side.

6. In the case of satellite, an initial down-conversion takes place in the antenna head (low noise converter, **LNC**), which brings the frequency into the 950–2150 MHz range (input of the IRD), where it undergoes a second down-conversion (after RF channel selection) to an intermediate frequency that is usually 480 MHz. For cable and terrestrial, there is only one down-conversion from the VHF/UHF channel to an IF of 36.15 MHz in Europe.

7. The coherent demodulation of this IF delivers the I and Q analog signals.

8. After A/D conversion, filtering and reformatting of I and Q (symbol demapping), the forward error correction recovers the transport packets of 188 bytes.

9. The demultiplexer selects the PES corresponding to the program chosen by the user, which may previously have been descrambled with the help of the ECM, EMM, and the user key (smart card).

10. The MPEG-2 decoder reconstructs the video and audio of the desired program.

## 8.2 Composition of the integrated receiver decoder (IRD)

We have seen above the main steps in the digital TV transmission and reception processes, which indicate the basics of the IRD architecture. We will now go into a little more detail, without, however, going down to the level of electrical diagrams since this would offer little, due to their very great complexity. In fact, without even taking into account the cost of such an enterprise, it is practically out of the question for any individual to build his or her own IRD. In addition to the great difficulty associated with finding, assembling, and testing the required components, even with the tools available to a clever electronic amateur (the main ICs can have more than 200 pins), the greatest difficulty is on the software side, which represents tens of person-years of work, involving very diverse specialities. Deep software layers are closely linked to the hardware, intermediate layers to the broadcast standard, and the highest layers to the network for which it is designed, and this is often partly defined by the broadcaster.

In addition, the technological evolution in this field is extremely rapid in order to take advantage of the continuous progress of integration (the lifetime of a hardware generation will probably not exceed a year, with overlaps between generations in production). This is required in order to reduce, as quickly as possible, the cost of the digital IRD, which is currently much more expensive than its analog predecessor, largely due to the cost of the memory required (fortunately, the cost of this memory has dropped a lot in recent months).

### 8.2.1   The satellite integrated receiver decoder

The block diagram in Figure 8.2 represents the main functional blocks of a 1995/96 satellite IRD and their interconnection. It does not necessarily correspond to the partitioning used by all chip makers for manufacture of the ICs. This partitioning can vary substantially from supplier to supplier, and depends on the integration level, which increases quickly between two successive hardware generations.

The signals received from the satellite (frequencies ranging from 10.7 to 12.75 GHz) are amplified and down-converted (in two bands) into the 950–2150 MHz range by the low noise converter (**LNC**) located at the antenna focus, and applied to the IRD's input.

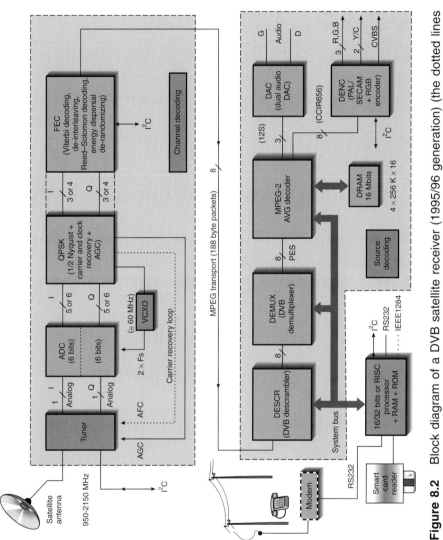

**Figure 8.2** Block diagram of a DVB satellite receiver (1995/96 generation) (the dotted lines represent functions which are sometimes combined).

147

## Tuner

The tuner (sometimes called the front end), generally controlled by an $I^2C$ bus, selects the required RF channel in the 950–2150 MHz range, converts it into a 480 MHz IF and achieves the required selection by means of a *surface acoustic wave filter* (**SAW**); the signal is amplified and coherently demodulated according to the 0° and 90° axes to obtain the analog I and Q signals. Recovery of the carrier phase required for demodulation is carried out in combination with the next stages of the receiver which lock the phase and the frequency of the local oscillator by means of a carrier recovery loop. Satellite tuners are nowadays of the *zero IF* (**ZIF**) type: the I/Q demodulation is directly performed at the input frequency from the LNB without frequency down-conversion, which allows a significant cost reduction mainly due to the removal of the SAW filter, the required selectivity being performed by means of a low-pass filter integrated in the IC.

## Analog-to-digital converter (ADC)

The ADC receives the analog I and Q signals which it converts at twice the symbol frequency $F_{SYMB}$ (of the order of 30 MHz in Europe). In most cases, this is done by means of a dual ADC with 6-bit resolution which has to work with a sampling frequency of more than 60 MHz. Here again, the sampling frequency is locked to the symbol frequency by means of a phase locked loop (clock recovery loop).

## QPSK

The QPSK block, in addition to its functions of carrier and clock recovery loops mentioned before, carries out the half-Nyquist filtering complementary to that applied on the transmitter side to the I and Q signals. Digitized I and Q signals are delivered on $2 \times 3$ or $2 \times 4$ bits of the next functional block (FEC).

## Forward error correction (FEC)

The FEC block distinguishes, by means of a majority logic, the 0's from the 1's and achieves the complete error correction in the following order: Viterbi decoding of the convolutional code, de-interleaving, Reed–Solomon decoding and energy dispersal de-randomizing; the output data are 188 byte transport packets which are generally delivered in parallel form (8 bit data, clock and control signals, of which one generally indicates uncorrectable errors).

The three blocks—ADC, QPSK, and FEC—now form a single integrated circuit (single chip satellite channel decoder).

## Descrambler

The DESCR block receives the transport packets and communicates with the main processor by a parallel bus to allow quick data transfers. It selects and descrambles the packets of the required program under control of the conditional access device. This function is sometimes combined with the demultiplexer.

## Demultiplexer

The DEMUX selects, by means of programmable filters, the PES packets corresponding to the program chosen by the user.

## MPEG

The audio and video PES outputs from the demultiplexer are applied to the input of the MPEG block, which generally combines MPEG audio and video functions and the graphics controller functions required, among other things, for the electronic program guide (**EPG**). MPEG-2 decoding generally requires at least 16 Mbits of **DRAM** (sometimes more for decoding 625-line signals, depending on the capabilities of the memory management).

## Digital video encoder (DENC)

Video signals reconstructed by the MPEG-2 decoder (digital YUV signals in CCIR 656 format) are then applied to a digital video encoder (**DENC**) which ensures their conversion into analog RGB + sync. for the best possible quality of display on a TV set via the

SCART/PERITEL plug and PAL, NTSC, or SECAM (composite and/or Y/C) mainly for VCR recording purposes.

### Digital-to-analog converter (DAC)

Decompressed digital audio signals in $I^2S$ format or similar are fed to a dual digital-to-analog converter (**DAC**) with 16 bits or more resolution which delivers the analog left and right signals.

### Microprocessor

The whole system is controlled by a powerful 32 bit **RISC** microprocessor (μP), which controls all the circuitry, interprets user commands from the remote control, and manages the smart card reader(s) and the communication interfaces which are generally available. The software amounts to many hundreds of kilobytes, which are partly located in a **flash EPROM** in order to permit optional updates during the lifetime of the product (off air or via the communication ports).

The four blocks—DEMUX, MPEG, DENC, and μP—are now integrated in a single IC, often referred to as a single chip source decoder.

### Smart card readers

The conditional access device generally includes one or two of these (one might be for a banking card, for instance). In the case of a detachable conditional access module using the DVB-CI common interface (manifested in the shape of PCMCIA slots), the conditional access circuits and the descrambler are located in the detachable PCMCIA module. The demultiplexer integrated into the IRD receives the packets "in the clear" (descrambled).

### Communication ports

The IRD can communicate with the external world (PC, modem, etc.) by means of one or more communication ports. The traditional RS232 (serial) and IEEE1284 (parallel) ports tend to be progressively replaced by a much quicker USB port. These ports, as well as a telephone line interface (via an integrated modem), are the necessary connection points required for interactivity and access to new services (pay per view, teleshopping, access to networks).

### 8.2.2   The cable integrated receiver decoder

### Basic receiver (without return channel)

The block diagram for this IRD is shown in Figure 8.3 and, in principle, differs from its satellite counterpart only in respect of the tuning, demodulation, and channel decoding parts which are suited to the cable frequency bands (UHF/VHF) and the QAM modulation prescribed. We will therefore limit the description below to those blocks specific to the cable application.

### Tuner

The tuner selects the desired channel in the cable band (VHF/UHF from 50 to 860 MHz), converts it into an IF frequency, $F_{IF}$, centered on 36.15 MHz, and achieves the appropriate selection by means of an SAW; after amplification, the IF signal is down-converted to the symbol frequency ($F_{SYMB} = 6.875$ MHz) by means of a mixer oscillator of which the frequency ($F_{OSC} = F_{IF} + F_{SYMB} = 43.025$ MHz) and phase are controlled by a carrier recovery loop from the following QAM demodulator. The recent QAM demodulators (from 2000 onward) can accept directly the IF at 36.15 MHz, which avoids the need of the above-mentioned down-conversion stage.

### ADC

In the traditional approach (dual conversion), the transposed QAM signal is applied to an analog-to-digital converter (**ADC**) with a resolution of 9 or 10 bits (<256-QAM) working at a sampling frequency generally equal to four times the symbol frequency $F_s$. The sampling frequency is locked to the symbol frequency by means of a clock recovery loop coming from the next block (QAM). In a single conversion application (direct IF sampling) the signal at 36.15 MHz is

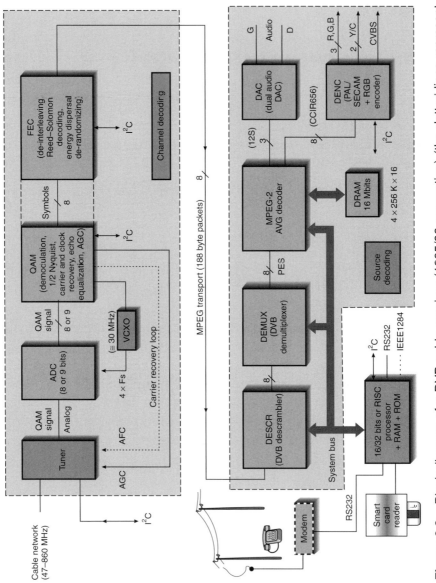

**Figure 8.3** Block diagram of a DVB cable receiver (1995/96 generation) (the dotted lines represent functions which are sometimes combined).

most often undersampled at a frequency in the order of 20 MHz, not necessarily linked to the symbol frequency.

## QAM

This is a key element in the channel decoding process: starting with the digital QAM signal, it performs digital demodulation and half-Nyquist filtering, echo equalization of the I and Q signals, and reformatting/demapping into an appropriate form for the FEC circuit (generally 8 bits parallel). It also plays a part in the clock and carrier recovery loops mentioned before, as well as generating the AGC for control of the IF and RF amplifiers at the front end.

## FEC

The FEC block performs de-interleaving, Reed–Solomon decoding, and energy dispersal de-randomizing; as is the case for satellite, the output data are the 188-byte transport packets in parallel form (8-bit data, clock, and control signals).

The three blocks—ADC, QAM, and FEC—now form a single integrated circuit (single chip cable channel decoder).

## Other functions

The processor, conditional access, descrambling, demultiplexing, MPEG-2 audio/video decoding and all other "secondary" functions (OSD, interfaces, modem, etc.) are, in principle, identical to those described above for the satellite for the same level of functionality.

## Interactive receiver (with cable return channel)

In principle, the interactive receiver differs from the basic receiver only by its "network interface" part (NIM), because of the need of an upstream for the return channel.

This needs, in addition to the existing circuitry of the downstream channel of the receiver described in the previous paragraph, specific functional blocks necessary for the emission of data to the network head-end station as well as software to control them.

In order that all receivers have the opportunity to send data to the head station, the frequency band allocated to the upstream (generally located between 5 and 65 MHz) is divided into channels on which time slots are dynamically allocated to receivers by the head station.

Management of the communication with the head station requires a sophisticated control software known as **MAC** (media access control), which requires significantly more important resources (processing power, FLASH, and RAM memory size) than a receiver without interactivity.

Three main standards exist today for bi-directional communication over cable:

- The **DOCSIS** standard, originating from the United States, is mainly intended for cable modems allowing high speed access to the Internet, but can also be used in an interactive digital TV set-top box. The upstream uses QPSK or 16-QAM modulation in the low VHF band (5 to 42 MHz). Interactive data use the native Internet Protocol (IP) with variable length frames. The downstream uses 6 MHz channels with 64- or 256-QAM and ITU-J83 Annex B FEC. It can in principle be placed anywhere in the UHF/VHF band (70 to 860 MHz). The original standard (DOCSIS 1.0) has been upgraded to DOCSIS 1.1 in order to ensure quality of service (QoS) required by voice over IP telephony.

- **Euro-DOCSIS** is a variant adapted to the European 8 MHz channels and frequency plan. The downstream complies with DVB-C specs (ETS 300 429/ITU-J83 Annex A FEC). The upstream uses QPSK or 16-QAM modulation in the low VHF band extended to 65 MHz, which increases substantially the return channel capacity over DOCSIS 1.x.

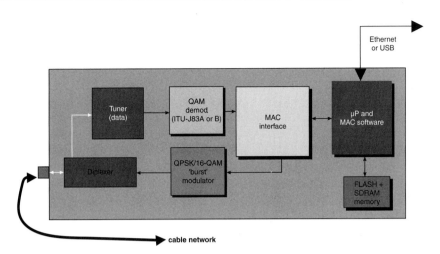

**Figure 8.4** Block diagram of a DOCSIS/Euro-DOCSIS cable modem.

The block diagram of a DOCSIS or Euro-DOCSIS cable modem can be seen in Figure 8.4. DOCSIS and Euro-DOCSIS can also be used in set-top boxes, but require in this case a second downstream channel (one for broadcast services and one for data).

- The **DVB/DAVIC** standard originates from Europe (specification ETS 300 800) and is mainly intended to bring interactivity to digital cable TV receiver–decoders. It adds to the conventional DVB-C downstream channel used for TV (so-called "in-band" channel) a second downstream at lower bit-rate (so-called "out-of-band" (**OOB**)) for data. The OOB channel use QPSK modulation in 1 or 2 MHz wide channels which can carry bit-rates of 1.5 or 3.0 Mb/s, and is situated in the mid-VHF range (70 to 130 MHz), but it can also use UHF channels (300 to 862 MHz), depending on the constraints of the network. The upstream channel uses differential QPSK (DQPSK) modulation in the European low VHF range (5 to 65 MHz) with channel widths of 200 kHz, 1 MHz, or 2 MHz. Interactive data use the Internet Protocol (**IP**) encapsulated in ATM cells.

The block diagram of a DVB/DAVIC cable receiver can be seen in Figure 8.5.

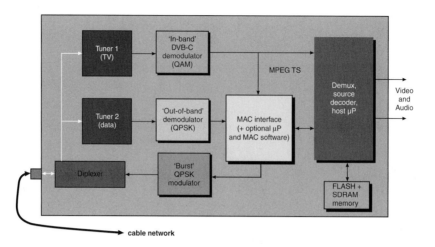

**Figure 8.5**  Block diagram of an interactive DVB/DAVIC cable receiver.

## 8.2.3  The digital terrestrial TV receiver (DVB-T)

The block diagram (Fig. 8.6, overleaf) differs from its cable (without return channel) and satellite counterparts only by its front-end (RF/IF, demodulation, and channel decoding parts). These parts have to be suited to the UHF and VHF frequency bands already used by analog television, and to the COFDM modulation prescribed

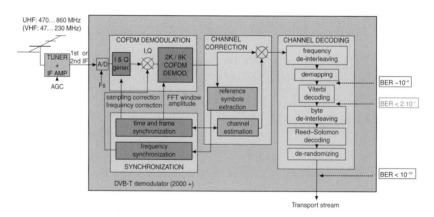

**Figure 8.6**  Block diagram of a DVB-T front-end (Source: Philips Semiconductors).

156

by the DVB-T standard. As it appears in Figure 8.6, the DVB-T front-end is much more complex than those of cable or satellite due to the COFDM modulation used. We will limit ourselves to the description of the blocks.

## Tuner

The tuner and IF part are functionally similar to the cable parts, but they have to satisfy more stringent requirements regarding the phase noise of the tuner's PLL and also the selectivity (because of the coexistence with adjacent analog channels, which can be more powerful than the desired channel). The tuner selects the desired channel in the VHF/UHF bands (47 to 230 and 470 to 860 MHz), transposes it into an intermediate frequency $F_{IF}$ centered on 36.15 MHz and realizes the required selectivity by means of two SAW filters (only one is required by some very recent COFDM demodulators); the AGC amplified IF signal is either transposed at a frequency $F_S$ in the order of 4.5 MHz by means of a "supradyne" mixer-oscillator ($F_{OSC} = F_{IF} + F_S \cong 40.65$ MHz), or directly applied to a recent COFDM demodulator (since 2001 products only) which accepts IF signals at 36.15 MHz at their input, thus avoiding an additional conversion stage.

## ADC

The COFDM signal, transposed or not, is applied to an analog-to-digital converter with a resolution of 9 or 10 bits, and digitized with a sampling frequency in the order of 20 MHz (undersampling when it is the IF signal at 36.15 MHz).

## COFDM demodulation

This block is the main element of the demodulation process. I and Q signals are reconstituted from the digitized IF signal, and the OFDM signal is demodulated by means of a fast Fourier transform (**FFT**) on 2K or 8K points, depending on the mode (number of carriers) of the received signal.

## Channel correction

This block performs the estimation of the transmission channel and its correction, and participates in the time and frequency synchronization.

## Synchronization

From the information it gets from the channel correction block, this block performs time and frequency correction of the COFDM demodulation.

## Channel decoding

This block performs frequency de-interleaving and demapping of the COFDM symbols. It is followed by a similar error correction to a satellite receiver (Viterbi decoding, Forney de-interleaving, RS decoding and energy dispersal removal).

The transport stream data at the output (188 bytes transport packets) are generally delivered in parallel format (8 bits data + control signals, one of which signals non-correctible packets). Recent circuits generally deliver the transport stream in a serial format.

All the functional blocks contained in the large gray rectangle in Figure 8.6 are now included in a single integrated circuit. The processor, conditional access, descrambling, demultiplexing, MPEG-2 audio/video decoding, and all secondary functions (OSD, interfaces, modem, etc.) are, in principle, identical to those described above for the satellite for the same level of functionality.

# Middleware and interoperability aspects

**9**

The size of investments required for setting up and running digital television transmissions as well as the bewildering increase in transmission rights of attractive contents (sports, recent movies) are such that the vast majority of digital TV programs are not free-to-air in countries where they have a significant penetration (the United States, United Kingdom, France, Italy, Spain). Even if the DVB consortium, like the GSM in the field of mobile telephony, played the role of a powerful unifier in Europe, it could not impose a common conditional access system or a unique user interface specification.

We saw in Chapter 5 that there were numerous conditional access systems using the DVB-CSA scrambling algorithm. These systems differ from one another due to the protocols used to manage and transmit access rights and keys, mainly by software embedded in the set-top box and the subscriber's smart card. Besides the conditional access system, the most important part of the software for ensuring complete interoperability between different operators of digital TV bouquets (beyond the simple passive reception of TV programs compliant with the DVB standard) is what is generally referred to as "middleware" or sometimes "interactivity engine" or, less often, just **API** (application programming interface). In fact, the term "middleware" is rather vague and does not mean anything more than that it is situated somewhere between the hardware and (application) software. The term API *stricto sensu* points only at the interface between an application and the software layer immediately below it. It is essentially made of a predefined set of function calls of the middleware.

The middleware can be functionally compared to a high-level operating system with graphical user interface (GUI) such as Windows, which is very different from a low-level real-time operating system (**RTOS**, such as pSOS, vxWorks, Nucleus to cite just a few), on which the middleware is based.

One of the crucial functions of most middlewares is to make the application independent of the hardware platform on which it is run, assuming it has sufficient resources (processing power and device functionality).

In order for the same hardware platform to relatively easily support many middlewares, which not only differ from one another by their upper API (to the applications), but also by their interface to the lower layers of the software (which we will name "middleware API"), the set-top box manufacturers most often interface the middleware to their own API (which we will name "platform API") through an adaptation layer. Figure 9.1 illustrates the different software layers of a set-top box using a middleware in comparison to the layers of a personal computer (PC).

It is the middleware that defines the look and feel of the user interface, the aspect and the possibilities of the Electronic Program Guide

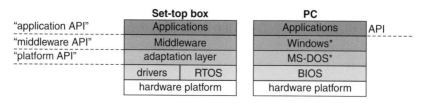

\* Windows includes the DOS functionality since Windows 95.

**Figure 9.1** Comparison of the software layers of a set-top box and a PC.

(**EPG**), the interactivity level of the applications which are offered to the user (pay-per-view programs, games, specific services requiring a return channel to the service provider, special functions such as hard disk recording, etc.). All middlewares generally offer two levels of interactivity:

- A local or off-line interactivity of the carousel type, which means that the user can only access data which are broadcast cyclically, in a manner similar to the Teletext information of analog TV transmissions (this is particularly the case with the Electronic Program Guide).

- An on-line interactivity, where the user is connected to a server by means of a return channel (telephone modem or cable return). The user can thus access remote data, either in a manner comparable to Videotex (e.g., Prestel or Minitel), the Internet, within the limits allowed by both the service provider, and/or from a terminal connected to a TV screen.

All middlewares allow downloading of data and software into the FLASH memory of the set-top box by means of the broadcast channel, which allows updating and upgrading (bug corrections, new functionalities) as well as downloading of applications.

Table 9.1 lists some proprietary middlewares in use today in the world of digital television.

**Table 9.1** Some popular middlewares used for digital TV

| Middleware | Type | Origin | Service providers (examples) |
|---|---|---|---|
| Betanova | V | Betaresearch (D) (obsolete) | Premiere World, Deutsche Telekom |
| Liberate | P | Liberate | CWC, Telewest... |
| MediaHighway | V/P | Canal+ Technologies (now NDS) | Canal+, Canal Satellite, DirecTV |
| Microsoft TV | P | Microsoft | TV Cabo, cable operators (U.S.) |
| OpenTV | P | OpenTV | BSkyB, Sky Italia, TPS |

Middlewares are classified as *proprietary* (P) when they belong to a company which is not linked to a pay TV operator, or as *vertical* (V) when a specific middleware has been developed by an operator or an affiliate company for its own use. They are noted P/V if they are both vertical and proposed to other service providers. However, independently of the middleware core, pay TV service providers (whose terminals are rented or subsidized most of the time) can personalize their own version of the middleware or restrain it in order that it cannot execute non-approved applications (for instance coming from a competitor), even if they are compliant to the middleware's API. Likewise, rented receivers are sometimes deliberately limited in order not to be able to receive transmissions (even free-to-air) from competitors who did not conclude an agreement with the service provider.

If this situation can be accepted in the context of pure pay TV (even if it is leading the customer to rent or buy one specific terminal for each service provider if he or she wants to access all the services), it is at least not desirable in view of "digital TV for everybody." In many countries, this should happen with digital terrestrial TV when it replaces analog TV at the end of the decade and include a large proportion of free-to-air transmissions. This is why alternative solutions are being developed to cover the needs of any service provider of pay or free-to-air TV, with different levels of functionality. These solutions are said to be horizontal, as opposed to vertical, integrated solutions of pay TV service providers (which range from the delivery of programs to specific set-top boxes).

Until boxes with such a standard middleware become available, it is possible to find on the market DVB-compliant receivers that do not use any middleware, commonly called "zapper boxes." These receivers have a proprietary control software, built directly on the RTOS and drivers of the hardware platform; most of the time they do not have a modem because its use would imply that it could run the application of a service provider requiring its middleware. So this proprietary software does not incorporate real interactive (on-line) functionalities, but it can usually be updated by downloading from satellite or from a PC connected to its serial port.

This software ensures the basic functions required for reception of TV programs, often with a mini-EPG limited to the information on the current program and the following one (sometimes called "*now and next*" function), assuming this information is transmitted in the EIT table of DVB-SI.

In addition to the free-to-air (**FTA**) transmissions some receivers are able to receive encrypted pay TV transmissions either by means of an embedded conditional access (Viaccess is one of the most common) or by means of an appropriate DVB-CI module. In both cases, of course, the appropriate smart card containing valid rights for the programs to be received is required. We will first have a brief look at three of the most common proprietary middlewares in use in Europe, then we will examine two open and standardized solutions.

## 9.1  Main proprietary middlewares used in Europe

### 9.1.1  MediaHighway: the middleware of the Canal+ "galaxy"

MediaHighway was developed in 1993 by the R&D department of Canal+ (which subsequently became Canal+ Technologies) initially for the launch of the first French digital TV service in April 1996: Canal Satellite Numérique (CSN).

MediaHighway is used by all the national variations of Canal Satellite which were launched shortly afterward (Spain, Italy, Poland, etc.). More recently it was proposed to service providers not belonging to the Canal+ group such as OnDigital (UK) in 1998, which later became ITV Digital, and some other satellite and cable operators in Europe, Asia, and the United States. Canal+ Technologies requires a tough certification process, which includes an important suite of unitary tests before allowing the marketing of products with the MediaHighway label.

Many versions of MediaHighway exist, which correspond to a **DLI** (device layer interface) number. The DLI is in fact the interface of the middleware to the lower layers of the software. The hardware platform together with its operating system and its drivers must comply with the DLI specification, generally via an adaptation layer. The DLI defines the functionalities supported by the middleware and ensures an independence (or abstraction) from the hardware platform and RTOS used.

MediaHighway supports near video-on-demand (NVoD) applications and impulse pay-per-view (IPPV) and allows downloading of data or applications. MediaHighway is usually used with MediaGuard, the in-house conditional access system, but can, in principle, be used with any embedded CA system; it also supports the DVB-CI interface standard for detachable conditional access modules. The DLI versions currently in use are

- **3.xx:** used by most satellite service providers of the Canal+ group, because of their early starting date. They have been enhanced by satellite downloads.

- **4.xx:** DLI version 4.1 was introduced at the beginning of the UK's DTT service (On Digital pay TV) in order to support the MHEG-5 API mandatory by law in the UK for digital terrestrial services. Other variants of the 4.xx DLI now include an Internet browser and management of a hard disk drive for recording TV programs and other data.

Recent versions of MediaHighway are based on "MediaHighway virtual machine" which can execute applications developed under many different standard languages (Java, etc., HTML, MHEG-5, etc.) by loading the appropriate interpreter.

This feature has allowed MediaHighway to be one of the first proprietary middlewares to be able to support applications compliant with the new DVB-MHP open standard, which is based on the Java language of Sun Microsystems. (See the website: www.canalplus-technologies.com.)

## 9.1.2 OpenTV: the most widely used middleware

OpenTV is a middleware proposed by a company (now independent) bearing the same name. It was originally a joint venture between Thomson MultiMedia and Sun Microsystems (Sun Interactive Alliance formed in 1994). The first digital TV service provider to use OpenTV was the French satellite bouquet TPS in 1996. OpenTV is now used by more than 30 digital TV service providers worldwide and is installed in more than 10 million set-top boxes produced by approximately 30 suppliers. Consequently, OpenTV has to support many different embedded conditional access systems as well as the DVB-CI interface standard for detachable conditional access modules.

OpenTV supports near video-on-demand (NVoD) applications, impulse pay-per-view (IPPV) and allows downloading of data or applications. Many OpenTV versions exist. Their numbers reflect their date of introduction:

- **OpenTV 1.0.x** is the version still used by the pioneers, mainly French cable and satellite service providers. It has no longer been proposed to new customers since early 2000. It has nevertheless been enhanced by many downloads over time.

- **OpenTV 1.2** is a specific derivative for the British satellite service provider BSkyB.

- **OpenTV EN** is the second generation of OpenTV.

- **OpenTV EN2** is the third generation, inheriting from both OpenTV EN and OpenTV 1.2.

OpenTV EN2 is based on two libraries:

- Basic functions are included in the core library, which is the heart of the middleware and is compatible with many real-time operating systems (RTOS).

- Optional functions are located in the extensions library, which allows service providers to personalize the middleware and extend its functionality by downloading.

OpenTV EN2 executes OpenTV applications written in O code (conceptually comparable to the byte code of Java) by means of a virtual machine (interpreter). This is why the architecture allows a relatively easy porting of MHP by means of adjunction of a second virtual machine (Java), which will enable the middleware to be compliant with both OpenTV and MHP applications. OpenTV functionalities extend now to the management of a hard disk and Internet browsing, notably thanks to the acquisition in 2000 of the company Spyglass. (See the website: www.opentv.com.)

### 9.1.3 Betanova: a very vertical middleware

Developed by Betaresearch, the technology branch of the big German media group Kirch, Betanova, in contrast to most other middlewares, does not pretend to be independent of the hardware platform or the RTOS upon which it runs. It is intimately linked to the "d-box," the set-top box developed for the satellite pay TV bouquet Premiere World. A cable variant of this platform has been adopted by Deutsche Telekom for its cable networks. Two generations of Betanova exist:

- **Betanova 1.xx:** this is the historical version, which runs on more than one million d-boxes. It supports NVoD applications, impulse pay-per-view (IPPV), and allows downloading of additional applications to the Electronic Program Guide (**EPG**). On the satellite d-box, Betanova also supports the DiSEqC antenna control system.

- **Betanova 2.xx:** this new version supports all the functionalities of the 1.xx version. It is written in Java, which simplifies adaptation and accelerates the writing of new applications. In addition, this new architecture is more flexible and foresees the support of the API of DVB-MHP (also based on Java), but it is still dedicated to the d-box. This new version of Betanova is also intended to support access to the Internet as well as home banking and home shopping applications.

Mainly due to the strict interdependence between Betanova and the d-box, both have found themselves limited to the German market,

166

on which their monopoly and lack of openness have been bitterly criticized by their competitors. However, things in favor of MHP and open platforms on the German market, among others, are changing due to the end of the *de facto* monopoly of Deutsche Telekom on the cable networks. Betaresearch is being dissolved after going bankrupt; this middleware does not evolve anymore.

## 9.2 The open European middlewares

### 9.2.1 MHEG-5: the first standardized middleware for digital TV

The **MHEG** (Multimedia and Hypermedia Expert Group) is a descriptive language of multimedia presentations, comparable to **HTML** (HyperText Markup Language) for hypertext pages. It is based on an object-oriented multimedia exchange format independent of the hardware and software (OS) platform on which it is executed. It is a declarative, as opposed to a procedural, language (such as Java).

The **MHEG-5** version, standardized under the ISO/IEC 13522-5 reference, is a subset of MHEG-1 particularly dedicated to digital TV receivers (set-top box or integrated digital TV receiver, iDTV) with limited processing power and memory size. It is practically the only MHEG version in real volume usage.

In the MHEG vocabulary, a multimedia presentation is an MHEG application or an MHEG scene. An MHEG application is a grouping of MHEG scenes. An MHEG scene is made up of three main groups of objects or ingredients:

- the interactive objects such as buttons, cursor, or other similar objects;

- the link objects (links) which define processes triggered by user actions on interactive objects;

- the presentation objects (objects) controlled by the above-mentioned link objects.

A certain number of other objects exist, which regroup many presentation objects. When an MHEG application is started, it generally expects an action from the user. If the user presses a button, the application generates the event "button selected." A link can be defined on this (interactive) object, for example in order to start a video sequence (presentation object). Objects themselves can in turn generate events which can trigger links. Relatively complex applications (video games, catalog sales, etc.) can be realized in this way.

An application is normally made up of scenes and some common objects and links. A scene is only made up of objects and links. Other versions of MHEG exist:

- MHEG-1 to 4: (for the record) the ancestors of MHEG-5— little used.

- MHEG-5: the most important, used by the digital TV services in the UK.

- MHEG-6: an extension of MHEG-5 by a virtual machine allowing the inclusion of applications based on a procedural language.

- MHEG-7: defines test and conformance procedures of MHEG-5 applications.

- MHEG-8: a project aimed at combining XML and MHEG.

The small amount of resources required to run MHEG-5 makes it a good candidate for the basic digital terrestrial receivers in countries starting transmissions.

### 9.2.2 DVB-MHP: the universal middleware for digital TV of the future?

From 1997 onward, since the standardization of coding of digital television signals was achieved, the DVB consortium decided to tackle the problem of software and hardware interoperability between digital TV services compliant with the DVB standard for broadcasting their signals. In addition to the initial assumption of interoperability, the main objectives of the development of **MHP** (Multimedia Home Platform) have been evolution (with the possibility of extending the functionality by downloading), backward compatibility, modularity, and stability.

The Internet has also been taken into account, as well as the integration to a local home network made up of various terminals (PC, telephones, domestic appliances, etc.). One of the prerequisites was that this new standard would be based on open standards in order to guarantee a non-discriminatory access to anybody desiring to use it. Another concern was to use an efficient format in terms of bandwidth requirements but still ensuring a complete separation between data and applications. A total neutrality versus the different optional conditional access systems, embedded or based on the DVB-CI interface, was another prerequisite.

MHP defines a generic software interface (API) between the interactive applications coming from different service providers and the terminals on which they should be run, independently of their hardware and software implementation. The performance level of these terminals can vary greatly. MHP can support various applications (in increasing order of interactivity):

- Electronic Program Guide (**EPG**);

- information services comparable to a super teletext;

- applications linked to the current TV program (betting on matches, games, etc.);

- electronic commerce (e-commerce) with secure banking transactions.

The MHP architecture has three levels: resources, system software, and applications (Fig. 9.2). Resources include all the essential parts of the set-top box: MPEG decoding, input/output devices, host processor, graphics subsystem, etc.

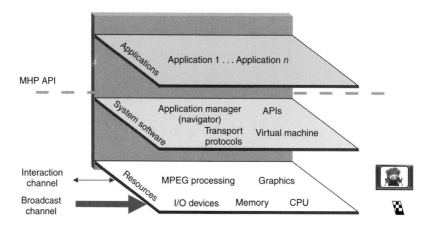

**Figure 9.2** The three levels of the MHP architecture (Source: © DVB 2000).

- System software enables presentation of an abstract view of the platform to the applications. It includes a navigator (or *application manager*) which takes control of the platform and applications which are run on it. The software kernel of MHP is called DVB-J (DVB-Java), based on the *Java Virtual Machine* defined by Sun Microsystems.

- MHP applications access the platform through the MHP API. A number of software interfaces required to make use of specific resources of the hardware platform are implemented by means of extensions. The task of any practical implementation of MHP is to ensure correspondence between the API and the hardware resources of the platform.

Three profiles have been defined for the MHP platform, by order of increasing functionality, which imply an increasing need for processing power and hardware complexity:

- enhanced broadcast profile—makes use of unidirectional broadcast services only;

- interactive broadcast profile—adds support for interactive services requiring only a low speed return channel (V22 modem for instance) via the telephone network;

- Internet access profile—adds the supplementary functionalities brought by Internet access within the limits of TV screen display. It requires a higher speed connection (e.g., V90 modem).

Other profiles or elements of profiles will be added in the future, for instance for the support of hard disk recording. Figure 9.3 illustrates the functionalities and the ascending compatibility between the three different profiles of MHP.

**MHP version 1.0** includes the first two profiles, and is now standardized by ETSI under the reference TS 101 812. **MHP version 1.1** covers the Internet access profile and thus adds the HTML functionality. It is specified in the ETSI document TS 102 812. DVB-MHP seems to be the only open standard which can deliver, at the same time, a unified user interface with different levels of functionality and a satisfactory evolution. These features can be seen as prerequisite conditions to a full switchover from analog to digital TV.

This is why MHP has obtained the support of many actors in the world of European television and beyond, especially in view of the generalization of digital terrestrial TV. However, MHP has not been

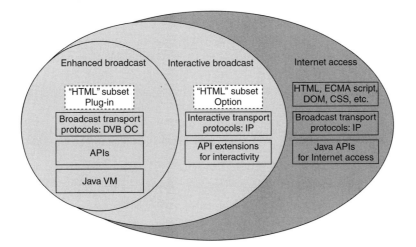

**Figure 9.3** Ascending functionality of the three profiles of MHP (Source: © DVB 2000).

made mandatory in the terminals because of a significant cost increase which is criticized by its detractors, due to the hardware resources (higher processing power and memory size) required by the Java virtual machine.

At time of writing (early 2006), MHP had not met the expected success in most countries where DTT has been launched, except in Italy where MHP interactive receivers have been strongly subsidized. But even there the interest has decreased after reduction of the subsidy after one year. MHP's relatively steep licensing fee also limits its general adoption. (See the website: www.dvb-mhp.org.)

# Evolution: state of the art and perspectives  **10**

Digital consumer applications (camcorders, MP3 players, DVD players/recorders and many other applications), which started in the mid-1990s by the first satellite TV transmissions in the United States and France, are now part of the consumer electronics landscape at the beginning of the third millennium. Digital cable television, and even digital terrestrial television in some countries, has now taken a significant share of the market. However, many evolutions in receiver functionalities as well as services proposed to the users are to be expected in the near future.

Given that we now have more than five years of experience since the beginning of digital television transmissions, it is probably less risky now (than at the time of the first edition of this book) to make some predictions of the evolution of services and receivers. This is what we will try to do in the following paragraphs, limiting our horizon to the next three to four years.

## 10.1  Digital terrestrial television

The European digital television system (standardized under the reference ETS 300 744) makes use of the OFDM modulation (also named COFDM), already used for the DAB digital radio system, in two variants (2 K and 8 K) which were described in Chapter 7. The United Kingdom was the first European country to start (end 1998) a digital terrestrial television service using the DVB-T standard (On Digital pay TV service, which after its bankrupcy was replaced by the Freeview free to air service).

Due to this early start, DVB-T demodulators were not available for 8 K COFDM at that time, so the 2 K mode of the DVB-T system was chosen; it is likely that the UK will be the only European country to use this DVB-T version (at least for services destined for fixed reception).

Sweden (service provider Senda) and Spain (service provider Quiero) have followed suit respectively at the end of 1999 and mid-2000, and use the 8 K mode of DVB-T. This enabled Spain to develop a single frequency network (**SFN**) on the whole territory, using the four highest channels of the UHF band (66 to 69) which were hitherto unused by analog television.

At the time of writing, the commercial success of these first transmissions is mixed, probably due to the fact that these almost entirely pay TV terrestrial bouquets can hardly compete with preexisting satellite and cable offers from the point of view of the number of programs (the diffusion capacity of digital terrestrial TV is in the order of ten times less than satellite or cable as long as analog television transmissions continue). This is why digital terrestrial television needs an important share of free-to-air transmissions to be successful, in order to reach the two-thirds to three-quarters of the population not yet prepared to pay a subscription to receive more television programs.

France has launched its terrestrial DTV service (Télévision Numérique Terrestre or TNT) in march 2005 with 5 multiplexes carrying a combination of MPEG-2 free-to-air services and MPEG-4 pay TV services. By the end of 2007, coverage is approximately 85% of the population and is due to reach 95% after complete analog switch-off (planned end 2011). Due to the relatively high number of free-to-air programs offered (18), TNT has quickly been successful (more than 5 M users by mid 2007).

Some countries like Italy had plans for a very early analog switch-off (2006), but this proved not to be realistic for the whole country, and only a few regions (Sardinia, Aosta) have followed this plan. The rest of the country is expected to switch off analog tansmissions just in time for the deadline fixed by the European Union (2012). Germany is introducing DTT region by region by replacing analog transmissions practically without simulcast.

The DVB-T system has already been selected by a number of non-European countries (such as Australia and Singapore), but for countries which have not yet made a choice, it is in competition with a new Japanese system (Integrated Services Digital Broadcasting – Terrestrial (**ISDB-T**)) which is also based on COFDM modulation with additions aiming at making it even more robust (especially for mobile reception) however, at the cost of an important increase in complexity and thus price (see Appendix C).

Digital terrestrial TV transmissions in the United States started in 1998, in high definition format based on the Advanced Television System Committee (**ATSC**) (see Appendix C), with the initial objective of stopping analog NTSC transmissions in 2008. However, its development has been very slow until now, mainly due to questionable technical and political choices (disappointing performances of the 8-VSB modulation chosen, high cost of high-definition-capable displays, absence of defined associated services), which makes the switch-off of analog transmissions in 2008 unlikely.

Generalized integration of digital television decoders in TV receivers will only happen when technical choices (standard middleware, a cheap and secure way of adding conditional access) as well as political choices (simulcasting, network deployment, subsidizing receivers) are very clear. As a first step, these receivers will have to be a hybrid (analog and digital), even if the 100% simulcast approach is followed, since the geographical coverage will be incomplete for a few years.

## 10.2   Evolution of the set-top box

### 10.2.1   Integration at (quasi) constant functionality

The block diagram of Figure 8.2 corresponds to the functional partitioning of the first generation (1996) of a European receiver/decoder—IRD. At that time, each block corresponded to a major integrated circuit. Most of these circuits were realized in CMOS technology with a $0.5\,\mu$ feature. Integration has progressed rapidly, and for the first time (1997–1999), one could observe a grouping of functions in circuits with a $0.35\,\mu$ feature, at (almost) constant functionality, following the scheme below:

- Integration of external interfaces (RS232, IEEE1284, etc.) and demultiplexer/descrambler with the main processor (often a RISC), with a maximum clock frequency in the order of 50 MHz.

- Integration of the video encoder with the MPEG audio/video decoder, to which more sophisticated graphics capabilities have been added (8 bits per pixel or more, sometimes a 2D accelerator).

- Reduction of the required (S)DRAM chips from four times $256\,\mathrm{K}\times16$ to a one $1\,\mathrm{M}\times16$ chip common to the MPEG decoder and to the graphics processor.

- Integration in a single channel decoder chip (first for satellite then for cable and later for terrestrial) of demodulation, error correction, and input ADCs.

- For the satellite tuner part, progressive adoption of the so-called "zero IF" or ZIF technology (also known as direct conversion) with a view to finally integrating it on the main board.

Functional integration continues inexorably, thanks to the availability of ever smaller geometries (0.25 then $0.18\,\mu\mathrm{m}$), which made possible, at the dawn of 2000, the integration of the processor (a 32-bit RISC with a clock frequency up to 100 MHz or more) and its peripherals with the source decoder, video encoder, and sometimes the audio DAC. A 32-bit unified memory architecture (UMA) for

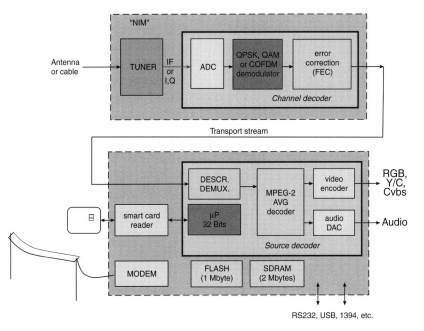

**Figure 10.1** Block diagram of a typical set-top box for pay TV (from 2000 onward).

the processor, MPEG audio/video decoding, and graphics functions reduce for most common applications the memory requirements to a unique SDRAM chip of 8 Mbytes (2 M × 32). Figure 10.1 illustrates the block diagram of such a receiver, commercially available in 2002.

## 10.2.2  Functional enhancements

Simultaneous to the integration of almost constant functionality, of which the main goal is cost reduction of the basic IRD, adjunction of new functions which increase its attractiveness is becoming common on mid- and high-end set-top boxes.

- A function missing from set-top boxes is the facility to record one program while watching another. This is all the more difficult to understand since it has always been possible with analog VCRs, which all include their own tuner. This deficiency and the concomitant phenomenal capacity increase and price decrease of hard disks (HDD) since the end of the 1990s have allowed set makers to integrate them in high-end set-top boxes. In order to be able to record a second program which is part of a different multiplex (transponder), a second front-end, or NIM (tuner+ channel decoder) is required, as well as a demultiplexer in order to record only the interesting part of the multiplex. This fuctionality is generally referred to as watch and record (**W&R**).

- Another, more innovating, functionality allowed by the hard disk (which has the advantage, over a tape recorder, of random access capability and simultaneous read and write) is what is generally called time shift recording (**TSR**). This allows a program to be stopped, for example to answer an incoming phone call, and resumed at the place where it was interrupted. From the moment the user stops watching, the hard disk records the program; the user can then resume watching from where he left while the hard disk continues recording in real time. The user watches from this moment with a time shift which is equal to the duration of the interruption. Figure 10.2 shows the block diagram of a satellite IRD with a dual front-end which allows a program to be watched, if required in time shift mode, and another one to be recorded not necessarily belonging to the same multiplex. This requires, of course, two front-ends, but also three

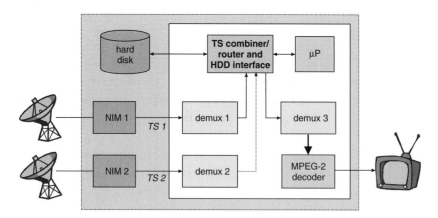

**Figure 10.2** Principle block diagram of a satellite receiver with HDD and dual front-end.

demultiplexers as well as a device (which we have named TS combiner) able to reconstruct a partial transport stream, since the information will usually have to be recorded in the form of a scrambled transport stream for copyright reasons.

- Another important advantage of the hard disk compared to the VCR is that the original quality of picture and sound is fully maintained, since the recorded bitstream does not undergo any bit-rate reduction before being written to the disk.

- Interfaces of the set-top box to the external world evolve, even if the analog PAL/SECAM output to an external recorder has not yet been replaced as expected by a high speed **IEEE1394** serial bus (see Appendix D), mainly due the very relative success of the digital D-VHS recorder. This situation is due both to the new possibilities brought by the hard disks discussed above and the opposition of the owners of rights (mainly of motion pictures) to allow digital recording of their works on a removable support. For the pure data interfaces, the current standards (RS232 serial and/or IEEE1284 parallel) tend to be progressively replaced by the USB interface, following (with some delay) the trend in the PC world.

- For decoders connected to a cable network, a high-speed return channel using the cable network instead of the telephone line becomes progressively standard, but it generally requires the upgrade of the network to make it bi-directional. The main standards used are DOCSIS in the United States and DVB-**DAVIC** (digital audio visual council) or EURODOCSIS in Europe. The set-top box can thus become an attractive way of accessing the data superhighways, enabling real interactivity, high speed access to the Internet on the TV set, as well as the possibility of using the set-top box as a high speed modem by a PC connected, for example, by a USB or Ethernet link.

## 10.3   New architectures

There are two main conflicting philosophies which are explained below about the long-term future of domestic digital TV receiving systems. It is likely that both solutions will have a share of the market, but will leave an important place to the classical set-top box for many years.

### 10.3.1 The integrated digital television receiver (iDTV)

Currently, the major players in analog television, as well as TV set makers, defend the integration of the digital decoder (essentially terrestrial) into the TV set—a first step to a hybrid receiver (analog and digital, see block diagram Fig. 10.3)—as long as analog terrestrial broadcasts continue. They see this as a way to phase in the eventual move to a digital-only receiver. This type of receiver is often referred to as the integrated digital television receiver (**iDTV**).

This relatively high-priced solution had until recently encountered little success (mainly in the United Kingdom) due to its lack of competitiveness because of the 100% subsidization of set-top boxes by pay TV operators (OnDigital for terrestrial TV as well as BSkyB for satellite) and also maybe because of a certain fear of obsolescence of the integrated decoder during the useful lifetime of a TV set. Actually, the features of a digital TV decoder evolve almost at the same

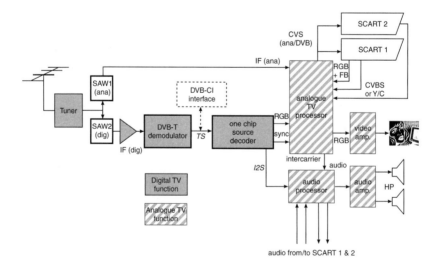

**Figure 10.3**  Example of a block diagram of a hybrid TV set.

speed as those of a PC (cycles in the order of 12 to 18 months) in comparison to a classical TV set, which appears not to evolve functionally anymore and has an average lifetime in the order of ten years. This reason, added to the new possibilities of interconnection through a home network (wired or wireless), tends to give weight to the "home gateway" concept as *the* access point to all external networks which pass the user premises.

### 10.3.2 The home gateway or the set-top box at the center of the home multimedia network

In order to allow equal access to all external information sources to all the terminals of a home with full interactivity, it is tempting to propose a client/server type of architecture as illustrated by Figure 10.4. In this concept, a set-top box (server) with an important processing power and equipped with high capacity hard disk(s) ensures interface with all external networks (cable, satellite, terrestrial, ADSL, and/or plain old telephone). It is directly connected to the main TV set or screen in the home and to simpler terminals (thin

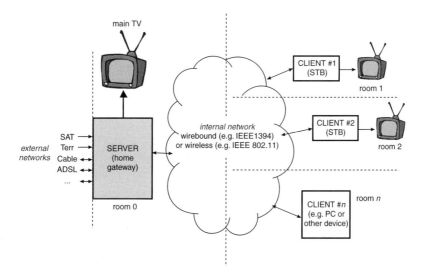

**Figure 10.4** Architecture example of a home multimedia network.

clients) by means of an internal high-speed network either wired (e.g., an extension of IEEE1394 as proposed by the HAVI committee) or wireless in the 2.4 or 5 GHz frequency band (e.g., one of the versions of **IEEE802.11** already used in the PC world).

One of the advantages of this solution is its evolution, which can be ensured mainly by updating or upgrading the server, since the clients are dumb terminals that are merely able to send requests to the server and to display the requested audiovisual services, whatever their origin (external networks or local disks) and their nature (audio/video, graphics, Internet pages).

However, this solution faces many obstacles, even if we assume the problems linked to the standardization of the communication network are resolved: for example, compatibility with the many middlewares and conditional access systems of pay TV operators, wiring constraints for the wired solution and bandwidth constraints for the wireless solution, as well as complete unavailability of all terminals in case of a problem at the server.

In a less ambitious approach, perhaps more realistic in the short term, a **Bluetooth** radio link (also at 2.4 GHz but at a lower bitrate than the various IEEE802.x standards—max. 1 Mb/s) is also proposed by some companies to link the set-top box to some peripherals. Originally developed by Ericsson to connect, wirelessly and at low cost, a mobile phone to its peripherals, Bluetooth is now supported by a consortium of participants belonging to all branches of the electronics industry.

A possible application is the connection to the set-top box of light terminals equipped with an LCD screen; this allows, for example, for the operation of the interactive functionalities of the set-top box without disturbing the display of the current program on the screen of the TV set. The same link allows a telephone (fixed or mobile) equipped with a Bluetooth interface to connect interactively and without additional wires, the set-top box to the external world.

## 10.4 High-Definition Television (HDTV)

The first tentative steps toward standardizing High-Definition Television (**HDTV**) in Europe date back to the end of the 1980s with HD-MAC, derived from and compatible with D2-MAC (a standard-definition D2-MAC receiver was able to receive an HD-MAC signal in standard definition).

However, because of the hybrid nature of this standard, the failure of the high-power satellites carrying these transmissions, and the then-exorbitant cost of screens capable of displaying such high resolutions, it has never been used except for experimental transmissions. The most prestigious instances of its use, and the last ones on a wide scale, have been the retransmissions of the Olympic Games of 1992 (Albertville, France, winter games and Barcelona, Spain, summer games).

The first digital HDTV system, which was standardized in 1998, is the American ATSC system, based on the MPEG-2 video compression standard. Besides many enhanced-definition formats, it comprises two high-definition resolutions: 720p60 ($1280 \times 720$, progressive scan, 60 frames per second) and 1080i30 ($1920 \times 1080$, interlaced scan, 30 frames per second). These two resolutions have since become the de facto standards for high-definition digital television. The European variant differs only by its refresh rates of 50 and 25 frames/second for 720 progressive and 1080 interlaced, respectively.

The recent progress of flat-screen technologies (LCD and plasma) from 2000 onward has resulted in a spectacular price decrease for HDTVs and monitors (from $1280 \times 720$ up), so it is now possible to envision a rapid, large-scale adoption of high-definition television.

Whichever technology its display uses (LCD, plasma, or CRT), a TV set or monitor intended for HDTV display will have to carry the "HD ready" logo (see Fig. 10.5) if one wants to be sure that it fullfills

**Figure 10.5** The "HD ready" logo.

the minimum required conditions fixed by EICTA for compatibility with HDTV broadcasts or records. These include the following:

- minimum display of 720 lines (vertical resolution) in widescreen format (i.e., 16:9)

- one analog HD input ($YP_BP_R$)

- one digital HD input (DVI or HDMI) with HDCP content protection

- the ability to accept 720p and 1080i formats at 50 Hz and 60 Hz on all HD inputs.

The development of HDTV will be also accelerated by the concomitant availability of new, more efficient compression standards than MPEG-2 (MPEG-4.10/H.264, WM9/VC1) as well as the new DVB-S2 satellite transmission standard which significantly increases the useful bit rate of a transponder, thanks to higher-order modulations and more powerful error-correction codes.

HDTV using these new standards started at the end of 2005 with Premiere, the German satellite pay-TV bouquet. Other big European pay TV operators (BskyB, Canal+, TPS, Sky Italia) started offering their HDTV services in the second quarter of 2006, in time for the World Cup football tournament. Free-to-air HDTV transmissions started slightly later in the second half of 2006, pushed mainly by public TV broadcasters (BBC, ARD/ZDF, France Televisions, RAI...). In the longer term, DTT might be the main vector of free-to-air HDTV, but with a relatively small number of channels until the analog switch-off is effective.

## 10.5 Digital TV over IP

A new way of transmitting digital TV to subscribers became a commercial reality at the beginning of the twenty-first century—over the phone line by **ADSL** (Asymmetric Digital Subscriber Line)—with a particular transport protocol known as IP (Internet Protocol).

The performance increase of ADSL technology for broadband connection to the Internet, the success it encountered following the decrease of subscription costs, and the opening to competition of local-loop unbundling have made IT possible to use the phone line as a new way of transmitting TV broadcasts to consumers. It is called TV over IP (Television over Internet Protocol), or more simply IPTV (Internet Protocol Television). It is sometimes referred to as Broadband TV.

In Europe, France has started delivering IPTV slightly earlier than its neighbors, mainly due to the aggressiveness of Free, a service provider which, in late 2003, launched the first wide-scale IPTV service over ADSL with its famous "Freebox." This "all-in-one" multi-function/multimedia terminal allows broadband connection to the Internet, telephony over IP (VoIP), and access to TV over IP in unbundled areas. Its initial maximum downstream speed of 8 Mb/s was upgraded to 20 Mb/s in 2004 with the introduction of ADSL2+ in unbundled areas. This multiple service offer is generally referred to as "triple play."

Other operators followed suit relatively quickly, most of them with a slightly different approach which separates the functions of access to the IP services performed by a kind of gateway to which the computer and an optional TV set-top box can be connected by Ethernet or WiFi, as well as an ordinary telephone set.

At the subscriber level, TV over IP differs from other transportation media (terrestrial, cable, satellite) in that, due to the limited bandwidth of the telephone line, all accessible channels are not transmitted simultaneously to the subscriber; only one channel at a time is transmitted on the subscriber's line. If the so-called Triple Play ADSL service provider (Internet access, voice over IP, television over IP) is not the incumbent telecom operator (telco), delivery of these services requires what is called "local loop unbundling," either partial (if the subscriber keeps a traditional switched telephony service from the incumbent telco) or total if it cancels the switched telephony service.

From an electrical point of view, partial unbundling consists of separating, by means of a filter located on the subscriber's line at its arrival in the telephone exchange building, the low frequencies (300–3400 Hz) and high frequencies (above 10 kHz) of switched telephony. The lower frequencies are directed to the incumbent's telephone exchange and the high frequencies (above 10 kHz) are directed to the **DSLAM** (Digital Subscriber's Line Access Multiplexer) of the ADSL service provider located in the same building.

Figure 10.6 illustrates schematically the connection of the subscriber's line at both sides (in the telephone exchange building and in the subscriber's premises) when a traditional telephony service is kept (similar to when all services are supplied by the incumbent telco or when the IP services are delivered by another service provider).

In case of total unbundling, the lines are directed without filtering directly to the service providers, which supplies the globality of communication services to their customers (sometimes even a switched telephony service). In this case, the service provider is the only point of contact for the customer, even in case of physical problems to the line. On the subscriber side, a low-pass filter is inserted on all "classical" phone equipment (fax, modem, telephones) in order that they do not disturb (and possibly are not disturbed by) the ADSL traffic. The ADSL modem or gateway itself is equipped with an internal high-pass filter which enables subscribers to be connected directly on the phone line.

Regarding TV over IP, only one TV program (the one which the subscriber has selected) is transmitted at any given moment

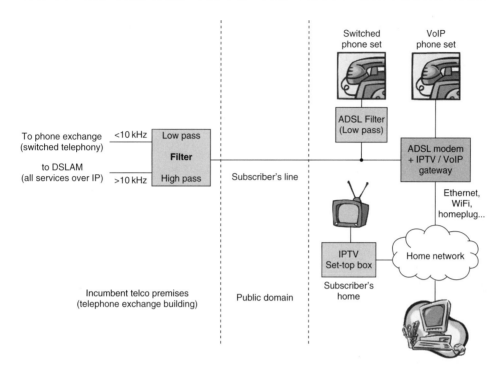

**Figure 10.6** Schematic view of an ADSL connection with VoIP and IPTV.

on the subscriber's line, the selection being performed at the DSLAM level. The fact that only the program selected by the user is transmitted is permitted by the bi-directional feature of the ADSL link, and allows *subscription* to pay TV and access to on-demand programs without requiring a conditional access system or encryption, since it is possible to check that the user has the required rights to access this program before delivering it. Some pay TV service providers nevertheless require that the IPTV terminal be equipped with a conditional access system to subscribe to it.

TV over IP also permits the delivery of true video on demand (VOD), since it is possible to send one specific video stream to only one subscriber at the time he or she has required it, without occupying the whole network with this stream.

## 10.5.1 Distribution of IPTV over a home network

Figure 10.7 shows the architecture of a home network based on a home reference model of the DVB. The various segments of the home network may use different technologies (Ethernet, WiFi, IEEE1394/FireWire, etc.) and the distribution networks may as well use different technologies (cable, satellite ADSL, and the like).

For our purpose here, we will concentrate only on the logical interfaces between the so-called home network end device (HNED) for television and the service provider via a home network, which we will assume are based on the DVB-IPI interface (Internet Protocol Interface) of the DVB and the home reference model defined in the ETSI technical specification TS 102 034 v1.1.1 (March 2005). In the most current cases, it's a simplified version of this model that will be put into practice with only one external access (the ADSL line)

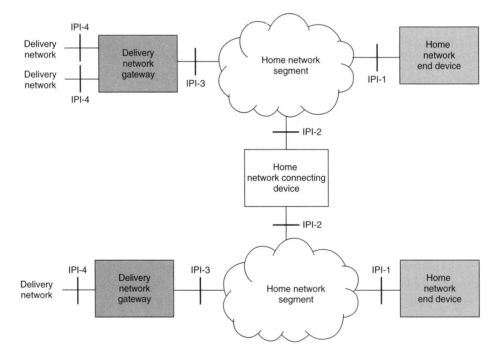

**Figure 10.7** Schematic representation of the DVB home network model (Home Reference Model).

and one or two network technologies for the home network (Ethernet and WiFi in most cases), as shown in Figure 10.6.

We will assume that the HNED which we consider here (the IPTV set-top box, or IPSTB) complies with the DVB-IPI-1 logical interface. Most IPTV solutions deployed so far correspond globally to this model, a notable exception being the Freebox (Freebox 1 to 4) which embeds the ADSL gateway and the TV terminal in one single box. However, the HDTV version of the Freebox (Freebox 5) launched in April 2006 separates these two functions in two distinct units interconnected by WiFi or Ethernet.

## 10.5.2   Main elements of the DVB-IP protocol

This protocol follows the model in layers of the OSI (Open System Interconnection). The highest layer corresponds to the services offered by the service provider (programs, information on programs, IP multicast, and/or unicast addresses).

The Home Network End Device is an IP terminal compliant with the requirements of the RFC1122 document, and it supports the following network and transport protocols: HTTP, TCP, UDP, and IP.

The information necessary for discovery and selection of available services are put together according to a protocol named Service Discovery and Selection (SD&S). They are transported following the DVBSTP protocol for multicast services and following the HTTP protocol (HypertText Transport Protocol) for unicast services. The RTSP protocol (Real Time Streaming Protocol) is used for control and delivery of TV and radio services, independently of their broadcast or on-demand nature. SD&S, DVBSTP, and RTSP are described in ETSI technical specification TS 102 034. This document specifies that the "transport stream" form must be used to transmit the audio, video, and Service Information (SI). We will examine below its encapsulation by the protocols mentioned above.

### 10.5.3 Transport of digital television over IP

Since it is required that audiovisual data are sent as messages compliant with the Internet Protocol (IP), it is necessary to encapsulate them according to the rules of this protocol. Because of the limited bandwidth of the transport medium (ADSL line in most cases), the Transport Stream to be sent sent over IP is usually made up of a single television program, but the DVB standard allows more than one program to be transmitted if the bandwidth permits it.

Due to the time-critical nature of the transported data, a so-called "real time" transport protocol has to be used: the **RTTP** (Real Time Transport Protocol). Each IP packet (or datagram) is made of a certain number of MPEG-2 transport packets of 188 bytes. The total number of transport packets is limited by the maximum length of an IP datagram (65535 bytes in the case of the IP v4 protocol in use today). This content is preceded by a standard IP header (20 bytes) followed by a UDP header (8 bytes) and an RTP header of 12 bytes (see Figure 10.8 to 10.11).

| IP header (20 bytes) | UDP header (8 bytes) | RTP header (12 bytes) | MPEG-2 Transport Packets (N * 188 bytes) |
|---|---|---|---|

< ------------------------------------------- 40 + N*188 octets ------------------------------------------- >

**Figure 10.8**  Global structure of an IP datagram for IPTB (IPv4).

| Version | IHL | Type of service | | Total Length | |
|---|---|---|---|---|---|
| Identification | | | 3 flags | Fragmentation offset | |
| Life time | | Protocol | | Checksum | |
| Source IP address | | | | | |
| Destination IP address | | | | | |

< ------------------------------------------- 32 bits ------------------------------------------- >

**Figure 10.9**  Detail of the IP header.

| Source port (16 bits) | Destination port (16 bits) |
|---|---|
| UDP length (16 bits) | Checksum (16 bits) |

< ------------------------------------------- 32 bits ------------------------------------------- >

**Figure 10.10**  Detail of the UDP header.

| V | P | X | CSRC | M | Payload Type | Sequence Number |
|---|---|---|---|---|---|---|

| Time Stamp |
|---|

| Sync Source (SSRC) |
|---|

< ---------------------------------------------------- 32 bits ------------------------------------------------------ >

**Figure 10.11**  Detail of the RTP header.

The V field (2 bits) indicates the version (RTP = 2).

The P field (1 bit) indicates whether there is padding.

The X field (1 bit) indicates whether there is a header extension beyond 12 bytes (ignored for IPTV).

The M field (1 bit) is a marker bit.

The CRSC field (4 bits) indicates the number of contributing sources (ignored for IPTV).

The Payload Type field (7 bits) indicates the nature of the payload. For IPTV, it should be set to decimal 33 (corresponding to an MPEG-2 transport stream).

The Sequence Number field enables the receiver to reorder packets which would not have been received in the original temporal order and to detect packet loss or multiple reception of the same packets.

The Time Stamp field is derived of a 90 kHz clock which can be optionally locked to the reference clock of one of the programs of the MPEG-2 transport stream. Locked or not, this clock must fulfill the requirements of the ISO/IEC 13818-1 specifications for the MPEG-2 system clock (accuracy and jitter).

The UDP header (8 bytes) is used to indicate the port numbers (always even) used by the UDP protocol as well as the number of transport packets from the UDP length field (Figure 10.10). The IP datagram length is in fact limited to a lower value than the value permitted by the IPv4 protocol because of the maximum size of the network transport unit (Maximum Transport Unit, MTU). This limit must not be exceeded in order to avoid a significant increase of lost packets and an overload of the routers and terminal equipment, which would have to fragment the IP packets to a size below the MTU and reassemble them. Ethernet networks have, in general, an MTU of 1500 bytes, which permits a maximum number of 7 transport packets (1316 bytes).

Depending on some options in the IP or RTP headers, the maximum number of transport packets may even be lower than 7. In order to avoid an RTP fragmentation that some terminals might not support, it is recommended that operators set the *don't fragment* bit to 1 in the IP header (one of the 3 flags). With this option set, routers will return an error message if the non-fragmentable length of the IP datagram exceeds the MTU of the destination network, which will enable the service provider to adjust the length of the payload to its capabilities. The minimum MTU that a network must support is 576 bytes, which permits only 2 transport packets per IP datagram.

### 10.5.4   Compression formats for digital TV over IP

The first implementations of television over IP by ADSL use (or have used) MPEG-2 for video compression with a bit-rate on the order of 3 Mb/s. This allows, depending on the characteristics of the telephone line, the service provider to offer the TV service up to a distance of about 2500 m of the DSLAM. Until the end of 2005, there was practically no other option because of the non-availability of efficient real-time encoders and affordable decoders for more efficient compression formats (H.264, WMV9, etc.).

From 2006 onward, it has become economically feasible to use these new video compression formats which will enable a division by two of the required bit-rate for video encoding at equivalent quality (around 1.5 Mb/s for standard definition).

This bit-rate reduction, combined with the ADSL2+ bandwidth increase, will permit an extension of the service area for standard definition TV over IP to the majority of households (lines of less than 4000 m). For shorter lines (mainly in towns and cities), this global efficiency increase will permit, for example, the transmission of two or three standard-definition programs or one high-definition program.

### 10.5.5   User Interface

The simplest user interface can in principle be a simple HTML browser allowing subscribers to send requests to the DSLAM by hitting active areas of an HTML page. However, the sophistication and the functionality of IP set-top boxes are increasing rapidly (reception of Digital Terrestrial Television, addition of a hard disk, media center functionality). Most boxes now use a true operating system (Linux or Windows CE, for example), which allows the easy porting of middleware and applications derived from the PC world. With each service provider trying to distinguish itself from its competitors by offering specific functionality, there is obviously no interoperability among their respective products, which in any event are rented to the subscriber in most cases.

## 10.6   Digital terrestrial television for mobiles

### 10.6.1   The European DVB-H standard

The DVB-H standard is a recent extension of the DVB-T standard. It is intended to allow reception of television programs with portable and mobile terminals of relatively small size (the H of DVB-H means "handheld," which indicates the primary type of devices targeted).

In most cases, the terminal will be a mobile phone. In fact, one of the main goals of DVB-H is to avoid the limitation inherent to UMTS of the number of terminals which can receive the same broadcast television program at one time (TV on UMTS is a *unicast* type of system where each receiver receives its own stream, so each receiver requires an independent bandwidth). The main extensions of DVB-H compared to DVB-T are as follows (their use is signaled by specific TPS bits):

- addition of a 4 k COFDM mode, better suited to the implementation of SFN networks of medium cell size and allowing a reduction of the power consumption of the terminal compared to the 8 k mode;

- addition of a longer time interleaving (double for the 4 k mode and quadruple for the 2 k mode), which improves the behavior in case of signal fading and resistance to impulsive noise;

- transmission of a given service in periodic bursts by a process known as "time slicing" which permits a subscriber to activate the receiver only during a fraction of the time (5 to 10%) in order to reduce the power consumption, thus increasing the battery operating time;

- the ability to increase robustness by means of an optional additional link layer error correction (MPE-FEC) to improve the reception with an integrated antenna of necessarily very limited performances.

In order to allow the best use of these extensions, TV programs or other broadcast services are transmitted to mobile terminals as elementary streams (**ES**) formatted as **IP** (Internet Protocol) datagrams. The use of the IP protocol is, however, different from the one in TV by ADSL using DVB-IP: in DVB-H, the IP datagrams are encapsulated according to the so-called multiprotocol encapsulation (**MPE**) and then inserted in an MPEG-2 transport stream for transmission (in DVB-IP, it's the transport stream which is IP encapsulated). This operation consists of encapsultaing the IP datagrams in DSM-CC sections by adding a header and a CRC termination. These sections are then segmented into MPEG-2 transport packets.

In order to realize the desired time-slicing, sections are not transmitted immediately, but are accumulated in order to form records of a maximum size of 191 kb, which will correspond to the duration of the time slice allocated to a service. These records can be represented as a table of 191 colums by a maximum of 1024 rows on which an optional additional error correction called "MPE-FEC" can be applied (Fig. 10.12).

This MPE-FEC consists of a Reed–Solomon coding RS (255,191) applied to words of 191 bytes made of the lines of this table. This will produce a second table made of an RS word of 64 bytes for each line of the original table. The result will be a new table of 255 colums by a maximum of 1024 lines which will be read column by column for transmission.

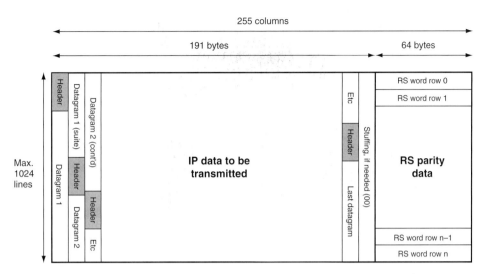

**Figure 10.12**   The MPE-FEC error correction table RS (255,191).

The correction words being also read column by column, each byte of an RS word will be distant by the number of lines of the table from the previous and following words, which creates de facto time interleaving and thereby increases the efficacy of the RS correction. The percentage of time allocated to each individual service, on the order of 5 to 10%, will depend on the number of services to be transmitted, of their individual bit-rate (on the order of 250 to 400 kb/s) and of the total bit-rate of the channel.

The DVB-H standard (Fig. 10.13) can be used in the UHF TV band with usual DVB-T channel widths (6, 7, or 8 MHz, depending on the region) or in other frequency bands (e.g., L-band in the United States around 1.67 GHz with other channel widths, 5 MHz in this case).

One of the problems with the use of the UHF band for TV reception in a GSM phone is the proximity of the high part of the UHF band (up to 862 MHz) to the GSM 900 transmit band of the terminal (880 to 915 MHz). Taking into account the current filtering capabilities, this prevents in practice the possibility of using the high UHF channels (>750 MHz) in a TV receiver integrated into an operating GSM phone.

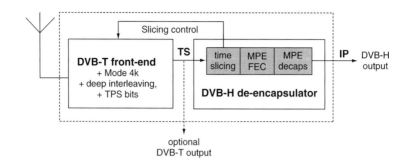

**Figure 10.13** Simplified block diagram of the DVB-H reception front-end.

The DVB-H standard can in principle use all the combinations of modulation parameters allowed by the standard (QPSK to 64-QAM, etc.) but, given the required robustness of this application, in practice only QPSK and 16-QAM with FEC of 1/2 or 2/3 are realistically usable, which permits bit-rates of 5 to 11 Mb/s in an 8 MHz channel (without MPE-FEC correction). The video encoding used will be mainly H.264 with a CIF or QCIF resolution and bit-rates in the order of 256 to 384 kb/s.

Various experiments took place in Europe from 2004 onward to test the technical performances of the system in order to define the characteristics of the network, and to find out the user acceptance and expectations in order to establish a viable business model. The reactions of the test sample have been positive or enthusiastic everywhere. The first commercial DVB-H services started in Finland and Italy in mid-2006.

## 10.6.2  Other mobile TV standards

Without entering into much detail, we will briefly mention the other significant mobile TV standards competing with DVB-H. All use COFDM modulation. The T-DMB standard is in fact a Korean adaptation of the T-DAB standard (Digital Audio Broadcasting) developed in the '90s with the intention of replacing FM transmissions (Eureka 147 project). The T-DMB standard as deployed in Korea uses the same modulation—COFDM—parameters, and channelization as DAB in VHF band III (channels or "blocks" of 1.5 MHz on a 1.75 MHz raster).

In Europe, the frequencies allocated to DAB are both the VHF band III (174–230 MHz) shared with television and the so-called L band (1452–1492 MHz). Given the very limited success of DAB in most European countries (except the UK since the early 2000s), most of this important frequency allocation is underused, therefore potentially usable by T-DMB, which could sometimes reuse an existing DAB network. Some European operators have shown interest in this system and have deployed field tests in VHF band III.

Unlike DVB-H, T-DMB does not use the Internet Protocol for transmission but a conventional MPEG-2 transport stream format. Video and audio codecs used are for the most part similar to those used in DVB-H. The ISDB-T standard (see Appendix C) was originally designed with portability in mind. To this end, it divides the 6 MHz channel into 13 segments and introduces time-interleaving. Mobile TV or sound broadcasting can use the central segment (430 kHz bandwidth), which allows a service provider to transmit only one TV program, or 3 adjacent segments (1.3 MHz bandwidth) to transmit more programs. The presence of time-interleaving in the standard allows it to withstand some "holes" due to blockage in the reception without the need for an additional error correction such as the MPE-FEC of DVB-H.

The MediaFLO™ "standard" is a proprietary system of the U.S. company Qualcomm. FLO™ stands for "Forward Link Only," which underscores the broadcast/multicast nature of the system. It uses 4 k COFDM (modulated in QPSK or 16-QAM). An optional layered modulation capability allows it to match the characteristics and availability of the services with the local coverage quality. A concatenation of turbocodes and Reed–Solomon is used for the Forward Error Correction and a suitable guard interval makes the system applicable to an SFN network configuration. A combination of time and frequency diversity for the insertion of the different components of the multiplex allows it to reduce the power consumption of the receiver's front-end. The audiovisual streams generally use a QVGA resolution encoded in H.264 and AAC+ audio compression. IP encapsulation is used only for non-real-time data delivery (text, graphics, files) but not for real-time AV streaming in order to reduce the encapsulation overhead.

In the United States, MediaFLO™ has been allocated a small portion of the UHF band (6 MHz to around 700 MHz). Qualcomm claims that MediaFLO™ is more spectrally efficient than other compcting systems, including DVB-H. More details can be found in Technology Briefs and white papers available on Qualcomm's website: http://www.qualcomm.com/mediaflo/news/resources.shtml.

We are now nearing the end of this book. In conclusion, the objective of this book will have been achieved if at this point readers have acquired a clear, global view of the new techniques used in digital television systems, which perhaps will give them the desire to investigate this subject further, as it rcmains in rapid evolution more than ten years after its start.

# Appendix A:
# Error detection and correction in digital transmissions

From the very first digital data transmissions, the need to detect and, as far as possible, to correct errors introduced by the transmission link has been recognized. Various more or less complex solutions are used, depending on the characteristics of the link, but they invariably consist of adding a calculated redundancy to the original message.

## A1.1  An error detecting code: the parity bit

The simplest means of detecting errors is the parity bit; it is still employed in short distance serial transmissions (for instance RS232), where it usually applies to words of 6–8 bits. On the transmission side, all the bits of the word to be transmitted are summed, and a supplementary "parity" bit is added at the end of the word; this supplementary bit is equal to 0 if the sum of the bits is even, and 1 if the sum is odd (even parity), or the reverse (odd parity).

On the reception side, the receiver does the same calculation and compares its result with the transmitted parity bit:

- if there is no error (or an even number of errors), the bits are identical,

- if there is one error (or an odd number of errors), the bits are different.

This system allows the detection, without being able to identify or correct it, of a 1-bit error in a word. The parity is only useful when the probability of more than one error per word is very low, as even numbers of errors are undetected, and when the communication link is bi-directional: in this case, the receiver which detects an error can ask the transmitter to retransmit the corrupted message. This principle of error correction is called *feedback error correction.*

## A1.2   Block error correction codes

The block error correction codes apply to finite length words composed of $k$ symbols (bits for instance) to which they add a calculated redundancy which increases the word's length to $n$ symbols (bits in our example), so that $n > k$. The coding algorithm therefore adds $n-k$ bits (called control or parity bits) to the end of the original word, and the redundancy comes from the fact that only $2^k$ combinations out of the $2^n$ possible from the resulting code are used. The ratio $k/n$ of the code (obviously $<1$) is called the *yield* of the code.

In order to be able to distinguish between them in the case of an error, all elements of the code should be as distant as possible from each other. The *Hamming distance* between two elements of a code is defined as the number of different bits situated in the same position. The *minimum* Hamming distance $d$ of the code is defined as the number of different bits between any two elements of the code; one can demonstrate that the number, $t$, of correctible errors in a word is equal to $t = (d-1)/2$.

The whole mechanism of the coding consists, therefore, of finding, for given $n$ and $d$ values (which define the correction capacity of the code), the coding algorithm giving the greatest $k$, and thus the best possible yield. This principle of error correction, which does not require a bi-directional link, is called *forward error correction* (**FEC**), in contrast to the preceding example (parity bit).

We will illustrate this principle by two simple codes (repetition and Hamming codes), in order to understand the philosophy of the more sophisticated codes used in digital video broadcasting (Reed–Solomon and convolutional codes) which we will not detail since they are based on rather complex mathematical concepts. The interested reader will, however, find some books entirely dedicated to these subjects in the bibliography.

## A1.2.1 Repetition

One of the simplest means of correcting error transmissions is to repeat the bits of the message and to use a majority logic (*vote*) on the reception side to decide whether the received bit is a 1 or a 0 in the case of an error. For example, with a repetition factor of 3 ($k = 1$, $n = 3$), the coding of a bit would be:

| Useful bit | Transmitted code |
|---|---|
| 0 | 000 |
| 1 | 111 |

In the above example, the code is made up of two words of 3 bits, all of which are different; the minimum Hamming distance is therefore $d = 3$, and the correction capacity of the code is $t = (3 - 1)/2 = 1$ erroneous bit per word.

On the reception side, if we assume that the transmission channel does not introduce more than one error per word, a majority logic will be able to correct it by deciding, according to Table A.1, where the corrupted, albeit correctible, messages (one erroneous bit out of three) are in the shaded area:

**Table A.1**

| Sent | | 000 | | | | 111 | | |
|---|---|---|---|---|---|---|---|---|
| Received | 000 | 001 | 010 | 100 | 011 | 101 | 110 | 111 |
| Decoded | 0 | 0 | 0 | 0 | 1 | 1 | 1 | 1 |

This type of error correction algorithm has a very low yield, as it triples the amount of information to be transmitted ($k/n = 0.33$), but it can correct high error rates (up to one bit out of three).

## A1.2.2 The Hamming code (7, 4, $d = 3$)

This code applies to 4-bit words ($k = 4$, $2^4 = 16$ code elements) to which it adds 3 bits of redundancy, thus $n = 7$); therefore the yield is $k/n = 4/7 = 0.57$.

It is used for, among other things, the coding of critical parts of teletext magazines, and it works as follows. Let $u$ be the original 4-bit words made up of the bits $u_1$, $u_2$, $u_3$, $u_4$. Let $c$ be the resulting 7-bit code composed of bits $u_1$, $u_2$, $u_3$, $u_4$, $v_1$, $v_2$, $v_3$, obtained by means of the generating matrix $\mathbf{G}$ below:

$$
\begin{array}{c|ccccccc}
u_1 & 1 & 0 & 0 & 0 & 0 & 1 & 1 \\
u_2 & 0 & 1 & 0 & 0 & 1 & 0 & 1 \\
u_3 & 0 & 0 & 1 & 0 & 1 & 1 & 0 \\
u_4 & 0 & 0 & 0 & 1 & 1 & 1 & 1 \\
\hline
 & u_1 & u_2 & u_3 & u_4 & v_1 & v_2 & v_3
\end{array}
$$

The parity bits $v_1$, $v_2$, $v_3$ (situated in the shaded area of the matrix) obey the following relations:

$$v_1 = 0 + u_2 + u_3 + u_4$$
$$v_2 = u_1 + 0 + u_3 + u_4$$
$$v_3 = u_1 + u_2 + 0 + u_4$$

On the receiving side, the decoder receives the message $y$ composed of bits $u_1'$, $u_2'$, $u_3'$, $u_4'$, $v_1'$, $v_2'$, $v_3'$, and does the same calculation as the encoder for the bits $u_1'$, $u_2'$, $u_3'$, $u_4'$, which yields the bits $w_1$, $w_2$, $w_3$:

$$w_1 = 0 + u_2' + u_3' + u_4'$$
$$w_2 = u_1' + 0 + u_3' + u_4'$$
$$w_3 = u_1' + u_2' + 0 + u_4'$$

The decoder calculates the *syndrome* $S = s_1$, $s_2$, $s_3 = v_1' - w_1$, $v_2' - w_2$, $v_3' - w_3$. The syndrome's calculation can be represented by the parity control matrix **H** below:

| 0 | 1 | 1 | 1 | 1 | 0 | 0 | $s_1$ |
|---|---|---|---|---|---|---|---|
| 1 | 0 | 1 | 1 | 0 | 1 | 0 | $s_2$ |
| 1 | 1 | 0 | 1 | 0 | 0 | 1 | $s_3$ |
| $u_1'$ | $u_2'$ | $u_3'$ | $u_4'$ | $v_1'$ | $v_2'$ | $v_3'$ | |

If we assume that there is a maximum error of 1 bit per received word, the results will be as follows:

- if there is no error, the syndrome will be $S = 0, 0, 0$;

- if the bit $u_4'$ is erroneous, the 3 bits $v_1'$, $v_2'$, $v_3'$ will be wrong, and the syndrome will be $S = 1, 1, 1$;

- if 1 of the 3 bits $u_1'$, $u_2'$, $u_3'$ received is erroneous, two of the three relations used to calculate $w_1$, $w_2$, $w_3$ will be wrong (as each bit is used once in two of the three equations); the syndrome $S$ will therefore have 2 bits at 1 and 1 bit at 0, the position of which will indicate which of bits $u_1'$, $u_2'$, $u_3'$ is in error;

- if the error affects a parity bit, its position will be indicated by the presence of only 1 in the syndrome.

From this, it can be seen that this code allows the detection and correction of one error in the received word ($t = 1$) which corresponds to a minimum Hamming distance of $d = 3$.

## A1.2.3 Reed–Solomon coding

This is also a block error correction code, the symbols of which are not bits but *finite field elements* (very often bytes); the mathematical theory of these codes can be found in specialized books, some of which can be found in the bibliography. We will therefore not present a theoretical description of the Reed–Solomon code, which would require long mathematical developments, but merely mention that it belongs to the cyclic class of codes and that it is a particular case of the so-called BCH codes (from their authors Bose, Ray-Chauduri, Hocquenghem). Like the two previous codes seen before, it is characterized by the three parameters ($n$, $k$, $t$) which define the size of the blocks on which it acts and the number of errors that it can correct:

- $n$ is the size (in symbols) of the block after coding;

- $k$ is the size (in symbols) of the original block;

- $t$ is the number of correctible symbols.

This code is well adapted to the correction of burst errors introduced by a transmission channel, which is why it has been chosen as the *outer coding* algorithm for all the variants of the DVB digital television standard, with a symbol size of 1 byte.

In the DVB case, the size of the original block is the transport packet ($k = 188$ bytes); the specified Reed–Solomon coding increases the block size by 16 bytes ($n = 204$ bytes), and the minimum Hamming distance is $d = 17$ bytes, which allows the correction of up to $(d - 1)/2 = 8$ erroneous bytes per block. This code is denoted RS (204, 188, $t = 8$), and its yield is $k/n = 188/204 = 0.92$. It is a shortened version of the RS(255, 239, $t = 8$) obtained at encoding by adding 51 null bytes before the 188 byte packets in order to form 239 byte blocks applied at the input of an RS(255, 239, $t = 8$) encoder. This coding adds 16 parity bytes to the end of the original blocks, thus forming new protected 255 byte blocks. After encoding, the first 51 null bytes added before coding are discarded, which gives the new protected transport packets of 204 bytes.

Decoding of the Reed–Solomon code uses a fast Fourier transform (FFT) to calculate the syndromes and a Euclidean algorithm to find the error evaluation and localization polynomials. Erroneous words are calculated by using the *Forney formula* and are corrected within the limit of a maximum of 8 bytes per block.

## A1.3   Convolutional coding

We will not develop the theory of these codes either, which is quite complex and requires high level mathematical explanations, and will again refer the interested reader to some of the references in the bibliography.

This coding acts on blocks of indefinite length: in practice it will be a *continuous bitstream* of arbitrary length. It is sometimes improperly called "Viterbi coding," from the name of the author of the decoding algorithm generally used. It is intended to correct random errors, most often as a complement to a block code.

The convolution coding transforms the input stream into $n$ output streams (two in the case of Fig. A.1), thus adding redundancy to it.

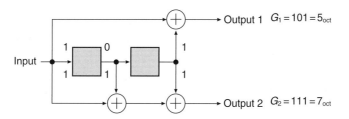

**Figure A.1**   An example of convolutional coding producing two bitstreams ($R_c = 1/2$, $K = 3$, $d_{free} = 5$).

There can be as many branches in parallel as one wants, but the most common case has two.

The incoming stream is applied to the input of a shift register which has intermediate outputs (taps) after each stage; the stream advances one stage in the shift register after each new incoming bit. The incoming stream is also applied to the input of the first modulo 2 adding machine of each branch, which receives the output of the first intermediate tap of the shift register at its other input. The output of this adding machine is applied to one of the inputs of the next adding machine, which receives the output of the next stage of the shift register at its other input, and so on. Some adding machines are omitted and are assigned a coefficient of 0, while those that are not omitted are given the coefficient 1. Each branch is then described by the binary or octal number formed by the sequence of 0's and 1's. Figure A.1 illustrates the process for a simple case with two outputs $X$ and $Y$ and three taps. The code is characterized by the following parameters:

- $R_c$, code rate: ratio between the input and output bit-rates (here 1/2)

- $K$, constraint length: number of usable taps (here 3)

- $G_1$, generator sum for $X$ (here $101_{bin}$)

- $G_2$, generator sum for $Y$ (here $111_{bin}$)

The generator sums $G_1$ and $G_2$ are obtained by assigning, from the left to the right, a 1 to the taps actually used and a 0 to the unused ones. The binary number obtained is generally represented in octal form (base 8). Hence, in the above example, the standard description is:

$$R_c = 1/2, K = 3, G_1 = 5_{oct}, G_2 = 7_{oct}$$

Another parameter, called the *free distance* ($d_{free}$), describes the correction capacity of the code: the higher the value of $d_{free}$, the more efficient is the correction (in the above example, $d_{free} = 5$).

The most standard method used to decode convolutional codes is based on the Viterbi algorithm, so named because of its inventor (1969). An explanation of the Viterbi algorithm would also be rather complex, and so we will simply indicate that its principle consists of finding the maximum likelihood route on a trellis representing the different possible states of the coder in order to find the most probable original message from the received stream.

# Appendix B: Spectral efficiency of cable and satellite transmissions with DVB parameters

The bandwidth occupied by an AM modulated signal is twice the bandwidth of the modulating signal, due to the two lateral bands generated by the modulation process. In the case of a digital signal of symbol period $T$ which is Nyquist filtered with a roll-off $\alpha$, the bandwidth will be:

$$BW = (1 + \alpha) \times 1/T$$

From this formula, we can now calculate the capacity of the channel and the spectral efficiency for various hypothetical cases.

## Cable

With a roll-off $\alpha = 0.15$, a European channel of bandwidth $BW = 8\,\text{MHz}$ can accept a maximum symbol rate $F_s = 1/T = BW/(1 + \alpha) = 8/1.15 \cong 7\,\text{MHz}$. A commonly used value is $6.875\,\text{MHz}$. The usable order of QAM will depend on the network quality which determines $E_b/N_o$. In the worst case, 16-QAM (4 bits/symbol) will have to be used, resulting in a *brutto* bit-rate of:

$$R_b = 6.875 \times 4 = 27.5\,\text{Mb/s (without Reed–Solomon coding)}$$

Hence the brutto spectral efficiency will be $27.5/8 = 3.437\,\text{b/s}$ per Hz. The *useful* bit-rate $R_u$ is the product of $R_b$ and the Reed–Solomon factor $r_{RS}$ (188/204), and hence:

$$R_u = R_b \times r_{RS} = 27.5 \times 188/204 \cong 25.34\,\text{Mb/s}$$

The *useful spectral efficiency* is therefore $25.34/8 = 3.16\,\text{b/s}$ per Hz. In the best case, 64-QAM (6 bits/symbol) will be possible, resulting in a brutto bit-rate of:

$$R_b = 6.875 \times 6 = 41.25\,\text{Mb/s} \text{ (without Reed–Solomon coding)}$$

Hence, the brutto spectral efficiency will be $41.25/8 = 5.156\,\text{b/s}$ per Hz. The useful bit-rate $R_u$ is calculated as before,

$$R_u = R_b \times r_{RS} = 41.25 \times 188/204 \cong 38.0\,\text{Mb/s}$$

The useful spectral efficiency is therefore $38.0/8 = 4.75\,\text{b/s}$ per Hz.

## Satellite

Theoretically with a roll-off $\alpha = 0.35$, a channel of $BW = 33\,\text{MHz}$ supports a maximum symbol rate $F_s = 1/T = BW/(1+\alpha) = 33/1.35 = 24.4\,\text{MHz}$.

With QPSK modulation (2 bits/symbol), the brutto bit-rate is therefore

$$R_b = 2 \times F_s = 48.88\,\text{Mb/s}$$

(without Reed–Solomon and inner codings).

In practice, this capacity can be slightly higher (a ratio $BW/F_s$ of 1.20 between bandwidth and symbol rates results in only a marginal degradation). The maximum symbol rate thus becomes $33/1.20 = 27.5\,\text{MHz}$; the brutto bit-rate $R_b = 55\,\text{Mb/s}$ and the brutto spectral efficiency is $55/33 = 1.66\,\text{b/s}$ per Hz.

The useful bit-rate depends on the code rate $r_c$ chosen for the inner coding; it is equal to the product of the brutto bit-rate $R_b$, $r_c$, and $r_{RS}$ (Reed–Solomon factor $= 188/204$). In the worst case (minimal $E_b/N_o$) the code rate $r_c = 1/2$ will have to be used to ensure a satisfactory service (BER $< 10^{-10}$); in this case the useful bit-rate is:

$$R_u = R_b \times r_c \times r_{RS} = 55 \times 1/2 \times 188/204 = 25.34 \, \text{Mb/s}$$

The useful spectral efficiency is therefore $25.34/33 = 0.76 \, \text{b/s}$ per Hz.

In the best case (maximal $E_b/N_o$), the same service quality can be obtained with $r_c = 7/8$; the useful bit-rate becomes:

$$R_u = R_b \times r_c \times r_{RS} = 55 \times 7/8 \times 188/204 = 44.35 \, \text{Mb/s}$$

The *useful* spectral efficiency is therefore $44.35/33 = 1.34 \, \text{b/s}$ per Hz. In fact, most digital satellite TV transmissions in use today on ASTRA and EUTELSAT (33 MHz channels) use this maximum symbol rate of 27.5 MHz and a code rate $r_c = 3/4$. This corresponds to a useful bit-rate of $27.5 \times 2 \times 3/4 \times 188/204 \simeq 38.0 \, \text{Mb/s}$, which allows transparent retransmission on a cable network with 8 MHz channels by using 64-QAM at a symbol rate of 6.875 MHz (best case example in our calculation for cable above). In this case, the spectral efficiency of the satellite channel is $38.0/33 = 1.15 \, \text{b/s}$ per Hz.

# Appendix C: The main other digital TV systems

Even if most countries in the world (in particular countries using PAL or SECAM systems for analog TV) have adopted the DVB system, the United States, Japan, and some other "NTSC countries" use it either partly or not at all. Other systems are also used or proposed, and the three main ones are briefly described below.

## C1.1 The DSS system (satellite, the United States)

**DSS** (Digital Satellite System), launched in 1994, is historically the first "direct to home" digital satellite TV broadcasting system and the most widely used in the United States. DSS started with the DirecTV® network, which was shortly after complemented on the same orbital position with the USBB® bouquet. These two networks, now merged, offer together more than 200 TV channels which can be received from anywhere in the United States with the same set-top box and a small 18" (45 cm) dish. Other satellites are also positioned 101° and 119° west.

Contrary to DVB which is an open system and an international standard, DSS® is the proprietary system of Hughes Electronics Corporation, the detailed specifications of which are not available to

**Table C.1**

| Parameter | Recall DVB-S | DSS | Remarks (DSS) |
|---|---|---|---|
| Video coding | MPEG-2 MP@ML | MPEG-1.5 | Format up to $720 \times 480$ |
| Audio coding | MPEG-1 level 2 | AC3 | Under licence of Dolby® labs |
| Multiplexing | MPEG transport | Proprietary | Statistical MPX allowed |
| Transport packet | 188 bytes | 130 bytes | Before channel coding |
| Scrambling | DVB-CSA | Proprietary | CA: Videoguard (NDS) |
| Energy dispersal | $G_{(15)} = 1 + X^{14} + X^{15}$ | None | |
| External coding | RS(204, 188, $T = 8$) | RS(204, 188, $T = 8$) | Sync byte not RS protected |
| Internal coding | Convolutive | Trellis | |
| Puncturing rates | 1/2, 2/3, 3/4, 5/6, 7/8 | 2/3 or 6/7 | Depending on transponder power |
| Modulation | QPSK | QPSK | |
| Roll-off factor | 35% | 20% | |
| Channel width | Up to 54 MHz | 27 MHz | Only one channel width |
| Symbol rate | From 1 to 45 Ms/s | 20 Ms/s | |
| Allocated Ku band | 10.7 to 12.75 GHz | 12.2 to 12.7 GHz | So-called DBS band |

the general public. Furthermore, as it was specified before the finalization of the MPEG-2 specifications, it uses an audio/video coding scheme sometimes called "MPEG-1.5" (somewhere in between MPEG-1 and MPEG-2, as the name suggests), an AC-3 audio coding (also known as Dolby® digital), and a specific multiplexing. Table C.1 summarizes differences between the DVB-S and DSS systems. The main competitor of DirecTV®, the DISH® Network from Echostar, uses the DVB system in the same band—DBS—and with the same channel width.

Table C.2 gives the frequency of the 32 DBS channels which use circular left (L) or right (R) polarization.

**Table C.2**

| DBS band (USA) 12.200–12.700 GHz | | | | | | | |
|---|---|---|---|---|---|---|---|
| Channel/ polar. | Frequency (MHz) | Channel/ polar. | Frequency (MHz) | Channel/ polar. | Frequency (MHz) | Channel/ polar. | Frequency (MHz) |
| 1 L | 12 224 | 9 L  | 12 341 | 17 L | 12 457 | 25 L | 12 574 |
| 2 R | 12 239 | 10 R | 12 355 | 18 R | 12 472 | 26 R | 12 588 |
| 3 L | 12 253 | 11 L | 12 370 | 19 L | 12 486 | 27 L | 12 603 |
| 4 R | 12 268 | 12 R | 12 384 | 20 R | 12 501 | 28 R | 12 618 |
| 5 L | 12 282 | 13 L | 12 399 | 21 L | 12 516 | 29 L | 12 632 |
| 6 R | 12 297 | 14 R | 12 414 | 22 R | 12 530 | 30 R | 12 647 |
| 7 L | 12 311 | 15 L | 12 428 | 23 L | 12 545 | 31 L | 12 661 |
| 8 R | 12 326 | 16 R | 12 443 | 24 R | 12 559 | 32 R | 12 676 |

## C2.1 The ATSC system (terrestrial, the United States)

The **ATSC** (Advanced Television System Committee) system is the result of work started in the mid-1980s which had as their original objective the specification of a high definition television system for terrestrial diffusion, in order to compete with the Japanese MUSE and the European HD-MAC systems. Many industrial interest groups were put in competition, out of which came three proposed digital solutions. In May 1993, they agreed to cooperate under the name of "Grand Alliance" in order to combine their individual proposals into a unique system, of which specifications were published in 1995 (Document ATSC A/53).

This system is based on the MPEG-2 standard for the video coding (MP@HL), and can transmit pictures at high definition (max. $1920 \times 1080$, 16/9), enhanced definition ($1280 \times 720$, 16/9) and standard definition ($720 \times 480$, 4/3 *or* 16/9). A $640 \times 480$, 4/3 format has also been foreseen in view of computer graphics compatibility (VGA). In all, no less than 18 different display formats (interlaced or progressive) have to be supported.

Audio compression uses the AC-3 process of the Dolby® laboratories (Document ATSC A/52). Multiplexing complies with the MPEG-2 system specification (ISO/IEC 13818–1), and 188-byte transport packets are thus identical to those used in the DVB system. Regarding channel coding and modulation used for terrestrial transmission, a process known as **8-VSB** (vestigial sideband with 8 states) has been retained. On the transmission side, after removal of the sync byte, energy dispersal followed by an internal coding RS(207, 187, $T = 10$) are applied to the 187 remaining bytes. The resulting 207-byte packets follow a convolutional interleaving followed by a trellis coding with a puncturing of 2/3.

A mapping forms segments of 828 symbols coded on 3 bits (8 levels) which are grouped in frames of 312 segments. Each frame starts by a synchronization segment formed with the synchronization bytes of the transport packets and each segment starts with a synchronization symbol. The structure obtained in this way resembles an analog television frame with a duration of 24.2 ms and is made of 313 segments (comparable to a TV line) of 77.3 μs.

The frames are grouped by two in a similar manner to an analog interlaced picture. This signal modulates a unique carrier (amplitude modulation with suppressed carrier), which can take eight discrete values during the useful duration of the segments. The signal is then Nyquist filtered (raised cosine with $\alpha = 0.1152$) in order to limit the upper sideband to 5.69 MHz and the lower sideband to 0.31 MHz. A pilot carrier with reduced amplitude is reinserted in place of the suppressed carrier.

One can see that this process is very different of the COFDM used in the DVB-T standard—it does not have its flexibility (all the parameters are fixed). More important, it does not have the same performance, especially in the presence of multiple echoes.

These unsatisfactory performances, added to the complexity and cost of the complete system due to the numerous display formats supported, including HD, mean that three years after its commercial launch in 1998, the ATSC system did not really take off (some tens of thousands of sets in 2001).

**Table C.3**

| Parameter | Recall DVB-T | ATSC | Remarks (ATSC) |
|---|---|---|---|
| Video coding | MPEG-2 MP@ML | MPEG-2 MP@HL | 18 formats, SDTV to HDTV |
| Audio coding | MPEG-1 level 2 | AC3 | License of Dolby® labs |
| Multiplexing | MPEG transport | MPEG-2 transport | Same as DVB |
| Transport packet | 188 bytes | 188 bytes | Before channel coding |
| Scrambling | DVB-CSA | Not specified | NRSS detachable CA module |
| Energy dispersal | $G_{(15)} = 1 + X^{14} + X^{15}$ | $G_{(16)} = X^{16} + X^{13} + X^{12} + X^7 + X^6 + X^3 + X + 1$ | |
| External coding | RS(204, 188, $T = 8$) | RS(207, 187, $T = 10$) | Sync byte not RS protected |
| Internal coding | Convolutive | Trellis | |
| Puncturing rates | 1/2, 2/3, 3/4, 5/6, 7/8 | 3-Feb | Fixed value |
| Modulation | COFDM 2K/8K | 8-VSB | 16-VSB mode for cable |
| Roll-off factor | NA | 0.1152 | Attenuation band: 0.31 MHz |
| Channel width | 6, 7, or 8 MHz | 6 MHz | No. 7 or 8 MHz variant |
| Useful bit-rate | From 5 to 31 Mb/s | 19.28 Mb/s | Fixed rate |

Table C.3 summarizes differences between the DVB-T and ATSC systems.

## C3.1   The ISDB-T system (terrestrial, Japan)

In 1999 Japan proposed another system for digital terrestrial television in view of standardization by the ITU. This system, named **ISDB-T** (Integrated Services Digital Broadcasting for Terrestrial transmission), is like DVB-T, based on COFDM modulation, and can be seen as a kind of extension of it. The input format (MPEG-2 transport stream) and the channel coding are identical to those of DVB-T. The philosophy behind this system is on the one hand to increase flexibility in allocating services by dividing the channel into segments capable of transmitting different services able to support different receiving conditions, and on the other hand to have the possibility of further increasing the signal's robustness for mobile reception by adding a time interleaving function.

The TV channel (which can have a 6, 7, or 8 MHz width) is divided in 14 segments, 13 of which (numbered 0 to 12) are effectively used, the 14th corresponding to a guard space between adjacent channels. Three COFDM modes are foreseen which are characterized by the number of carriers per segment:

108 carriers/segment (corresponding to a 2K mode in a single segment)

216 carriers/segment (corresponding to a 4K mode in a single segment)

432 carriers/segment (corresponding to a 8K mode in a single segment)

The segments are associated in groups (maximum three groups per channel), which have the same purpose as the hierarchical modes of DVB-T. The minimum size of a group is one segment. In order to ensure different receiving conditions, each segment group can use different internal coding parameters (puncturing rate) and modulation orders (dQPSK, QPSK, 16-QAM, 64-QAM) as well as different time interleaving depths. The system thus allows partial, narrowband reception (single segment, which has to be the central segment), for example, for mobile audio reception.

Figure C.1 represents the 13 segments and their positions in the channel, where three groups can be seen, of which segment 0 in the middle of the channel is intended for narrow-band reception.

The only significant improvement of ISDB-T over DVB-T is the robustness if a relatively long time interleaving is used, which allows it to withstand relatively long reception holes or disturbances. However, this feature is balanced by a considerable cost increase, mainly due to the RAM capacity required by time interleaving.

**Figure C.1**   Segmentation of the ISDB-T Channel

**Table C.4**

| Parameter | Recall DVB-T | ISDB-T | Remark |
|---|---|---|---|
| Multiplexing | MPEG-2 transport | MPEG-2 transport | Same as DVB-T |
| Transport packet | 188 bytes | 188 bytes | Same as DVB-T |
| Energy dispersal | $G_{(15)} = 1 + X^{14} + X^{15}$ | $G_{(15)} = 1 + X^{14} + X^{15}$ | Same as DVB-T |
| External coding | RS(204, 188, $T = 8$) | RS(204, 188, $T = 8$) | Same as DVB-T |
| Internal coding | Convolutive | Convolutive | Same as DVB-T |
| Puncturing rates | 1/2, 2/3, 3/4, 5/6, 7/8 | 1/2, 2/3, 3/4, 5/6, 7/8 | Same as DVB-T |
| Modulation | COFDM 2K/8K | Segmented COFDM | 108, 216, 432 carriers/seg. |
| Modulation orders | 4, 16, or 64 | 4d, 4, 16, or 64 | dQPSK supported |
| Segment number | 1 | 13 useful | segment width = channel/14 |
| Hierarchical modes | By constellation | By segmentation | 3 groups max. |
| Time interleaving | No | Yes | Improvement of mobile rec. |
| Guard interval | 1/4, 1/8, 1/16, 1/32 | 1/4, 1/8, 1/16, 1/32 | Same as DVB-T |
| Channel width | 6, 7, or 8 MHz | 6, 7, or 8 MHz | Same as DVB-T |
| Useful bit-rate (8 MHz) | From 5 to 32 Mb/s | From 5 to 31 Mb/s | Slightly less than DVB-T |

At the time of writing, ISDB-T is still not in commercial use in Japan and no consumer circuit is available for this system, which does not prevent its promoters from strong lobbying actions that put it in direct competition with DVB-T in countries which have as yet not chosen a system for digital terrestrial TV. Table C.4 shows the comparison of the main parameters of DVB-T and ISDB-T.

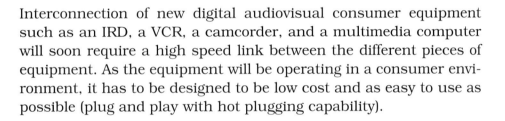

# Appendix D: The IEEE1394 high speed serial AV interconnection bus

Interconnection of new digital audiovisual consumer equipment such as an IRD, a VCR, a camcorder, and a multimedia computer will soon require a high speed link between the different pieces of equipment. As the equipment will be operating in a consumer environment, it has to be designed to be low cost and as easy to use as possible (plug and play with hot plugging capability).

The recently standardized IEEE1394 (1995) high speed serial bus fulfills these requirements. It is based on Apple computer's Fire-Wire bus and allows communication at up to 400 Mb/s (an upgrade to more than 1 Gb/s is under study). Three standard speeds are defined (100, 200, and 400 Mb/s), but most current implementations only cover the first two speeds.

The IEEE1394 bus architecture enables the construction of a kind of network, made up of multiple (up to 63) participants called **nodes**. Each of the nodes has three basic functional components:

- a physical layer interface (PHY) which carries out the physical interfacing to the cable, bus arbitration, and an active repeater function;

- a link layer controller (LINK) which assembles/disassembles data packets and handles handshaking and acknowledgment;

- a host controller (MCU) which deals with the higher levels of the bus protocols.

Figure D.1 shows an example of a three node IEEE1394 network where the three above-mentioned components can be seen.

In the first implementation of IEEE1394 chipsets, the blocks denoted "LINK" and "PHY" generally correspond to two different integrated circuits. The IEEE1394 specification defines two kinds of data transfer which can coexist on the bus:

- **Isochronous** transfers are reserved for time-critical data, such as audio and video streams which need to be real time, as delays in audio or video frames cannot be tolerated. These types of transfer are allocated a guaranteed bandwidth and use time division multiplexing.

- **Asynchronous** transfers are reserved for non-time-critical data, which are used, for instance, for data interchange or storage and employ a more conventional process of handshaking and acknowledgment.

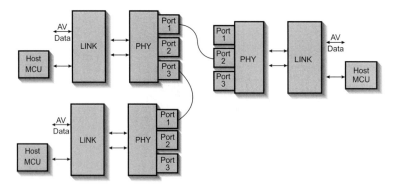

**Figure D.1** Structure of an IEEE1394 network (example with three nodes).

The proportion of bus bandwidth reserved for isochronous data packets is defined during the initialization phase by electing as the root node a node which includes an isochronous resource manager (IRM). The IRM is then responsible for allocating isochronous resources for a whole session, based on 125 μs cycles on the bus. However, this is not sufficient to guarantee the very low jitter required to transmit, for example, an MPEG-2 transport stream over the bus (a variation in transport delay of less than 500 ns is required in this case).

In the case of a DVB set-top box, the AV data interface of the link circuit in Figure D.1 would be connected to the transport stream path (i.e., between the output of the channel decoding part and the input of the source decoding part, before or after descrambling). This would allow, for example, the non-descrambled transport stream to be sent to a digital VCR, and in this case playback would require suitable access rights for viewing.

In order to enable the receiver to compensate for the delays introduced by the bus, an AV layer has been defined and standardized in the IEC1883 specification. It adds a 32-bit header (a quadlet in IEEE1394 terminology) to the 188-byte MPEG-2 packets which then become 192 bytes long, the header quadlet containing a time stamp which allows resynchronization at the receiving end. In addition, if a 192-byte packet (= 48 quadlets) cannot be transmitted in one 125 μs cycle, the AV layer allows it to be split into two, four, or eight smaller equal parts (or blocks) which then can fit within one cycle.

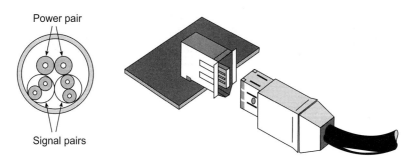

Power pair

Signal pairs

**Figure D.2** Cable and connector for IEEE1394 cabling (six pin version with power).

Electrically, the bus is made up of two signals (DATA and STROBE), which are both transported in differential mode at low impedance on a shielded pair of conductors. An optional third pair is used for power distribution over the bus. Each branch of the network between two nodes can be up to 4.5 m long and is terminated at both ends by two 56 Ω resistors connected to a common DC reference. A low cost six pin connector (similar to those used on Nintendo Game Boy® consoles) and a specific cable have been standardized (see Fig. D.2). A version of the bus with only two pairs (without the power pair) has also been standardized.

# Appendix E: The DiSEqC bus for antenna system control

Back in 1995, EUTELSAT proposed, in cooperation with the satellite receiver and antenna industries, the introduction of a control bus using the coaxial cable of a satellite antenna called **DiSEqC**™ (**Di**gital **S**atellite **Eq**uipment **C**ontrol).

This solution is compatible with the most common switching system in use today in recent individual satellite installations (14/18 V for the polarization and 22 kHz for the band). It is royalty free and the DiSEqC™ label may be used, provided the EUTELSAT specifications are fulfilled.

## E1.1  The DiSEqC levels

DiSEqC has three implementation levels: ToneBurst, DiSEqC 1.0, and DiSEqC 2.0 and above.

- The ToneBurst is a short-term, simple extension to the 22 kHz tone intended to allow switching of two antennas (or LNBs fitted on the same dish, e.g., for Astra 19.2°E and Eutelsat 13°E).

**Table E.1**  Minimum functionality of receiver for the various DiSEqC levels

| Level | Communication | Minimal receiver functionality |
|---|---|---|
| ToneBurst | Unidirectional | 14/18 V + 0/22 kHz + A/B switch control |
| DiSEqC 1.0 | Unidirectional | Idem ToneBurst + control of 4 committed switches |
| DiSEqC 1.1 | Unidirectional | Idem 1.0 + additional controls + repetition (x 3) |
| DiSEqC 1.2 | Unidirectional | Idem 1.1 + positioner control + optional polarized |
| DiSEqC 2.x | Bidirectional | Idem 1.x + reading of data from slave |

- The first true DiSEqC level (DiSEqC 1.0) is a unidirectional, relatively simple implementation allowing more sophisticated controls, sufficient for most consumer installations.

- Upper levels (DiSEqC 2.0 and above) use a bi-directional communication between the master (set-top box) and slaves, with a view to longer-term plug and play installation.

For each DiSEqC level, a minimal functionality has been defined by EUTELSAT for receivers (Table E.1) and peripherals.

## E2.1  DiSEqC basic principles

DiSEqC is an extension to the 22 kHz tone control in use today (mostly for bandswitching of Universal LNBs) which simplifies its implementation in existing receivers. It is a system with a single master (the satellite receiver) and many slaves (peripheral devices such as switches, LNBs, etc.); the master is the only one to have the capability of starting a communication on the bus, slaves can only react to a command from the master.

DiSEqC philosophy has some similarities with the popular I²C bus from Philips. DiSEqC messages are obtained by PWK (pulse width keying) modulating the duty cycle of the 22 kHz with two values: 0 corresponds to two-thirds duty cycle and 1 to one-third duty cycle (Fig. E.1).

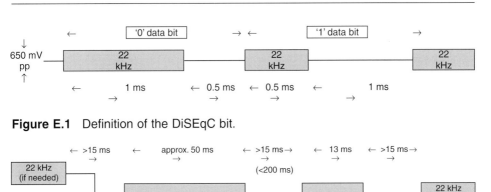

**Figure E.1** Definition of the DiSEqC bit.

**Figure E.2** DiSEqC sequence compatible with Universal LNB and ToneBurst.

The bit period is 33 cycles of 22 kHz (1.5 ms ± 20% taking into account the 22 kHz tolerance). Each DiSEqC message must be followed by at least 6 ms "silence." The 22 kHz level superimposed on the LNB supply voltage is nominally 650 mV pp. Above level 2.0, the master should have a source impedance of 15 Ω at 22 kHz in order to be able to receive the response from the slaves. DiSEqC is specified in a way which is compatible with existing hardware:

- In order to be compatible with existing peripherals (14/18 V, 0/22 kHz, ToneBurst) new receivers must first apply the appropriate voltage for polarization control and the 22 kHz tone if required, then after a short "silence" the true DiSEqC message is followed by the ToneBurst (see Fig. E.2).

- In order that new DiSEqC peripherals be at least partly controllable by existing (non-DiSEqC) receivers, they will initially have to respond to traditional 14/18 V and 22 kHz controls.

## E2.1.1 DiSEqC ToneBurst

The ToneBurst consists of either a plain 22 kHz burst of 12.5 ms (satellite A selection) or of a sequence of nine 1's (one-third duty cycle) for satellite B selection (see Fig. E.3).

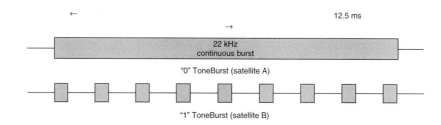

**Figure E.3**  Definition of the ToneBurst.

## E2.1.2  DiSEqC 1.0 and above formats

DiSEqC messages are made of one or more bytes (MSB first) each followed by an odd parity bit in order to be able to detect transmission errors.

- Commands from *master* consist of a minimum of 3 bytes (framing, address, control), followed by a certain number of data bytes for some commands. The general format is illustrated below:

| FRAMING | P | ADDRESS | P | CONTROL | P | DATA | P | DATA | P |
|---------|---|---------|---|---------|---|------|---|------|---|

In order to keep the duration of a message within acceptable limits, a maximum of 1 byte of data is used with level 1.0, and a maximum of 3 for levels 2.0 and above.

- The response from a *slave* is at the master's discretion, and occurs only if they are both at level 2.0 or above. It is made of a framing byte (used as acknowledge) optionally followed by one or more data bytes carrying the message content. Its format is shown below:

| FRAMING | P | DATA | P | DATA | P |
|---------|---|------|---|------|---|

Slave response must occur within 150 ms after the master's command end. The error recovery method is not defined by the specification; the most usual strategy consists of repeating the message, but is entirely at the master's software discretion.

## E3.1   Different fields of the DiSEqC message

### E3.1.1   Framing byte

The framing byte is the first byte of a master's command or a slave's response.

- The 4 MSBs are used for synchronization (*run-in*) and recognition (*framing*) of a DiSEqC message. They are currently fixed at 1110, but the two last bits might be affected later.

- The 5th bit is reserved (currently 0); it might be used later.

- The 6th bit indicates the origin of the message: 0 if it comes from the master, 1 if it comes from a slave.

- The 7th bit is set to 1 if a response is expected, 0 otherwise. In the case of a slave response, it can be set to 1 to ask repetition of the message in the case of a transmission error.

- The 8th bit is set to 1 by the master if it is a retransmission. In the case of a slave response, it indicates the reason of non-execution of the command: 0 in the case of a parity error asking for retransmission, 1 if the command is not supported by the slave.

The meaning of framing bytes is described in Table E.2; only the first two lines apply to level 1.0.

### E3.1.2   Address byte

The second byte sent by the master indicates the slave to which the message is destined; it is subdivided into two nibbles. The MS nibble indicates the family to which the slave belongs (LNB, switch, positioner, etc.); the LS nibble divides the family into subgroups.

**Table E.2**

| Hex. | Binary | Meaning |
|------|--------|---------|
| E0 | 1110 0000 | Master command, no response expected, 1st transmission |
| E1 | 1110 0001 | Master command, no response expected, 2nd transmission |
| E2 | 1110 0010 | Master command, response expected, 1st transmission |
| E3 | 1110 0011 | Master command, response expected, repetition |
| E4 | 1110 0100 | Slave response, repetition unnecessary, no error |
| E5 | 1110 0101 | Slave response, repetition unnecessary, command not supported |
| E6 | 1110 0110 | Slave response, repetition required, parity error |
| E7 | 1110 0111 | Slave response, repetition required, command not recognized |

For each nibble the value 0000 indicates a value for all families (MS nibble) or all subgroups of a family (LS nibble). The address hex. 00 is recognized by all peripherals.

Table E.3 indicates addresses currently specified (addresses above hex. 20 are only used by levels 2.0 and above).

**Table E.3**

| Hex. address. | Binary | Category |
|---------------|--------|----------|
| 00 | 0000 0000 | All families, all subgroups (general call) |
| 10 | 0001 0000 | Switch (all types, including LNB or SMATV) |
| 11 | 0001 0001 | LNB |
| 12 | 0001 0010 | LNB with loop-through and switching |
| 14 | 0001 0100 | Switch without DC pass-through |
| 15 | 0001 0101 | Switch with DC and bus pass-through |
| 18 | 0001 1000 | SMATV |
| 20 | 0010 0000 | Polarizer (all types) |
| 21 | 0010 0001 | Linear polarization control (full skew) |
| 30 | 0011 0000 | Positioner (all types) |
| 40 | 0100 0000 | Installation support (all types) |
| 41 | 0100 0001 | Signal intensity adjustment support |
| 6x | 0110 xxxx | Reserved for address reallocation |
| 70 | 0111 0000 | Slave intelligent interface (all type) |
| 71 | 0111 0001 | Interface for subscriber-controlled head station |
| Fx | 1111 xxxx | Manufacturer extensions |

## E3.1.3 Control (or command) byte

This byte allows up to 256 basic commands, optionally controlled by one or more data bytes. DiSEqC specification (version 4.2 of 25/02/98) defines around 50 commands, divided into three status categories: mandatory (M), recommended (R), and suggested (S). For the 1.0 level, only three commands are taken into account, out of which only one is mandatory (38 "write N0"). "Reset command (00)" is mandatory only when the receiver is equipped with an antenna loop-through function. Commands 38 and 39 use an additional byte to define the status of the outputs of a slave microcontroller defined by Eutelsat and intended to be integrated in peripherals. Commands 20 to 2F (optional) control each of the microcontroller outputs individually, but are of little interest because they are redundant with commands 38 and 39, followed by an appropriate data byte.

From level 1.1 up, commands 38 (write N1) and 58 (write frequency) are mandatory. This last command, followed by 3 bytes indicating the transponder frequency (in BCD coding), is intended for use in SMATV systems using a user-controlled frequency transposer in the head station. DiSEqC 1.1 foresees the repetition of commands (up to 2 times after the first) in order to allow control of cascaded switches. DiSEqC 1.2 adds the commands of a positioner and (optionally) of a polarizer.

For the 1.0 level, only the first two commands of Table E.4 are mandatory (M), the third is recommended (R). These commands determine the state of the output ports of a specific microcontroller defined by EUTELSAT by means of the byte which follows them.

## E3.1.4 Data bytes

Commands 38 and 39 must be followed by a byte, of which each bit at 1 of the MS nibble (clear) clears individually one of the four outputs of one of the two ports of the slave microcontroller, the LS nibble (set) setting them individually in the same way.

**Table E.4**

| Hex. | Status | From level | Bytes | Name | Function |
|------|--------|-----------|-------|------|----------|
| 00 | M / R | 1.0 | 3 | Reset | Reset DiSEqC microcontroller (peripheral) |
| 03 | R | 1.0 | 3 | Power On | Supply peripheral |
| 38 | M | 1.0 | 4 | Write N0 | Write port 0 (committed switches) |
| 39 | M | 1.1 | 4 | Write N1 | Write port 1 (uncommitted switches) |
| 48 | R | 1.2 | 4 | Write A0 | Polarizer control (skew) |
| 58 | M | 1.1 | 5 or 6 | Write Freq. | Tune to transponder frequency |
| 60 to 6B | M | 1.2 | 3 or 4 | divers | Positioner commands |

| CLEAR | SET |
|-------|-----|
| $b_7 b_6 b_5 b_4 = 1111 = F_h$ | $b_3 b_2 b_1 b_0 = xxxx = x_h$ |

A DiSEqC 1.0 message intended to control an output port of the slave microcontroller will follow the general form below:

| FRAMING (E0 or E1) | ADDRESS (10 to 18) | COMMAND (38 or 39) | DATA (Fx) |
|--------------------|--------------------|--------------------|-----------|

For command 38h, three of the four outputs of the "committed" port are dedicated to a predefined function (the fourth one being usable freely) according to Table E.5.

Command 39h functionality depends on the use of the "uncommitted" switches by the manufacturer.

**Table E.5**

| Bit | $b_3$ | | $b_2$ | | $b_1$ | | $b_0$ | |
|---|---|---|---|---|---|---|---|---|
| Function | OPTION (1) | | SATELLITE (2) | | POLARIZATION | | BAND | |
| State | 1 | 0 | 1 | 0 | 1 | 0 | 1 | 0 |
| Result | $\beta$ | $\alpha$ | A | B | Horiz. | Vert. | High | Low |

(1) Example: $\alpha$ = satellites group ASTRA/EUTELSAT, $\beta$ = satellites group TELECOM 2A/2B.
(2) Example: A = Astra, B = Eutelsat (group $\alpha$), A = Telecom 2A, B = Telecom 2B (group $\beta$).

## E3.1.5 Upper levels of DiSEqC

DiSEqC levels above 2.0 imply a bi-directional communication between the master and the slave(s), which must always respond at least by a framing byte used as acknowledgment, followed for certain commands by one or more data bytes.

One of the most interesting possibilities offered to the receiver is to "interrogate" the antenna configuration by which it is connected at switch-on to configure itself. For instance, command 51h makes it possible to know the LNB characteristics (LO frequency among others). Other commands make it possible to interrogate the status of the committed and uncommitted switches, to read analog values such as the position of a motorized antenna, etc. In the longer-term, if DiSEqC is generalized to all peripherals (switches, LNBs, positioners, etc.), the retro-compatibility will no longer be required, and a "true" bus structure will be possible (standardized address allocation, permanent bus and power supply distribution to all peripherals which will have a standby mode).

## E3.1.6 The USALS antenna-pointing system

The pointing of a motorized satellite antenna, even controlled by means of DiSEqC 1.2, is not very easy; it requires a precise adjustment. If this adjustment is not optimal, the pointing accuracy of satellites will degrade when the pointing direction is far from the reference direction (true South).

In order to ease the adjustment of a motorized satellite dish by non-specialists and the accurate pointing of all satellites receivable at a given place, the Italian satellite accessory manufacturer STAB has developed a software named Universal Satellite Automatic Location System (USALS), which makes use the DiSEqC 1.2 protocol by completing it.

USALS is designed to calculate the rotation of the DiSEqC 1.2 motor from the coordinates of the place of reception and the position of the satellites on the Clark Belt chain. The USALS software is intended to be embedded in satellite receivers, and STAB gives a free-of-charge license to the manufacturers who want to use it, provided they submit their receiver to the approval of STAB before putting their product on sale with the USALS logo on it (Fig. E4).

The coordinates of the main satellites receivable in a given world region are stored in a table which, of course, the user can modify in order to add or remove satellites. Regarding the installation procedure, the motor-positioner is fixed on the mast (which has to be perfectly vertical) at an angle that depends on the latitude of the place of reception. The antenna is fixed with a predefined elevation angle on the rotor's tube; these two operations are eased by means of graduations engraved on the antenna rotor's fixation.

This being done, the user has to input the coordinates of the place of reception in the USALS installation menu of the receiver and then select a satellite as near as possible to the true South of this place. The only remaining adjustment is then the fine tuning of the azimuth

**Figure E.4**  The Stab-USALS logo (courtesy STAB Srl, Italy).

to obtain the best possible reception. If the mast is really vertical and if the positioning of the motor on the mast and the antenna on the motor have been made with sufficient care, the system is ready for reception of all the satellites visible from the place of reception, within, of course, the limits imposed by the size of the dish.

# Appendix F:
# The common interface (DVB-CI)

In order to allow access to pay TV transmissions scrambled according to the DVB standard with a non-service provider specific terminal, the DVB consortium has defined a standardized interface known as **DVB-CI** (DVB common interface) which allows adjunction of detachable conditional access modules with a PC-Card (former PCMCIA) form factor, of which DVB-CI is an extension.

This interface is defined in the European standard EN 50221 and the ETSI extension TS 101699 and a few additional documents (implementation guides).

The DVB-CI interface can in principle also be used for other purposes, for example to increase the functionality of the set-top box by means of FLASH memory containing software extensions, to add an NIM for another transmission medium, or even add some modules from the PC world (modems or others) if the set-top box software can exploit them. Conditional access, however, is by far the main use, which is why we will describe briefly its principle of operation.

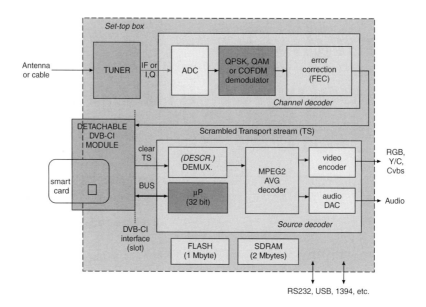

**Figure F.1** Block diagram of a receiver with a DVB-CI interface and CA module.

Figure F.1 represents the block diagram of a set-top box equipped with a DVB-CI conditional access module, where it can be seen that the module receives the scrambled transport stream at its input, and, assuming that a subscriber's smart card with valid access rights is inserted in it, delivers it "in the clear" to the source decoder. The module is, in addition, connected to the main processor by means of a conventional address, data and control bus to exchange control and OSD information.

Figure F.2 represents a more detailed view of the DVB-CI module and its communication with the set-top box and the subscriber's smart card. The CA module includes mainly a DVB-CSA descrambler (or possibly another one) and a microcontroller, on which the conditional access software is executed. The microcontroller is connected to a smart card reader via the ISO 7816 interface and to the host processor of the set-top box via the DVB-CI interface. Operation of the CA module is similar to that of an embedded CA (see Chapter 5).

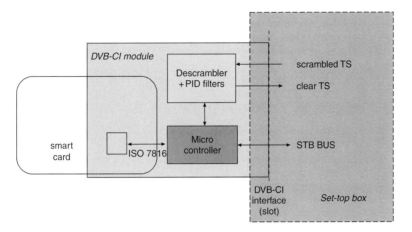

**Figure F.2** Simplified block diagram of a DVB-CI CA module.

The microcontroller receives, after selection by a PID filtering, the encrypted control words transmitted in the ECM messages and returns them to the descrambler after decryption by means of the keys contained in the smart card, on the condition that it has the required access rights which are sent by the EMM messages. This process allows the module to return a transport stream partly or fully descrambled (depending on the level—program or transport— of the scrambling at the transmission side). More than one DVB-CI (most often two) may be present in a set-top box. In this case, the transport stream interfaces are connected in cascade (daisy chain).

The set-top box's internal DVB-CI interface circuitry contains switches which enable a direct path for the transport stream when no module is inserted in a slot, or when the transmission is in the clear or scrambled with a system not supported by the module.

In addition to the physical interface, the DVB-CI specification also defines a communication protocol between the module and the host processor, in order that (in principle) all modules are compatible with all DVB-CI compliant boxes, which is, unfortunately, not always the case. The internal software of the DVB-CI module is, of course, dependent on the conditional access supported, whereas the hardware implementation of the module can be common to many systems based on the DVB-CSA scrambling algorithm.

Modules are available today for most conditional access systems used in Europe, and the presence of at least one DVB-CI slot is mandatory for terrestrial digital TV receivers in most countries where these transmissions are available.

# Appendix G: DVI and HDMI links for interconnecting digital audiovisual equipment

If one wants to make best use of matrix displays (LCD, plasma, DLP projectors) the link between the digital video source and the display system must be in digital form in order to avoid any quality loss resulting from unnecessary digital-to-analog and analog-to-digital conversions.

With the advent of high definition TV, this digital point-to-point link must be able to transmit very high bit-rates (at least up to 2.2 Gb/s for 720p or 1080i resolutions). In addition, video content rights holders (Hollywood studios, for example) require that an efficient copy protection system is put in place in order to prevent users from copying high-definition content in digital quality at the level of the link with the display device.

The Digital Visual Interface (**DVI**) link used in recent personal computers fulfills these requirements. It exists in two forms:

- DVI-I: includes 24 pins for the digital part (on the left in Fig. G.1a) and 5 separate pins enabling compatibility with the analog VGA connector (on the right).

- DVI-D (digital only): includes only the 24 digital pins (Fig. G.1b).

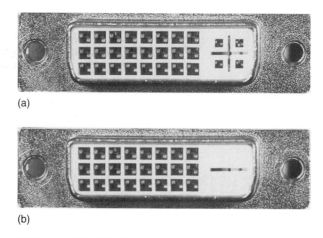

(a)

(b)

**Figure G.1**  (a) DVI-I and (b) DVI-D connectors (female).

The DVI connection is, however, not really optimized for a consumer application. Thus, some additional requirements have to be taken into account:

- necessity of a compact connector, easy to manipulate (no screws) and cost-effective (the analog part of the DVI-I is not necessary).

- carriage of digital audio and video on the same cable.

- exchange of configuration and control information.

The High Definition Multimedia Interface (HDMI) link takes all these requirements into account. It uses the same principles and has the same electrical characteristics as the digital video part of the DVI link (Fig. G.2), with which it is compatible by means of a simple mechanical adapter. It is a unidirectional link regarding the audio and video signals. In HDMI jargon, the signal generator (HDMI output) is called the *source* and the receiver (HDMI input) is called the *sink*.

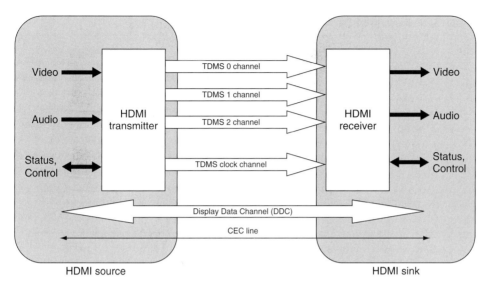

**Figure G.2** Schematic view of the link between a DVI or HDMI source and sink.

Like the DVI link, HDMI uses a transmission protocol named Transition Minimized Differential Signalling (TMDS) using four differential pairs:

- Three channels (TDMS 0, 1, and 2) transmit the audio and video signals and auxiliary data.

- A fourth channel (TDMS clock) transmits the pixel clock signal.

- A display data channel (VESA DDC) enables information exchange between the source and the sink to inform the source of the display capabilities of the sink, according to the VESA standard Enhanced Extended Display Identification Data (E-DID).

If necessary, an optional additional bi-directional data line—CEC—permits the exchange of control information between the various interconnected audiovisual devices.

The four TDMS channels are transmitted by means of shielded differential pairs. The VESA DDC channel is transmitted by means of an I2C bus (Philips Semiconductors). Video is transmitted as a

**Table G.1** Pinning of the type A HDMI connector

| Pin | Signal | Pin | Signal |
|---|---|---|---|
| 1 | TDMS data 2+ | 2 | TDMS data 2 shield |
| 3 | TDMS data 2− | 4 | TDMS data 1+ |
| 5 | TDMS data 1 shield | 6 | TDMS data 1− |
| 7 | TDMS data 0+ | 8 | TDMS data 0 shield |
| 9 | TDMS data 0− | 10 | TDMS clock+ |
| 11 | TDMS Clock shield | 12 | TDMS clock− |
| 13 | CEC | 14 | Réserved (NC) |
| 15 | I2C SCL (DDC) | 16 | I2C SDA (DDC) |
| 17 | DDC/CEC ground | 18 | +5V supply |
| 19 | | hot plug detect | |

stream of pixels coded in 24 bits on the three TDMS channels (8 bits per channel for each of the three components, which can be RGB or $YC_BC_R$).

Using a BCH error-correction code, the TDMS encoding protects these 8 bits per channel, which it converts into a 10-bit sequence (or packet) with minimum transition, transmitted on each of the three differential pairs at the rate of 10 bits per pixel clock period. Pixel clock frequencies range from 25 MHz to 165 MHz depending on picture resolution (largely covering the range from 480p to 1080i). Formats with lower pixel clocks (e.g., 13.5 MHz for 480i or 576i interlaced pictures) can be transmitted by repeating every pixel, which doubles the apparent pixel clock. The pixel coding format can be RGB, $YC_BC_R$ 4:4:4, or $YC_BC_R$ 4:2:2.

Audio and auxiliary data are transmitted according to the same 10-bit packet format and are also protected by the same BCH encoding. The original audio stream can be a simple IEC60958 stereo stream sampled at 32, 44.1, or 48 kHz, but it is also possible to transmit multichannel audio streams with a higher sampling frequency (up to 8 audio channels sampled at 96 kHz or one stereo stream at 192 kHz).

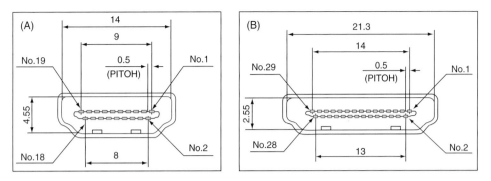

**Figure G.3** Details of the type A and B HDMI receivers.

HIGH-DEFINITION MULTIMEDIA INTERFACE

**Figure G.4** The HDMI logo.

Regarding the connectors, there are two types (Fig. G.3 A & B):

- The so-called type A connector with 19 contacts (by far the most common, See pinning table H1) allows the transport of pictures up to a 1080i resolution (pixel clock up to 165 MHz).

- The so-called type B connector with 29 contacts allows the transport of pictures with higher resolution (1080p, for example) requiring a pixel clock of more than 165 MHz. In practice, it is a dual HDMI link for the TDMS part, the DDC and CEC part being not duplicated. To our knowledge, this connector is not used for the time being in consumer applications.

**Note:**
The latest revision of the HDMI spec (logo shown in Figure G.4) to date (rev. 1.3 of 2006/06/22) has added many new features, among them a new mini-connector (type C, intended mainly for portable devices such as camcorders), higher link-speed capabilities, deeper color spaces (up to 48 bits per pixel), enhanced colorimetry (xvYCC), and additional audio formats.

# Appendix H: Sample chipset for DVB receivers/decoders

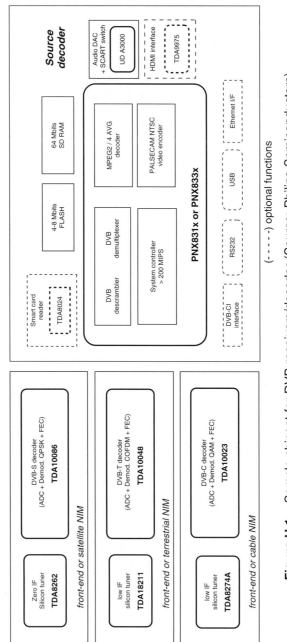

**Figure H.1**   Sample chipset for DVB receivers/decoder (Source: Philips Semiconductors).

# Glossary of abbreviations, words, and expressions

## Abbreviations

**1080i** – 1080 interlaced (high-definition interlaced format with 1080 lines and 1920 pixels/line).

**720p** – 720 progressive (high-definition progressive format with 720 lines and 1280 pixels/line).

**AAC** – Advanced Audio Codec (a digital audio encoding/compression format also known as MPEG-2 Part 7; more efficient than MP3. A later improvement known as AAC+ or HE-AAC further improves compression efficiency).

**AC-3** – multichannel digital audio system developed by the U.S. company Dolby®.

**ADC** – analog-to-digital converter (device converting an analog voltage into a binary number).

**ADSL** – Asymmetric Digital Subscriber Line (system exploiting the high-frequency transmission capabilities of a telephone line to enable an asymmetric broadband link method (up to 20 Mb/s for the downlink and 1 Mb/s for the uplink with ADSL2+).

**AF** – adaptation field (data field used to adapt the *PES* to transport packet length).

**API** – application programming interface (programming interface of middleware for its compatible applications; sometimes used to designate the middleware itself).

**APSK** – Amplitude and Phase Shift Keying (modulation in which phase and amplitude can both take more than two states). The DVB-S2 standard foresees usage of 16-APSK and 32-APSK for point-to-point links.

**ASK** – amplitude shift keying (digital amplitude modulation with two states).

**ATSC** – Advanced Television System Committee (U.S. digital terrestrial TV system supporting *HDTV* and using 8-*VSB* modulation).

**AVC** – Advanced Video Coding (alternate name of *MPEG*-4.10 or H.264).

**AU** – access unit (*MPEG* coded representation of a presentation unit: picture or sound frame).

**B** – bi-directional (picture): MPEG picture coded from the preceding and the following picture.

**BAT** – bouquet association table (optional table of *DVB-SI*).

**BCH** – Bose-Chauduri Hocquenghem (*external* error correction code used in *DVB-S2* instead of the Reed-Solomon code of *DVB-S*). Also used to protect DVI and HDMI connections.

**BER** – bit error rate (ratio of the number of erroneous bits to the total number of bits transmitted).

**BPSK** – bi-phase shift-keying (two-state phase modulation, carrying one bit per symbol).

**CA** – conditional access (system allowing to limit the access to pay TV broadcasts).

**CABAC** – Context-Adaptive Binary Arithmetic Coding (the most efficient entropy coding of the H.264 standard). Used only in the main and high profiles as it requires important computing resources.

**CAM** – conditional access message (specific messages for conditional access: *ECM* and *EMM*).

**CAT** – conditional access table (*MPEG-2* table indicating the *PID* of conditional access packets).

**CAVLC** – Context-Adaptive Variable Length Coding ("standard" entropy coding used in H.264).

**CAZAC/M** – constant amplitude zero auto correlation (reference symbol in the *DVB-T* proposal).

**CBR** – constant bitrate. Simplest operating mode of an MPEG encoder, generally used when its output stream is not multiplexed with other MPEG sources.

**CCIR** – Comité Consultatif International des Radiocommunications (now IUT-R).

**CCIR-601 (ITU-R 601)** – recommendation for digitization of video signals ($F_\text{s} = 13{:}5\,\text{MHz}$, YUV signals in 4:2:2 format).

**CCIR-656 (ITU-R 656)** – recommendation for interfacing CCIR-601 signals (most common variant: 8 bits parallel multiplexed YUV format).

**CCITT** – Comité Consultatif International du Télégraphe et du Téléphone (now *ITU*-T).

**CIF** – common intermediate format ($360 \times 288@30\,\text{Hz}$).

**CNR** – carrier-to-noise ratio (or C/N) ratio (in dB) between the received power of the carrier and the noise power in the channel bandwidth.

**COFDM** – coded orthogonal frequency division multiplex (see *OFDM*).

**CSA** – common scrambling algorithm (scrambling algorithm specified by *DVB*).

**CVBS** – Color Video Baseband Signal (color composite video, e.g., *NTSC*, *PAL*, or *SECAM*).

**Dl** – professional digital video recording format in component form (*CCIR-656*).

**D2** – professional digital video recording format in composite form (*NTSC, PAL*, or *SECAM*).

**D2-MAC** – duobinary multiplex analog components (hybrid standard used on satellite and cable).

**DAB** – digital audio broadcasting (new European digital audio broadcasting standard).

**DAC** – digital-to-analog converter (device converting a binary value into an analog voltage or current).

**DAVIC** – digital audio visual council, a non-profit making association based in Geneva with members from all industries involved in digital technologies applied to audio and video, from content producer to service provider to hardware manufacturer. One of its goals is to define and specify open interfaces allowing maximal interoperability across countries, applications, and services.

**DBS** – direct broadcast satellite (satellite in the 11.7–12.5 GHz band reserved for TV broadcast).

**DC** – direct current (coefficient of the null frequency in the *DCT*).

**DCT** – discrete cosine transform (temporal to frequency transform used in *JPEG* and *MPEG*).

**DiSEqC**™ – digital satellite equipment control (control protocol allowing a bidirectional digital communication between the set-top box and the antenna for complex switching functions by modulating the 22 KHz tone with digital messages). Two versions (1.0 and 2.0) currently exist.

**DLI** – device layer interface.

**DOCSIS** – data over cable service interface specifications (main standard of U.S. cable modems).

**DPCM** – differential pulse code modulation (coding of a value by its difference to the previous one).

**DRAM** – dynamic random access memory (read/write memory requiring a periodic refresh of the information, the most widespread due to its low cost).

**DSLAM** – Digital Subscriber Line Access Multiplexer (device for multiplexing a few hundreds of ADSL lines and linking them to the internet by means of a very high-bit rate link; it is located in the telephone exchange of the incumbent telecom operator).

**DSM** – digital storage medium (mass storage devices such as hard disk, tape, or CD).

**DSM-CC** – Digital Storage Media-Command and Control (a toolkit intended for developing control channels associated with MPEG streams, defined in part 6 of the MPEG-2 standard, ISO/IEC 13818-6). Initially mainly intended for providing VCR like features, it is in fact mainly used to provide pseudo-interactivity features by means of data and object "carousels" sending these data repetitively (as in teletext).

**DSNG** – Digital Satellite News Gathering (point-to-point satellite link, generally temporary and transportable, intended for coverage of events).

**DSP** – digital signal processor (processor specialized in processing of digitized analog signals).

**DSS** – Digital Satellite System (main direct-to-home digital satellite TV system in the United States).

**DTS** – decoding time stamp (indicator of the decoding time of an MPEG access unit).

**DVB** – digital video broadcasting: European digital TV standard with three variants, DVB-C (cable), DVB-S (satellite), DVB-T (terrestrial).

**DVB-C** – Digital Video Broadcasting–Cable (cable digital TV standard using 16 to 256-*QAM*).

**DVB-CI** – common interface (DVB interface for conditional access modules in PCMCIA form).

**DVB-H** – Digital Video Broadcasting–Handheld (terrestrial digital TV standard intended for reception on mobile terminals, derived from *DVB-T*; it uses 2 k, 4 k, or 8 k *COFDM* and a time-slicing mechanism to reduce the power consumption of the mobile terminal).

**DVB-S** – Digital Video Broadcasting–Satellite (satellite digital TV standard using *QPSK* modulation).

**DVB-S2** – Digital Video Broadcasting–Satellite 2nd generation (new transmission standard more flexible and bandwidth-efficient than *DVB-S* due to the possibility to use higher-order 8 k to 32-state modulations and more powerful *LDPC+BCH* channel coding).

**DVB-SI** – Service information (group of tables specified by *DVB*, additional to *MPEG-2 PSI*).

**DVB-T** – Digital Video Broadcasting–Terrestrial (terrestrial digital TV standard using 2 k or 8 k *COFDM*).

**DVD** – unified optical disc format with 4.7–19 Gbyte capacity.

**DVI** – Digital Visual Interface (digital interface intended for connection of computer displays; it is electrically compatible with HDMI, with a different connector and without audio support).

**$E_b/N_o$** – ratio between the average bit energy $E_b$ and noise density $N_o$ (related to C/N).

**EBU** – European Broadcasting Union (French: Union Européenne de Radiodiffusion, UER). Organization grouping the main European broadcasters which, among other things, works on new broadcasting standards (ex: *DAB, DVB*) which are then approved by the ETSI.

**ECM** – entitlement control message (first type of conditional access message of the *DVB* standard).

**EICTA** – European Information & Communications Technology Association (European interest group representing the Information Technology, Telecommunications, and Consumer Electronics industries).

**EIT** – event information table (optional table of *DVB-SI* indicating a new event).

**ELG** – European Launching Group (group at the origin of the *DVB* project in 1991).

**EMM** – entitlement management message (second type of conditional access message of the *DVB* standard).

**EPG** – electronic program guide (graphical user interface for easier access to *DVB* programs).

**ES** – elementary stream (output stream of an *MPEG* audio or video encoder).

**ETSI** – European Telecommunications Standards Institute (organization issuing the European standards in the field of telecommunications, ETS).

**FCC** – Federal Communications Commission (regulatory authority for telecommunications in the United States).

**FEC** – forward error correction (addition of redundancy to a digital signal before transmission, allowing errors to be corrected at the receiving end; synonym: channel coding).

**FFT** – fast Fourier transform (digital Fourier transform on sampled signals).

**FIFO** – first in, first out (type of memory often used as a buffer).

**FRExt** – Fidelity Range Extensions (extensions to the coding toolbox of H.264 used only in the "high" profiles of the standard).

**FSK** – frequency shift keying (digital frequency modulation with two states).

**FSS** – fixed service satellite (satellite in the 10.7–11.7 GHz or 12.5–12.75 GHz bands originally reserved for telecommunications).

**FTA** – free-to-air (or free-to-view; designates free access TV programs).

**GOP** – group of pictures (MPEG video layer: succession of pictures starting with an I picture).

**H.261** – compression standard used for ISDN videotelephony (bitrate of $p \times 64$ kb/s).

**H.264** – alternative video compression standard to MPEG-2 chosen by the DVB to improve coding efficiency, for example for HDTV applications. Also known as AVC (Advanced Video Coding) or MPEG-4 part 10.

**HDCP** – High-Bandwidth Digital Content Protection (content protection standard ecrypting the data transmitted on a *DVI* or HDMI link to prevent illegal copying).

**HD-MAC** – high definition MAC (high definition extension to the D2-MAC standard with 1250 lines).

**HDTV** – High Definition Television (television system with a picture resolution of $1280 \times 720$ or more).

**HTML** – HyperText Markup Language. The main coding standard used for creating web pages. Tags (codes) are used, for example, to specify text styles and color, display images, include links to other web pages and/or websites etc.

**I** – in-phase; for QAM, designates the signal modulating the carrier following the 0° axis.

**I** – intra (picture); MPEG picture coded without reference to other pictures.

**I²C** – inter-integrated circuits (serial interconnection bus between ICs developed by Philips).

**I²S** – inter-integrated sound (serial link between digital sound ICs developed by Philips).

**iDTV** – integrated digital TV (hybrid TV set able to receive analog and digital transmissions).

**IDTV** – Improved Definition TeleVision (TV system with a resolution between standard TV and *HDTV*).

256

**IEC** – International Electrotechnical Commission (international organization for standardization in the field of electrotechnics, electricity and electronics).

**IEEE802.11b** – wireless LAN standard at 2.4 GHz and 11 Mb/s.

**IEEE1284** – bidirectional high speed parallel interface (enhanced Centronics interface).

**IEEE1394** – high speed serial interface (up to 400 Mb/s) which is the likely future standard for consumer digital A/V links (already used in some digital video recorders and camcorders).

**IP** – Internet Protocol (protocol used to transmit data in the form of IP datagrams by means of an encapsulation which, among other benefits, ensures source and destination addressing).

**IRD** – integrated receiver decoder; popular synonym: set-top box.

**ISDB-T** – Integrated Services Digital Broadcasting–Terrestrial (Japanese digital terrestrial TV and multimedia system also based on *COFDM* modulation).

**ISI** – inter-symbol interference (interference between successive symbols in a digital transmission).

**ISO** – International Standards Organization (international standardization organization within the UNO).

**ITU** – International Telecommunications Union (world regulation organization for telecommunications, previously *CCITT*).

**JPEG** – Joint Photographic Experts Group (standard for fixed pictures compression).

**LDPC** – Low-Density Parity Code (internal error correction code code used in *DVB-S2* instead of the *Viterbi* convolutional coding of *DVB-S*).

**LNC** – low noise converter (down-converter situated at the focus of a satellite antenna). Synonym = LNB (low noise block).

**LSB** – Least Significant Bit. The bit which carries the lowest power of two ($2^0 = 1$) in a multibit word.

**MAC** – media access control (designates hardware and software parts of a network adapter or of an interactive cable receiver, in charge of management of network access and bandwidth sharing between users).

**MBAFF** – MacroBlock Adaptive Frame Field (coding option of H.264 allowing a better processing of interlaced pictures).

**MHEG-5** – Multimedia and Hypermedia Expert Group version 5 (standard middleware based on the MHEG decriptive language requiring only limited resources; used in the UK for digital terrestrial TV).

**MHP** – multimedia home platform (standard, open middleware proposed by the DVB consortium for interoperability of all digital TV transmissions in Europe).

**MP3** – MPEG-1 level 3 (audio compression format approximately two times more efficient than level 2; MP3 is the de facto standard for exchange of music files on the Internet).

**MP@ML** – main profile at main level (main video format of the DVB standard).

**MPEG** – Motion Pictures Experts Group (group which developed the MPEG-1 and MPEG-2 standards, currently working on MPEG-4 for very low bit-rate compression).

**MSB** – Most Significant Bit. The bit which carries the highest power of two in a multibit word.

**MUSE** – Japanese high definition television system (analog system with digital assistance).

**MUSICAM** – masking universal sub-band integrated coding and multiplexing (coding process of MPEG-1 audio, layer 2 used by *DAB* and *DVB*).

**NICAM** – near instantaneous companded audio multiplexing (digital sound system for analogue TV using a *QPSK* modulated carrier at 5.85 or 6.55 MHz).

**NIT** – network information table (optional table of *DVB-SI*).

**NTSC** – National Television Standard Committee (color TV system used in the United States and most 60 Hz countries).

**OFDM** – orthogonal frequency division multiplex (digital modulation system based on a high number of carriers used for *DAB* and proposed for terrestrial *DVB-T*).

**OOB** – out of band (additional medium bit-rate downstream channel used for user interaction and signalling data in the *DVB/DAVIC* interactive cable standard).

**P** – predictive (picture) MPEG picture coded with reference to the preceding I or P picture.

**PAL** – phase alternating line (color TV system used in most European and 50 Hz countries).

**PAT** – program allocation table (*DVB* table indicating the *PID* of the components of a program).

**PCM** – pulse code modulation (result of the digitization of an analog signal).

**PCMCIA** – (now renamed PC-Card)–Personal Computer Memory Card Association (designates the format used for PC extension modules and proposed by *DVB* for the detachable conditional access modules using the *DVB-CI* common interface).

**PCR** – program clock reference (information sent at regular intervals in *MPEG-2* to synchronize the decoder's clock to the clock of the program being decoded).

**PES** – packetized elementary stream (*MPEG* elementary stream after packetization).

**PID** – packet identifier (*PES* identification number in the *DVB* standard).

**PMT** – program map table (*DVB* table indicating the *PID* of the *PAT* of all programs in a transport multiplex).

**PRBS** – pseudo-random binary sequence (used for signal scrambling).

**PSI** – program specific information (*MPEG-2* mandatory tables: *CAT, PAT, PMT*).

**PSK** – Phase-Shift Keying (multistate phase modulation with constant amplitude). DVB-S2 allows the use of four state modulations (QPSK or 4-PSK) and 8 states (8-PSK) for broadcast applications.

**PTS** – presentation time stamp (information indicating the presentation time of a decoded image or sound).

**PU** – presentation unit (decoded picture or audio frame in *MPEG*).

**PVR** – Personal Video Recorder (hard disk-based recorder allowing conventional and time shift recording. It include most of the time a dual tuner receiver).

**Q** – quadrature; for QAM, designates the signal modulating the carrier following the 90° axis.

**QAM** – quadrature amplitude modulation (modulation of two orthogonal derivates of a carrier by two signals).

**QCIF** – quarter common intermediate format ($180 \times 144 @ 15$ Hz used for videotelephony).

**QEF** – quasi error-free (designates a channel with a $BER < 10^{-10}$).

**QPSK** – quadrature phase shift keying (phase modulation with four states, equivalent to 4-*QAM*).

**RISC** – reduced instruction set computer.

**RLC** – run length coding (data compression method exploiting repetitions).

**RS(204, 188, 8)** – abbreviated notation of the Reed–Solomon coding used by DVB.

**RS232** – standardized asynchronous serial communication interface (relatively slow).

**RST** – running status table (optional table of *DVB-SI* informing on the current transmission).

**RTTP** – Real Time Transport Protocol (transmission protocol used to transmit time critical data such as TV over *IP*).

**SCR** – system clock reference (information sent at regular intervals in *MPEG*-1 to synchronize the decoder's clock to the system clock).

**SDRAM** – synchronous dynamic random access memory (a new kind of high speed *DRAM* (16 bits organized) used with recent *MPEG* decoders).

**SDT** – service description table (optional table of *DVB-SI*).

**SECAM** – séquentiel couleur à mémoire (color TV system mainly used in France and in eastern European countries).

**SFN** – single frequency network (terrestrial TV transmitter network using the same frequency on all its coverage area; it uses the 8 K *COFDM* mode of the *DVB-T* standard and a relatively long guard interval).

**SIF** – source intermediate format ($360 \times 288$@25 Hz or $360 \times 240$@30 Hz; basis for *MPEG*-1).

**ST** – stuffing table (optional table of *DVB-SI*).

**STC** – system time clock.

**STD** – system target decoder (hypothetical reference decoder used in *MPEG* standards).

**TDT** – time and date table (optional table of *DVB-SI*).

**TPS** – transmission parameter signalling (modulation and channel coding parameters transmitted on pilot carriers of the *OFDM* multiplex in the *DVB-T* proposal).

**TSR** – time shift recording (facility to watch a complete live TV transmission in spite of interruptions thanks to the simultaneous record and playback capability of a hard disk).

**USALS** – Universal Satellite Automatic Location System (software developed by the Italian STAB company and embedded on top of *DiSEqC*™ 1.2 in satellite receivers in order to calculate the rotation of a motorized antenna from the coordinates of the receiver's location and the orbital position of the satellite).

**USB** – universal serial bus (high speed serial bus—up to 11 Mb/s for version 1.1 and 480 Mb/s for version 2—replacing progressively the RS232 and IEEE1284 in PCs and now digital TV STBs).

**VBS** – video baseband signal (monochrome composite signal).

**VBR** – variable bitrate. When many programs are multiplexed to form a stream of a fixed bitrate, it is advantageous to use **statistical multiplexing** to improve bandwith usage, which results in a variable bitrate for each of the components of the stream.

**VLC** – variable length coding (data compression method consisting of coding frequent elements with fewer bits than infrequent ones).

**VLIW** – very long instruction word (new type of processor using parallelism).

**VSB** – vestigial sideband (AM with one of the two sidebands truncated); used by all analog TV standards and proposed for the terrestrial broadcasting of the digital "Grand Alliance" US HDTV system (8 or 16-VSB).

**W & R** – watch and record.

**WSS** – wide screen signalling (signalling information on line 23 of the *PALP* signal, also used on standard *PAL* or *SECAM*, to indicate the format and other characteristics of the transmission).

**ZIF** – see *zero IF*.

## Words and expressions

**aliasing** – disturbance caused by spectrum mixing when sampling a signal with a bandwidth exceeding half of the sampling frequency (during an A-to-D conversion, for instance).

**asynchronous** – in IEEE1394 terminology, designates the mode specified for the transport of non-time-critical data (used, for example, for function control or storage).

**baseband** – original frequency band of an analog or digital signal before modulation or after demodulation.

**block** – in JPEG and MPEG this designates the portion of an $8 \times 8$ pixel picture to which the DCT is applied.

**Bluetooth** – RF communication standard at 2.4 GHz for short distances (in the order of 10 m) and medium bit-rate (max. 1 Mb/s) allowing interconnection of up to seven participants forming a piconet. Different piconets can communicate between each other by means of participants belonging to two piconets.

**burst errors** – multiple errors occurring in a short time with relatively long error-free periods in between.

**channel coding** – addition of redundancy to a digital signal before transmission, allowing errors to be corrected at the receiving end (synonym: *FEC*).

**comb filter** – filter used in NTSC or PAL with "teeth" corresponding to the stripes in the chrominance and luminance spectra for optimum separation of chrominance and luminance.

**components video** – color video made of three elementary signals (e.g., RVB or YUV).

**composite video** – coded color video using one signal only (*NTSC, PAL*, or *SECAM*).

**compression layer** – in MPEG, designates the information at the output of the individual encoders (elementary streams, *ES*s).

**constellation** – simultaneous display in I/Q coordinates of the points representing all the possible states of a quadrature modulated signal (*QAM, QPSK*).

**convolutional coding** – inner part of the channel coding for satellite and terrestrial transmissions, increasing the redundancy by providing two bitstreams from the original one; it corrects mainly random errors due to noise.

**digitization** – conversion of an analog value into a (generally binary) number (synonym: analog-to-digital conversion, *ADC*).

**downlink** – communication link from a satellite to earth station(s) or consumer receivers.

**echo equalizer** – device designed for cancellation or attenuation of the echoes introduced by transmission (cable transmission mainly).

**encryption** – encoding of information with a key to control its access.

**energy dispersal** – logic combination of a digital bitstream with a pseudo-random binary sequence (*PRBS*) to obtain an evenly distributed energy after modulation.

**entropy coding** – coding principle using variable length words to encode information elements depending on their probability of occurrence (synonym: variable length coding, *VLC*); the most well-known method for VLC is the Huffmann algorithm.

**Eurocrypt** – conditional access system mainly used with the D2-MAC standard.

**flash EPROM** – non-volatile, electrically erasable and rewritable memory (in blocks).

**flicker** – disturbing periodic variation of the luminance of a picture when its refresh frequency is too low (below 50 Hz).

**frame (audio)** – elementary period during which the psychoacoustical coding is performed (corresponds to 12 times 32 PCM samples); its duration varies from 8 to 12 ms depending on the sampling frequency; (*DVB-T*)-7 series of 68 OFDM symbols; four consecutive frames form a superframe.

**granule** – in MPEG audio (layer 2), designates a group of three consecutive sub-band samples (corresponds to 96 PCM samples).

**HD-ready** – label defined by the EICTA and granted to audiovisual equipment compatible with the minimum requirements of HDTV.

**interlaced scanning** – scanning of a picture in two successive fields, one with odd lines and the other with even lines, in order to reduce by a factor of 2 the bandwidth required for a given resolution and a given refresh rate compared to a progressively scanned picture.

**isochronous** – in IEEE1394 terminology, designates the quasi-synchronous mode used to transport time-critical data (real time audio and video).

**joint_stereo** – MPEG audio mode exploiting the redundancy between left and right channels with two submodes (*MS_stereo:* coding of L + R and L − R; *intensity_stereo:* coding of common sub-band coefficients for high bands of L and R).

**layer** – in MPEG audio, defines the algorithm used for compression (there are three different layers).

**layer** – in MPEG video, corresponds to the hierarchical decomposition (from sequence to block).

**letterbox** – broadcast format used to transmit wide screen films (16/9 or more) on a standard 4/3 TV screen, leaving two horizontal black stripes at the top and bottom of the picture.

**level** – in MPEG-2, defines the spatial resolution of the picture to be coded.

**line-locked clock** – clock synchronized by a PLL loop to the line frequency of a video signal.

**lossless compression** – same as reversible coding (see this phrase; opposite: lossy compression).

**lossy compression** – compression process which discards some imperceptible or hardly perceptible information elements (opposite: lossless or reversible compression).

**macroblock** – picture area of $16 \times 16$ pixels used for motion estimation. A macroblock is made up of six blocks: 4 $Y$, 1 $C_b$ and 1 $C_r$.

**masking** – occultation of the perception of a sound by a more powerful one at a near frequency (frequency masking) and/or time (temporal masking).

**Mediahighway** – middleware developed and promoted by Canal+ Technologies and used among others by ITV Digital.

**mini-DiSEqC** – see *Toneburst*.

**Monoblock (LNB)** – specific type of dual universal LNB for the reception of two satellites located on nearby orbital positions (for example, Astra1 and Hotbird, distant from 6.2°) with the same dish and cable.

**motion estimation** – determination of a motion vector allowing an area of a picture to be deduced from an area of a previous picture.

**multicrypt** – one of the conditional access options in DVB, based on a detachable CA module connected via the common interface DVB-CI.

**node** – in IEEE 1394 terminology, designates a participant connected to the bus.

**OpenTV** – middleware developed and promoted by the company OpenTV and used among others by BSkyB.

**orthogonal sampling** – sampling of a video signal by means of a clock locked to the line frequency in order to obtain samples with fixed positions on a rectangular grid.

**orthogonality** – property of a digitally modulated multiple carrier system when the spacing between consecutive carriers is equal to the inverse of the period of the modulating signal, so that the spectrum of any carrier presents zeroes for the central value of the neighboring carriers (*OFDM* modulation).

**padding** – non-significant bits added to adjust the duration of an audio frame (padding bits), or non-significant stream added to adjust the bit-rate of a bitstream (padding stream).

**payload** – for MPEG-2 transport packets (188 bytes), this designates the "useful" 184 bytes following the header.

**peritel** – 21 pin audio/video connector (also known as SCART plug or EUROCONNECTOR) used to interconnect audiovisual equipment (TV, VCR, set-top box, etc.).

**pixel** (or pel) abbreviation of picture element – the smallest element of an imaging or display device. In digital TV, it corresponds to the visual representation of one sample of a digitized picture.

**profile** – in MPEG-2, defines the toolbox used for video encoding.

**progressive scanning** – scanning of all the lines of a picture in numerical order in only one frame containing all picture lines (type of scanning used for computer monitors).

**psychoacoustic model** – mathematical model of the behavior of the human auditive system, based, among other things, on the frequency and temporal masking effects.

**puncture** – operation consisting of taking only a part of the bits generated by the convolutional coding to reduce its redundancy, at the expense of a reduced robustness (used in *DVB-S* and *DVB-T*).

**quantization** – measurement of a quantity with a limited number of discrete values (distant from the quantization step), for instance in an analog-to-digital conversion or a compression process.

**quantization noise** – noise introduced by an analog-to-digital conversion process, mainly due to the uncertainty on the least significant bit (representing the quantization step).

**Reed–Solomon coding** – outer part of the DVB channel coding, which adds 16 parity bytes to the 188 byte packets and allows correction of up to 8 bytes per packet; it is denoted RS(204, 188, 8).

**reversible coding** – coding allowing the recovery of the exact original information by applying the reverse process (synonym: lossless coding; opposite: lossy coding).

**roll-off factor** – characteristic of the steepness of the filtering applied to a digital signal in order to limit its bandwidth, generally with a view to modulation.

**sampling** – periodic acquisition of the value of an analog signal, generally with a view to converting it into a digital number.

**scalable profile** – MPEG-2 profile allowing different levels of quality to be obtained from the same bitstream (in terms of resolution for *spatially scalable profiles* or signal-to-noise ratio for *SNR scalable profiles*).

**scaling factor** – in MPEG audio, a 6-bit multiplying factor applied to each sub-band coefficient for the duration of a frame (giving a 128 dB range with 64 values in steps of 2 dB).

**sequence** – in MPEG, an uninterrupted series of GOP defined with the same basic parameters.

**set-top box** – popular denomination of an integrated receiver decoder (*IRD*).

**simulcast** – simultaneous transmission of a program in two or more standards (e.g., *PAL* and *DVB*), generally during a transition period between these standards.

**simulcrypt** – principle consisting of sending ECM and EMM for more than one conditional access system for one program, in order to allow reception by different types of decoder.

**slice** – in MPEG, a slice is a portion of the picture made up of horizontally consecutive macroblocks (most of the time a complete row). It is used for intra-frame addressing and resynchronization.

**source coding** – ensemble of coding operations aiming to reduce the quantity of information delivered by a source (synonym: compression).

**spectral efficiency** – ratio (in bits/s per Hz) between the bit-rate of a bitstream and the bandwidth occupied by the RF signal modulated by this bitstream.

**square pixels** – name given to the pixels obtained when sampling results in an equivalent resolution along the two axes of the picture (e.g., $640 \times 480$ for a 4/3 picture).

**statistical multiplexing** – when many TV programs are multiplexed in a single channel, it is possible to improve bandwidth efficiency based on the assumption that all programs do not need a maximum bitrate all at the same time. The bitrate of each of the programs is made variable (**VBR**) by changing the quantization step of the

MPEG encoders according to the instaneous requirements of the video contents. The gain of statistical multiplexing increases with the number of programs of the multiplex.

**sub-band sample** – in MPEG audio, output signal of one of the 32 sub-band filters (duration: 32 PCM samples, corresponding to 1 ms at 32 kHz sampling rate).

**symbol** – in a digital transmission, this is the modulating information element. The number of bits/symbol depends on the modulation type (e.g., 2 bits/symbol for *QPSK*, 6 for 64-*QAM*).

**symbol rate** – number of symbols transmitted per second.

**system layer** – in MPEG-1, designates the form of the packetized information after multiplexing.

**table (MPEG-2 PSI and DVB-SI)** – descriptive information necessary to access DVB transmissions or making this access easier.

**thresholding** – elimination of values below a given threshold (used in video compression to reduce the amount of information to be transmitted).

**Toneburst** – (or Mini-DiSEqC) early and simplistic version of the DiSEqC™ protocol allowing switching between two orbital positions only. Equipment supporting only Toneburst are not permitted to carry the DiSEqC™ logo.

**transponder** – electronic device in a communication satellite receiving information from an earth station and re-sending it after frequency conversion and amplification to earth station(s) or consumers; there is generally one transponder per RF channel.

**transport packet** – packet of 188 bytes (4 header bytes P184 payload bytes) forming the elementary blocks of an MPEG-2 transport bitstream to which the error correction is applied.

**uplink** – communication link from an earth station to a satellite, supplying the information to be rebroadcast by one or more transponder(s).

**zero IF** (or direct conversion) – designates the concept of recent satellite tuners able to recover I and Q baseband signals by coherent demodulation directly at the incoming frequency, resulting in a "zero IF" instead of the 480 MHz IF of the conventional "superheterodyne" concept.

# Bibliography

## Books

Bic, J.C., Duponteil, D., Imbeaux, J.C. 1991. *Elements of digital communication.* Paris: Wiley (in English).

Brémaud, P. 1995. *Signal et communications.* Paris: Ellipses (in French).

Chambers, W.G. 1985. *Basics of communication and coding.* Oxford: Clarendon Press (in English).

Cohen, G., Dornstetter, J.L., Godlewski, P. 1992. *Codes correcteurs d'erreur.* Paris: Masson (in French).

Hill, R. 1986. *A first course in coding theory.* Oxford: Clarendon Press (in English).

Moreau, N. 1995. *Techniques de compression des signaux.* Paris: Masson (in French).

Petersen, D. 1992. *Audio, video and data telecommunications.* London: McGraw-Hill (in English).

Poli, A., Huguet, L. 1989. *Codes correcteurs.* Paris: Masson (in French).

Reimers, U., Fechter, F., Jaeger, D., Johansen, C., Ladebusch, U., Ricken, C., Roy, A., Verse, A. 1995. *Digitales Fernsehtechnik.* Berlin: Springer (in German).

Sandbank, C.P. 1990. *Digital Television.* Chichester: Wiley.

Viterbi, A.J., Omura, J.K. 1979. *Principals of digital communication and coding.* New York: McGraw Hill (in English).

Ziemer, A., *et al.* 1994. *Digitales Fernsehen.* Heidelberg: R. von Decker (in German).

## Official documents (in English)

BT 601 (ITU-R) Studio encoding parameters of digital television for standard 4:3 and wide screen 16:9 aspect ratios (Recommendation CCIR-601).

BT 656 (ITU-R) Interfaces for digital component video signals in 525 line and 625 line television systems operating at the 4:2:2 level of Rec. 601 (Recommendation CCIR-656).

EN 300 468 (ETSI): Specification for Service Information (SI) in DVB systems.

EN 302 304 (ETSI) Transmission System for Handheld terminals (DVB-H).

EN 302 307 (ETSI) Second Generation framing structure, etc., for satellite applications (DVB-S2).

EN 50221 (CENELEC) Common Interface Specification for Conditional Access and other DVB decoder applications (DVB-CI).

ETR 154 (ETSI/EBU) Implementation guidelines for the use of MPEG-2 systems, audio and video in satellite and cable broadcasting applications.

ETR 162 (ETSI/EBU) Allocation of SI codes for DVB systems.

ETS 300 421 (ETSI/EBU) Framing structure channel coding and modulation for satellite services.

ETS 300 429 (ETSI/EBU) Framing structure channel coding and modulation for cable services.

ETS 300 468 (ETSI/EBU) Specification for Service Information (SI) in DVB systems.

ETS 300 472 (ETSI/EBU) Specification for conveying ITU-R system B Teletext in DVB bitstreams.

ETS 300 744 (ETSI/EBU) Framing structure channel coding and modulation for terrestrial services (DVB-T).

ETS 300 748 (ETSI/EBU) Framing structure, channel coding and modulation for Multipoint Video Distribution Systems (MVDS) at 10 GHz and above (based on ETS 300 421 DVB-S).

ETS 300 749 (ETSI/EBU) Framing structure channel coding and modulation for MMDS below 10 GHz (based on ETS 300 429, DVB-C).

ETS 300 800 (ETSI/UER) DVB interaction channels for cable TV distribution systems (CATV).

EUTELSAT DiSEqC Bus functional specification (version 4.0, 22/03/96).

EUTELSAT DiSEqC Update and recommendations for implementation (version 1.0, 22/03/96).

HDMI Specification version 1.2 (HDMI).

IEEE1394, 1995 Standard for a high performance serial bus.

ISO 10918 (ISO/IEC) Digital compression and coding of continuous tone still images (JPEG).

ISO 11172-1, 11172-2, 11172-3 (ISO/IEC) Coding of moving pictures and associated audio for digital storage media up to about 1.5 Mb/s (MPEG-1 system, video, audio).

ISO 13818-1, 13818-2, 13818-3 (ISO/IEC) Coding of moving pictures and associated audio (MPEG-2 system, video, audio).

ISO 13818-6 (ISO) Extension for Digital Storage Media Command and Control (DSM-CC).

TR 101 190 (ETSI) Measurement guidelines for DVB systems.

TR 101 200 (ETSI) A guideline for the use of DVB specifications.

TR 102 377 (ETSI) Transmission to Handheld terminals; DVB-H Implementation Guidelines.

TR 102 401 (ETSI) Transmission to Handheld terminals; Validation Task Force Report.

TS 101 154 (ETSI) Implementation guidelines for the use of video and audio coding in broadcast applications based on the MPEG-2 transport stream.

TS 101 812 (ETSI) Multimedia Home Platform (MHP revision 1.0).

TS 102 005 (ETSI) Specification for the use of video and audio coding in DVB services delivered directly over IP.

TS 102 034 (ETSI) Transport of MPEG-2 based DVB services over IP-based networks.

## Press articles and other publications

FARIA Gérard (Teamcast, France), DVB-H: Digital TV in the hands! (2005).

Schäfer, Ralf *et al*: The emerging H.264/AVC standard (EBU technical review, January 2003).

Sullivan, Gari G. *et al*: The H264/AVC Advanced Video Coding Standard, Overview and Introduction to the Fidelity Range Extensions (SPIE Conference, August 2004).

Morello Alberto et Mignone Vittoria: DVB-S2 ready for take-off (EBU technical review, October 2004).

## Some useful Internet addresses

| | |
|---|---|
| ASTRA: | http://www.astra.lu |
| ATSC: | http://www.atsc.org |
| Bluetooth: | http://www.bluetooth.org |
| Cable labs: | http://www.cablelabs.org |
| Digitag: | http://www.digitag.org |
| DTG: | http://www.dtg.org.uk |
| DVB: | http://www.dvb.org |
| DVB-H: | http://www.dvb-h.org/ |
| EBU (UER): | http://www.ebu.ch |
| EICTA: | http://www.eicta.org |
| ETSI: | http://www.etsi.fr |
| Eurocablelabs: | http://www.eurocablelabs.com |
| EUTELSAT: | http://www.eutelsat.org |
| HDMI: | http://www.hdmi.org |
| IEC (CEI): | http://www.iec.org |
| IEEE: | http://www.ieee.org |
| ISO: | http://www.iso.ch |
| Liberate: | http://www.liberate.com |
| Mediaflo: | http://www.qualcomm.com/mediaflo |
| MHP: | http://www.DVB-MHP.org |
| Open Cable: | http://www.opencable.com |
| Open TV: | http://www.opentv.com |
| SCTE: | http://www.scte.org |
| Tcomlabs: | http://www.tcomlabs.com |
| TV Anytime: | http://www.tv-anytime.org |

# Index

FEC (forward error correction) (*Continued*)
- energy dispersal, 106–8
- inner coding, 111–13
- outer coding, 108–9
- satellite IRD, 148–49
- temporal spreading of errors, 109–11
- virtual channel, 106

Feedback error correction, 200
FFT (fast Fourier transform), 157, 205, 255
FIFO buffer, 51, 255
Finite field elements, 204
Flash EPROM, 150, 264
Flicker, 264
Forney convolutional interleaving, 109–11, 205
Frame formats, MPEG audio, 68–69
- granules, 69, 264
- layer I, 68–69
- layer II, 69

Frames, 264
- ATSC, 216
- DVB-T, 136

Framing byte (DiSEqC message), 229
Frequency masking, 62, 63
FRExt (Fidelity Range Extensions), 60, 255
FSK (frequency shift keying), 119, 255
FSS (fixed service satellite), 255
FTA (free-to-air) transmissions, 163, 255

GERBER standard, 4–5
Glossary, 249–70
GOP (group of pictures), 46, 255
Granules, 69, 264
Guard interval, 131, 132

H.261, 256
H.264, 60–61, 128–29, 256
Hamming code, 202–4
- defined, 202
- parity bits, 203
- parity control matrix, 203
- results, 203–4

Hamming distance
- defined, 200
- minimum, 200, 201

HDCP (High-Bandwidth Digital Content Protection), 256

HD-MAC, 11, 183, 256
HDMI (High Definition Multimedia Interface), 242–45
- A connector, 244, 245
- B connector, 245
- defined, 242
- link schematic view, 243
- logo, 245
- receiver details, 245
- sink, 242
- source, 242
- TDMS, 243–44

HDTV (high-definition television), 183–84
- broadcast compatiblity, 184
- defined, 256
- displays, 183
- formats, 24–25
- free-to-air transmissions, 184
- HD-MAC, 11, 183
- "HD ready" logo, 183–84
- standards, 184

HNED (home network end device), 188–89
Home gateway, 181–82
Huffmann coding algorithm, 33–34
- application, 34
- efficiency, 34
- functioning of, 33

Iconoscope, 2
iDTV (integrated digital television receiver), 180–81, 256
IEC (International Electrotechnical Commission), 257
IEEE 801.11, 182, 257
IEEE 1394, 179, 221–24, 257
- asynchronous transfers, 222
- bus architecture, 221
- cabling, 223
- defined, 221
- isochronous transfers, 222
- network structure, 222
- nodes, 221–22

iFFT (inverse Fast Fourier Transform), 134
I (intra) pictures, 45, 256
Inner coding, 111–13
- defined, 111
- DVB, characteristics, 112